How to Negotiate Anything with Anyone Anywhere around the World

THIRD EDITION

Frank L. Acuff

MJF BOOKS
NEW YORK

Published by MJF Books
Fine Communications
322 Eighth Avenue
New York, NY 10001

How to Negotiate Anything with Anyone Anywhere around the World (Third Edition)
LC Control Number: 2010934706
ISBN-13: 978-1-60671-031-9
ISBN-10: 1-60671-031-1

This edition is published by MJF Books in arrangement with AMACOM, a division
of American Management Association.

Publisher's Note: This publication is designed to provide accurate and authoritative
information in regard to the subject matter covered. It is sold with the understanding
that neither the original publisher nor Fine Communications is engaged in rendering
legal, accounting, or other professional service. If legal advice or other expert assistance
is required, the services of a competent professional should be sought.

Printed in the United States of America.

MJF Books and the MJF colophon are trademarks of Fine Creative Media, Inc.

QF 10 9 8 7 6 5 4 3 2 1

To my children,

Kristin and **Ryan**,

both tough negotiators

Contents

Preface

This book is for the person in the trenches, who needs practical guidelines to get the very best deal possible with people and organizations that have very different backgrounds and experiences. This book is for the practitioner—for the person who faces an international negotiating challenge and who perhaps should have done his or her homework earlier, but didn't. I wrote this book largely from a "lessons-learned" perspective: These are the kinds of things I wish someone had told me before I entered into global negotiations.

If you will be interacting with people from different cultures in either business or travel, this book is for you. If you find that you are uncomfortable in dealing with people from different cultures and want to understand why, this book is for you. Or, if you are an experienced negotiator who is getting less-than-excellent results from your international negotiations, this book is for you. This book is for anyone who works or travels abroad, and for those who must deal with people in their own country who have recently come from other countries. It is for managers, sales representatives, marketers, traders, diplomats, military personnel, attorneys, entrepreneurs, and other professionals whose success will depend on their ability to influence others.

Objectives

This book has four main objectives:

1. To help you to avoid the typical mistakes and pitfalls of international negotiating

2. To enable you to build on your current negotiating strengths

3. To help you to understand the process of international negotiations

4. To lead you to strengthen your cultural awareness and skills

This book will help protect you from making an agreement you should reject, and it will help you make the most of your assets.

In years past, it was typical to court our negotiating counterparts in one's own country. We now must ask, "Your place or mine?" Regardless of our personal knowledge of international business, many negotiating parties have, in fact, moved overseas. We can sit outside and wonder what's going on inside the dance hall, or we can join the party. This book will help you not only to show up, but also to dance every dance.

Overall Approach

We will briefly review negotiations in any language, an overview of the negotiations process as a whole, regardless of culture. Global negotiations will then be examined: what to look for in other cultures; how these cultural factors affect negotiations; challenges faced by global negotiators; how to deal with your boss; and how to be prepared for the phases of international adjustment. The term *TOS* refers to "The Other Side" in the negotiation.

This book is divided into three parts. Part One explores key aspects of the negotiating process. Part Two addresses the unique aspects of global negotiations and explores practical strategies to help you on your global journey. Part Two also examines the most difficult negotiating problems that you are likely to experience internationally and offers solutions that you can use on the job.

Part Three takes you on an intercultural journey to sixty-three countries. Specific guidelines, called "Negotiating Primers," are given for virtually anywhere in the world you are likely to do business. A profile of typical negotiators and specific negotiating strategies will be presented for seven regions of the world: Western Europe, Eastern Europe, Latin America, North America, the Middle East and North Africa, Asia and Pacific Rim, and Sub-Saharan Africa. For each of these regions, you will learn such critical factors as pace of the negotiation, negotiating style, emphasis on personal relationships, decision making, and contractual and administrative issues. You will strengthen your negotiating skills for these regions, learning the dos and don'ts of global negotiating that will most affect you on a day-to-day basis.

Let's get busy on putting you on the international map!

Acknowledgments

Distilling the many extraordinary aspects of global negotiating into an understandable and practical form is indeed challenging and, thankfully, stimulating and fun. This undertaking could not have happened, however, without the help of many people. It is impossible to acknowledge appropriately all the many individuals whose experiences, insights, and support influenced the development and writing of this book. But there are specific people to whom I especially owe a great deal of thanks. Although these individuals share in the quality of the book, any errors or limitations are mine alone.

My thanks to: Kristin Acuff and Ryan Acuff, who were very helpful in sourcing information and reviewers; Salvador Avila of Exxon Company, U.S.A.; Desi Bakalis of the American Management Association; Adelaide Bannon; Miriam Ben-Yoseph; Catherine Boudes of Axcan Pharma; Susan Cherion of the Billy Graham Evangelistic Association; Edward Cline; Robert Coshland of Tribol; Moira E. Crean of MasterCard International, Inc.; Ken Ellis and Alex Neyin of Chevron U.S.A.; Viktor Gorbach of FactSet Research; Ron Hansek of McDonald's Corporation; Robert Hentzen of Baxter Healthcare Corporation; Hein Huyghe; Rajika Jayatilake of the Embassy of Sri Lanka, Washington, D.C.; Zhang Jian; Douglas Kincade of P & H Mining Co.; Mohammad Shoaib Khan; Muge Kilinc; Rochelle Kopp of Japan Intercultural Consulting; Susan Koscis; Isa Laurinsilta of Genencor; Wilbert Law; Ursula E. Lentz of TAP Pharmaceutical Products; Foster Lin of the Far East Trade Service; Fiona Lorenz; Mamdough Mahfouz of Agiba Petroleum; Mike McMahon; Derek Mills of the U.S. Navy Defense Institute

of International Legal Studies; Aigul Moldadekova of the Embassy of Kazakhstan, Washington, D.C.; Ali Mounadi; Andrea S. Mounadi; Lee Meader; Louis Mitra of TAP Pharmaceutical Products; Isobel Morgan; Maggie Neale of Stanford University; Ken Nelson of Yokohama Academy USA; Bruce Peer of the Canadian Management Centre; Elaine Re; Lois Toolan; Bill Usner of Pennzoil; Paul Uzureau; Tom Wilson; Beryl York; and Jian Zhang of the School of Economics and Management, Beijing.

The contributions of Ellen Kadin, executive editor, and Andrea Pedolsky, acquisitions editor, at AMACOM Books, were enormous. Their many perceptive questions and comments always moved the book toward relevance and clarity. The research and writing of others was helpful in preparation of the country-by-country Negotiating Primers and other aspects of the book. The following resources were particularly helpful: Nancy J. Adler, *International Dimensions of Organizational Behavior* (Cincinnati, OH: South-Western, 2002); Borgna Brunner, ed., *Time Almanac 2008* (Pearson Education Company: Boston, MA, 2007); Lennie Copeland and Lewis Griggs, *Going International* (New York: Random House, 1985); *CultureGrams™ 2007 World Edition* (Provo, UT: ProQuest Information and Learning Company, 2006); *Harvard Business Review on Doing Business in China* (Boston, MA: Harvard Business School Publishing, 2004); Marlene L. Rossman, *International Business of the '90s: A Guide to Success in the Global Market* (New York: Praeger, 1990); John W. Wright, ed., *The New York Times 2008 Almanac* (New York: Penguin Group, 2008).

Global Negotiating

Let's get started on our journey! Chapter 1, "Negotiating in Any Language: How Negotiations Work," reviews the common ingredients of effective negotiations, regardless of the culture involved. This basis is important to the ensuing discussion of the international aspects of negotiations and to the negotiations process as a whole.

Negotiating in Any Language: How Negotiations Work

"Have more than thou showest, speak less than thou knowest."
—SHAKESPEARE, *KING LEAR*

- Negotiating Defined
- The Importance of Win-Win, or Interest-Based, Negotiations
- The Stages of Negotiation
- Planning Your Negotiation
- What It Takes to Close a Deal

The subject of negotiations is both timely and timeless. It is timely because almost everything about our society in general, and our workplace in particular, is increasingly complicated. Today there is more litigation, more cultural diversity, more regulation, more technology, and—in line with the focus of this book—more globalization among businesses. The subject is timeless because life is a series of endless negotiations.

Moses, for example, was more than an Old Testament prophet. He was an ace negotiator. He had been up on the mountain for forty days negotiating the Ten Commandments with the Supreme Other Side. His buddies asked, "Hey Mo, how'd it go up there?" "It was really rough up there," Moses answered, quite exhausted. "The good news is, I finally got Him down to ten. The bad news is, adultery's still in there!"

Certain fundamentals of negotiations apply whether you are negotiating in Toronto, Brussels, New York, Buenos Aires, Istanbul, Shanghai, or Dubai. It is

important to understand these fundamentals: They are the foundation on which you will later build your international negotiating strengths. These fundamentals include understanding the concept of negotiation, appreciating the importance of the win-win approach, understanding the stages of negotiation, being able to plan your negotiation, and knowing what it takes to close a deal.

In many ways, the negotiating skills we seek to master are those you practiced as a child but forgot as you became older and more sophisticated. Anyone with a six-year-old is reminded of this on a daily basis. Children are excellent negotiators:

- They are persistent.
- They don't know the meaning of the word *no*. They know that when we say no, we often mean maybe.
- They are never embarrassed.
- They often read *us* better than we read *them*.

Let's begin relearning these skills by defining our subject.

Negotiating Defined

Negotiating is the process of communicating back and forth for the purpose of reaching a joint agreement about differing needs or ideas. Negotiating has to do with persuasion rather than the use of crude power. What's more, negotiating has to do with the other side feeling good about the outcome of the negotiation. As such, negotiating is a collection of behaviors that involves communications, sales, marketing, psychology, sociology, assertiveness, and conflict resolution. Above all, it has to do with the clear understanding of our own motivations and those of the other side as we try to persuade them to do what we want them to do.

A negotiator may be a buyer or seller, a customer or supplier, a boss or employee, a business partner, a diplomat, or a civil servant. On a more personal level, a negotiator may be your spouse, friend, parent, or child. In all these cases, your negotiating skill strongly influences your ability to get ahead in both your organizational life and in your other interpersonal relationships.

Some negotiations involve business counterparts outside your organization, while others involve those within your organization, such as the boss, top management, attorneys, accountants, and other technocrats. With both internal and external situations, the main objective of a negotiation is to help you get what you want.

Since the focus of this book is international business negotiations, we refer to our counterpart from a foreign culture as TOS (The Other Side). TOS can be a negotiating counterpart in a foreign country (or host country) where the negotiation is taking place or a negotiator visiting your country to do business with you.

What Can You Negotiate About?

Although the details of business negotiations can be quite complex, there are really only nine subjects about which you can negotiate. Everything else is a variation on these themes:

1. Price
2. Terms (e.g., how and when payment will be made)
3. Delivery
4. Quality
5. Service
6. Training
7. Resources (people, money, materials)
8. Scope
9. Process (who is going to do what to whom)

Many negotiations are centered on price. Negotiations that involve the other eight items relate to the return on investment, or the value added.

The Importance of Win-Win, or Interest-Based, Negotiations

Almost any book about negotiating written in the past couple of decades includes great tributes to the virtues of win-win, or interest-based, negotiations. This means that both you and The Other Side (TOS) win in the negotiation. After having conducted seminars on negotiating with thousands of participants around the world, I can tell you that virtually every individual is quick to agree publicly with the idea of win-win negotiations. Yet in real-life—particularly in the United States—negotiations are often conducted with an "I win, you lose" type of behavior. Intellectually, we know that the cool, even-handed, interest-based approach is appropriate, but this is sometimes difficult to remember when the heat is on.

You might ask, "What's so bad about win-lose negotiations, as long as I make sure that I'm not the loser? I mean, I'm under a lot of pressure, so if the

other person bleeds a little, this is not one of my life's great problems. It's nothing personal, but I'm not in the charity business." Using that rationale, we put our foot right on the other person's neck and proceed with the negotiation.

The problem with win-lose negotiations is this. The loser usually behaves quite predictably and tries to get even. The loser's thinking goes something like this: "I'm going to get you. It may not be today. It may not be tomorrow, but I *will* get you. You will bleed and not even know it." Losers usually wind up pouring much of their energy into all kinds of dysfunctional behavior, aimed at getting out of the losing position. Sometimes the result is even lose-lose.

You can see much evidence of win-lose problems on the geopolitical level. The conflicts that have been sustained for decades, or sometimes even centuries, are really unresolved conflicts from previous win-lose situations. The Middle East antagonisms are a good example—a series of situations where the various parties have sought to *win*, only at the expense of TOS.

Interest-based negotiation is critical, not for you to be a wonderful, kind human being, but because it is the practical thing to do. It will help you get more of what you want. And how is this achieved? In two key ways:

1. *Meet the needs of TOS*. Switch to the frequency that others can tune in to, which is known as WIIFT (what's in it for them). The idea here is that in helping others, we can often help ourselves.

2. *Focus on interests and not positions*.[1] Positions are almost always irresolvable: "Our position is that we don't really need your product," is a dead end. Finding out interests, by contrast, helps you access the real needs of TOS: "Let's see what we can do to make this deal good for you and good for us," opens the door to fuller conversation.

It is sometimes difficult to establish an interest-based framework, even in a domestic business negotiation, and even when one has honorable intentions. Your counterpart may doubt your sincerity, or the condition under which you are negotiating may not lend itself to a feeling of collaboration and mutual trust. Achieving an interest-based outcome can be especially difficult, however, in global business negotiations. The different cultural backgrounds of negotiators may cause them to bring different expectations to the bargaining sessions, create stereotypes of TOS, and develop a climate of suspicion or distrust.

Thousands of such examples abound in international business negotiations. Achieving interest-based negotiations, and tuning in to WIIFT, takes an enormous amount of empathy, understanding, listening, patience—and skill. A California-based distributor of computer software relates the frustration she felt during her first trip to the Pacific Rim. "I left California for ten days to accom-

plish some fairly routine business in Japan and more complicated business in Singapore. I knew that business takes longer in Japan than in the United States, but I had no idea it would take several days to really get down to business in Tokyo. The tone of the negotiation was very bad, because I really felt they were dragging their feet." The situation changed in Singapore. "I was equally surprised to find that in Singapore I was in and out of there in no time. Things got off to a bad start because I felt I should make small talk—I'd been doing it for five days in Japan—and I think the Singaporeans felt I was being evasive and not really wanting to move ahead on the deal. I finally convinced them that we had the same objectives. I had scheduled five days there, but I needed only a morning. The Singaporean buyers wanted to talk business as much as I did. After a nice lunch with them, I headed for the airport, mission accomplished."

WIIFT for the Japanese negotiators in this case was patience on the U.S. negotiator's part—patience that indicated interest and respect for the long-term relationship. WIIFT for the Singaporeans was different. They were looking for the U.S. negotiator to demonstrate interest by moving along crisply in the business deal.

The Stages of Negotiation

In both domestic and international negotiations, there are six stages through which negotiations proceed: (1) orientation and fact-finding; (2) resistance; (3) reformulation of strategies; (4) hard bargaining and decision making; (5) agreement; and (6) follow-up. Knowledge of these stages helps you understand the overall shape of the negotiating process and gives you a bearing as you proceed through each negotiation. Here is a summary of the six stages:

1. *Orientation and Fact-Finding.* This first stage is critical for what is to come in the negotiations. The saying, "Information is power," is never more true than in the early stages of the negotiation process. The more information you can obtain here, the bigger the dividends will be in the negotiation's later stages. Unfortunately, many U.S. negotiators pay little attention to this critical stage of the negotiation. Orientation and fact-finding should begin even before you sit down with TOS. Orientation may mean learning about the organization of TOS, the history of similar negotiations with TOS, or the individual styles of your counterparts. Does the organization have a good reputation? Are there any recent management shake-ups? How much power do you think your negotiating counterpart has within his or her organization? How are negotiating issues to be addressed: individually, or as a group? How important will a written contract be? Are these people generally easy to do business with?

2. *Resistance.* This can be a painful, if predictable, part of any negotiation. Indeed, TOS is usually not devoted to showing you a good time. Try not to be upset by the resistance you encounter in your negotiations. In fact, if you encounter no resistance, this could be a signal that there is little genuine interest in meaningful negotiations. As long as there is resistance, there is interest, and knowing the source of the resistance allows you to work on overcoming TOS's objections. To break through this resistance, we must again tune in to the frequency that TOS can understand: WIIFT—what's in it for them. This means finding ways to meet the needs of TOS. Here are typical reasons why you may encounter resistance from TOS:

- *Logic:* "Your price is too high." "We need it sooner."
- *Emotion:* "I really don't like doing business with these people."
- *Change:* People are usually more comfortable with predictable, familiar situations than the changes you want them to adopt, such as a different product line or price.
- *Testing Your Limits:* "How far is this person willing to go?" "Is this really her bottom line?"
- *Organizational Constraint:* A budget, policy, or boss overrules TOS's decision.
- *Personal Rule:* "No concessions will be made at the first meeting."

3. *Reformulation of Strategies.* You develop negotiating strategies when you plan the negotiation. As you gain new data, it is important to reassess earlier strategies. What is the motivation of the parties to do this deal? What strategies worked? What didn't work? This is the time to put your creativity and ingenuity to work.

4. *Hard Bargaining and Decision Making.* Concentrate on the real needs of both sides, not just on the formal positions being taken at the negotiating table. Here you concentrate on the determination of real objectives. What are TOS's main objections? How can they be overcome? What are the key issues involved? Determining WIIFT becomes critical. Here is the time to invent options for mutual gain that will result in a win-win outcome.[2]

5. *Agreement.* Here you work out the details of the negotiation and ensure understanding. The negotiators ratify the agreement with their respective sides. In your case, ratification may be by your boss, attorneys, or financial management.

6. *Follow-Up.* This stage is often forgotten by negotiators. You work hard to sign the contract, then it's *adios, au revoir, syanora, arrivederci*—I'm outta here. But by effective follow-up, you set the stage for the next negotiation. Use this follow-up as an opportunity for relationship building. Be sure to remind TOS that they made a good decision in negotiating the agreed-upon deal.

Exhibit 1-1 outlines the stages of negotiation and the activities within each of these stages. Note that there are both task (or content) issues and relationship (or process) issues in each stage. The content issues have to do with logic or facts, while the process issues have more to do with emotions and feelings. For example, the task aspects of stage 1, *orientation and fact-finding,* are to introduce the parties to the negotiation and to define the negotiating issues. The relationship aspects of stage 1, however, include setting the climate for the negotiations and building rapport with TOS. It is important to address both task and relationship issues in order to have a successful negotiation.

Planning Your Negotiation

Intellectually, negotiators know that proper planning is important. Practically, however, many negotiators would rather take a beating than write a business plan of any kind. This resistance stems from three negative fantasy scripts: (1) "Someone might actually hold me responsible for this plan"; (2) "Once I write it down, I can't change it"; and (3) "I know what I want to say, but I just can't say it." None of these fantasies need be true. With regard to the third one, psychologists tell us that when we have this script, we in fact *don't* know what it is we are trying to say, and trying to write it down can make this painfully clear. Planning your negotiation means doing your homework. Without this vital preparation, you will concede the power that comes from making informed business decisions.

Planning your negotiation is a straightforward, four-step process that must be applied to both your side and TOS. For both sides, you must: (1) identify all the issues; (2) prioritize the issues; (3) establish a settlement range; and (4) develop strategies and tactics. Let's look at each of these steps in detail.

1. Be sure to *identify all the issues* you can think of for both your side and TOS. Brainstorm the issues with your colleagues—aiming for quantity, not quality—to compile your lists. Be postjudicial, not prejudicial, in this process, thereby allowing a free flow of ideas from you and your negotiating team or other relevant players. The idea is to get a long list of every issue that *could* arise during the negotiations, for both your side and TOS.

Exhibit 1-1. Issues in the stages of negotiations.

Task (or Content) Issues	*Relationship (or Process) Issues*

1. Orientation and fact-finding

- Introductions
- Opening statements
- Overview of the situation
- Defining issues
- Prioritizing

- Setting the climate
- Building rapport
- Defining roles
- Asking more questions

2. Resistance

- Position taking
- Logical points of view
- Debating/arguing
- Speech making

- WIIFM (what's in it for me)
- Protecting turf

3. Reformulation of strategies

- Introduction of new data
- Redefinition of issues
- Reassessment of original strategies

- Problem solving
- Trying another approach

4. Hard bargaining and decision making

- Determination of real objectives
- Probing alternatives
- Creating options for both parties
- Determining what it will it take to close this deal

- WIIFT (what's in it for them)
- Collaboration
- Mutual problem solving

5. Agreement

- Finding areas of agreement
- Ensuring understanding
- Drafting and reviewing the agreement
- Ratification

- Recapping
- Little ambiguity
- Getting a done deal

- Noting that it's good doing business together

6. Follow-Up

- Checking the implementation of the negotiated agreement

- Setting the stage for future negotiations
- Agreeing that you made a good deal

2. *Prioritize the issues* for both sides in the negotiation. This will, of course, be an estimate as to the priorities of TOS. Don't worry about perfection. The key point is to start thinking in terms of TOS's needs.

3. *Establish a settlement range*, defining the areas within which agreement is possible:

- *Above goal position.* The agreement that you want under ideal conditions, and to which some degree of logic can be attached.
- *What I'm really asking.* The agreement you really want.
- *Least acceptable agreement.* The agreement that can be accepted if the going gets really rough. Your bottom line.

The settlement range is discussed further in the next section.

4. *Develop strategies* that help you achieve your goals and that meet the needs of TOS. Strategies determine the overall approach your side plans to take. Strategies may include which of your priorities you choose to emphasize and the overall emphasis you give to each of the subjects being negotiated.

Tactics are sometimes viewed as having to do with being manipulative, playing games, or having a hidden agenda. That is not the intent here. Rather, tactics are meant to be the "how-to" part of achieving the overall negotiating strategies. Tactics may include whether to make the first offer, how much to offer, when to make concessions, and the speed at which you plan to make concessions. Many strategies and tactics are discussed in this book—not for you to be manipulative, but rather for you to avoid being a victim and to be aware of manipulations.

In order for a negotiating subterfuge or game to be successful, an unscrupulous TOS needs a victim—some poor slob who doesn't know any better. For example, TOS may ask for your airline ticket when you first get to Yokohama in order to help you with further flight arrangements. This may be an act of courtesy on the part of TOS, but it also provides TOS with valuable information on pacing the negotiations. TOS knows you will be there for eight days, piling up large expenses, and if TOS can be patient, you will probably be willing to agree to almost anything come the eighth day if little progress has been made. (Many U.S. negotiators have found that little content was discussed until the ride back to the airport.) In this case, be alert to TOS's game and avoid being a victim by trying not to be specific about return travel plans and being aware that TOS's patience is putting you at a disadvantage. At the same time, be careful not to read too many games into every TOS action: TOS may not always be trying to manipulate you, any more than you are always trying to manipulate them.

Let's return to the issue of the settlement range, since you will be operating within it throughout the negotiation.

The Zone of Doability Within the Settlement Range

Is the negotiation doable? That is, is a successful conclusion of the negotiation possible, given your settlement range and that estimated for TOS? The answer is yes, if the settlement ranges overlap. In terms of the planning steps just discussed, the *zone of doability* is the area of agreement that is possible when the least acceptable amount is less or equal for the seller compared to the buyer—in other words, if the seller will accept an amount less than or equal to that which the buyer is willing to pay. For example, if a seller will accept $20,000 for a concrete block machine, and the buyer is willing to pay $21,000, then the deal is doable. Exhibit 1-2 illustrates negotiations that are doable. In Situation A, there is a range of doability of $2,000 (between $38,000 and $40,000). In Situation B, this range is $22,000 (between $38,000 and $60,000). Anything beyond the least acceptable amounts is not doable because that would be a deal breaker. Situation B should be particularly doable because the buyer is really asking even more ($50,000) than the seller is really asking ($40,000) for this product or service.

Remember, establish your settlement range and then estimate the settlement range for TOS. Will you guess wrong sometimes? Of course. The key point here is not one of precision but of empathy and understanding. It is critical to get in the mind-set of thinking about the needs of TOS, of what they may be after. You can always readjust your estimate of TOS's settlement range with new information from the negotiation.

There are two important rules for effective use of the settlement range. First, prepare your settlement range before the negotiation. Second, have a logical reason for moving from your *above goal* position to your *really asking* position and so on through the range. Let's look at these two rules.

Exhibit 1-2. Doable negotiations.

Doable

	Situation A		Situation B	
	Yours (Seller)	Theirs (Buyer)	Yours (Seller)	Theirs (Buyer)
Above goal	$50K	$25K	$50K	$40K
Really asking	$40K	$35K	$40K	$50K
Least acceptable	$38K	$40K	$38K	$60K

☐ Zone of doability

Preparation of the Settlement Range Prior to the Negotiation

You must decide your settlement range before the negotiation takes place. This is important for one key reason: It prevents you from making concessions you would not have wanted to make had not the pressures of the moment been so great during the negotiation process. This is particularly true in international negotiations. For example, let's say you have been in Jakarta for three weeks and have a perpetual stomachache. The work is piling up on your desk back at the office, and your boss wants to know the hold-up on the deal. Meanwhile, you're a week late in negotiating another agreement, your travel expenses are beginning to look like the national debt, your friends at home have found a permanent replacement for you on your softball team, and your significant other hasn't exactly shown the greatest compassion in the world for your plight. It would be very tempting at this point to make a deal simply to get on with your organizational and personal life. Developing a settlement range in advance helps keep you focused when these type of pressures mount.

What It Takes to Close a Deal

There are both logical and emotional aspects to each stage of the negotiation. With these points in mind, there are three things you must do in order to close a deal successfully: (1) satisfy the logical needs of TOS; (2) satisfy the emotional needs of TOS; and (3) convince TOS that you are at your bottom line.

1. *Satisfy logical needs.* The logical, hard-data world is a very potent one, predictable and certain. Most U.S. negotiators tend to focus on logical issues, thinking, "If I can show TOS the force of my logic, then I will prevail in the negotiation by the very force of this reasoning." It is true that we must convince TOS that $2 + 2 = 4$ in order to conclude the negotiation. For example, TOS may like you personally, but unless the equipment you are selling does what you say it will do, you are unlikely to consummate the negotiation. However, while logic is a key part of the playing field, it is by no means the only part.

2. *Satisfy emotional needs.* Although we almost always pay attention to the logical needs of TOS, we often neglect the emotional needs. "If $2 + 2 = 4$, then what do emotions have to do with it?" you may ask. Everything. In fact, emotions are often more important in negotiations than logic. If TOS's emotional needs aren't met, this can block TOS's willingness to deal fully with the facts you have gathered. Think of your own reaction when negotiating with someone you really detest, compared with negotiating with someone you trust and respect. You may say, "It doesn't really matter, because business is business." But

if you're like most people, you will behave very differently in these two cases. You can bet that there is a much better chance of successfully concluding a deal in the second situation.

Consumers routinely defy logic in their purchase decisions. For example, in the purchase of luxury cars, the incremental cost of producing a Cadillac is not much more than that of producing General Motors' companion cars. So why do consumers love to pay big bucks for a Cadillac? Because of prestige and status. This is not very logical, but certain key emotional needs are being met.

3. *Convince TOS that you are at your bottom line.* The final step in successfully closing a deal is to convince TOS that this is as far as you are willing to go. This has a lot to do with the emotional climate and trust that you have developed with TOS. If you have established a positive climate of believability, then you will have a much better chance of convincing TOS that this is as far as you can or will go with your offer.

Which of these three actions are the most important to concluding a negotiation? The answer lies in a remark made by Andrew Carnegie: "Which is the most important leg of a three-legged stool?" They are all important: Each of the three factors is critical in closing a deal.

Remember, though, that it is not always necessary to close a deal and reach agreement with TOS. If you have to exceed your least acceptable position in order to conclude the negotiation, you may decide it is better not to make the deal. Ask these questions often: "Is this deal a must?" and, "What is the cost of walking out?" Keep in mind that sometimes the best deal is no deal.

In this chapter, we have examined key elements of the negotiating process that can be applied to negotiations: (1) the win-win, interest-based approach; (2) knowing the stages of negotiation; (3) planning your negotiation; and (4) closing the deal. Though we will explore the differences among cultures throughout the balance of this book, these fundamentals of negotiating apply anywhere in the world. The specific styles and methods of the negotiators involved differ significantly, however, from culture to culture.

Notes

1. Roger Fisher and William Ury, *Getting to Yes: Negotiating Agreement Without Giving In* (New York: Penguin, 1983), pp. 40–55.

2. Ibid, pp. 56–80.

How Global Negotiations Work

There are forces that tend to minimize differences among international business negotiators. These forces include a common purpose (such as profit) and, gradually, common references (as both parties learn to work with each other). Generally, however, there are wide differences between what constitutes effective negotiating strategies in the United States versus other cultures.

It is difficult enough to be persuasive and get what we want when we know the players, understand the game, and have a home-field advantage. But when we lose the familiar guideposts of how to deal with others and of how to do business, we experience not only culture shock, but—from a negotiating viewpoint—a "we-got-clobbered" shock. In fact, we may bleed and not even know it.

Chapter 2, "What Makes Global Negotiations Different?" examines the key factors that make international negotiations different from domestic negotiations. Specifically, cultural differences and their effects on international negotiations are applied to a negotiating model used for the individual countries examined. Chapter 3, "Ten Powerful Strategies for Negotiating Around the World," explores the ten specific negotiating strategies that work anywhere in the world.

There are unique problems associated with international negotiating. In Chapter 4, "The Four Most Difficult Challenges Faced by International Negotiators (and How to Deal with Them)," we identify these problems and suggest specific actions for their resolution.

What Makes Global Negotiations Different?

"Human beings draw close to one another by their common nature, but habits and customs keep them apart."

—Confucian saying

- Cultural Factors That Affect Global Business Negotiations
- How Negotiations Differ from Region to Region
- Gender Issues in Global Business Negotiations

There are numerous "macrofactors" that influence your international business negotiations, such as the politics and economic climate of the region involved. There are also organizational aspects that impact TOS (The Other Side), such as upsizings or downsizings or the organizational clout of your negotiating counterpart. Attention to these factors helps you assess the overall business and organizational climate in which the negotiation is taking place. More important than any other key influences, however, are cultural factors. In this chapter we first examine the cultural factors that affect international negotiations and then explore more specifically how pace, style, strategies, and other factors of the international negotiation process can differ from culture to culture. We also explore the part played by gender issues in international negotiating.

Cultural Factors That Affect Global Business Negotiations

There are four cultural factors that most affect negotiations among cultures: (1) use of time; (2) individualism versus collectivism; (3) role orderliness and

conformity; and (4) patterns of communication. Let's examine each of these factors and how they affect negotiations.

Use of Time

Cultures differ in their use of time. The Americans, Swiss, Germans, and Australians are usually fast-paced and exact in their approach to time. Their professional and personal lives tend to be closely calibrated. A negotiating session that is scheduled for 9:30 a.m. on Tuesday is expected to start at 9:30 a.m. on Tuesday.

U.S. negotiators, especially, are noted for time-consciousness. ("Will we be able to complete the project by March 1? Yes, but would it help you make a decision in our favor if we were to guarantee completion by February 1?") Much of this time emphasis is related to the technological roots of Western society. The demands of machinery, the interrelationships of information software and hardware, and other issues all make time a critical factor. Can you imagine the New York Stock Exchange opening every business day "sometime between 9:00 and 10:00 a.m."? Or the second shift of a factory starting at "three-ish"?

To those in many other cultures, Americans, particularly, seem obsessed with time—prisoners of clocks and time constraints. In Latin America, starting a negotiating session a half hour after the appointed time may be considered normal, and even expected. A manager from a U.S.–based organization found this to be the case when negotiating a contract to buy television time. She notes, "I had an appointment with the minister of communications in Argentina for an interview. Because of his position, we were told that we'd better be there a little earlier. We wanted to make sure we were not putting ourselves in a position of wasting his time. Nevertheless, we waited for two hours and he never showed up." A Middle East project delayed for two months may be more usual than unusual. The thinking may be, "Our country has done without this new equipment for many centuries, and it will be okay if we don't have it for another two months."

Individualism vs. Collectivism

Individualism refers to the "I" consciousness found in some cultures, as contrasted with the "we" (or group) consciousness found in others. A classic study done by Dutch researcher Geert Hofstede found a wide difference among countries. With 100 the highest on the scale, U.S. managers score 91, making them the most individualistic of all surveyed countries. This includes other Western countries such as Australia (90), Great Britain (89), and Canada (77). Most Pacific Rim cultures score much lower on the scale, indicating the collective,

group consciousness: Japan (46), Hong Kong (25), Singapore (20), and Taiwan (17). This is also true to a lesser extent in Latin American countries, where scores range from 46 (Argentina) to 16 (Venezuela).[1]

Americans want an individual winner to emerge. This can be seen in the way Americans structure the prize system of athletic contests. If, for example, the first prize in a golf or tennis tournament this weekend is $150,000, how much is the second prize? Well, the right answer isn't $149,900. The second prize is usually half the first prize—about $75,000.

The emphasis on the group helps explain why the Japanese are so slow at making negotiating decisions. It takes time to ensure that there is buy-in from all members of the team. The group emphasis also influences whom you are trying to convince at the negotiating table. North American negotiators bargaining with other North Americans usually look for the top person who represents TOS. They don't want to waste precious time on anyone who isn't a key decision maker. In we-oriented cultures, however, it is the group, not an individual, that you must convince. This is why you might feel like you have become best friends with sushi before you ever meet the senior Japanese negotiator, let alone convince him of your point of view. This group emphasis also explains why the Japanese pack the negotiating table with fourteen people while you have only three—and that includes your driver.

Role Orderliness and Conformity

Some cultures, such as those in the Pacific Rim, are characterized by a high need for role orderliness and conformity. Often, more emphasis is put on the form or structure of behavior than on content. *How* things are done is of paramount importance. Other cultures, typified by the United States, have a low need in this regard and are much more at ease with ambiguity.

This factor helps explain why the Japanese emphasize the relationship with one's counterpart. Getting to know the other person helps to bring orderliness and predictability to the negotiating process. On the one hand, the Japanese pay great attention to ritual, such as presenting business cards. Little is left to guesswork. On the other hand, negotiators from the United States, Canada, Germany, and Switzerland tend to put more emphasis on the content of the negotiations than on the procedures for achieving the end results. This is evident in the legal and administrative aspects of the negotiation process, where detailed contracts to legitimize the content are common. North American negotiators generally have a much more informal negotiating style than those from other nations, with relatively little rigid status distinction when dealing with others. You, for example, are probably comfortable using first names when addressing business associates. And if you are like most American negotiators, you

may find it difficult to adapt to the flowery language, complex methods of address, and ritualistic manners that reflect the hierarchical social structure in many other cultures.[2]

Patterns of Communication

In one way, the communications process is very simple. A sender is trying to get a message through to a receiver. The model shown in Exhibit 2-1 represents this basic concept. The responsibility of the sender is to send a clear message. The responsibility of the receiver is to listen. Notice that this simple process becomes more complicated as the sender encodes the message sent, and the receiver decodes the message received. For example, as the seller of a new machine, you might say to TOS: "I'd like to review with you the detailed calibrations of our new X-15 model. You'll be pleased to know that output has been increased by 16.23 percent, and conformance to standards is now 99.74 percent at close-tolerance machining. Here's a schematic of the X-15." The message you might have encoded in this example is the importance your company attaches to productivity and quality. But no matter how noble your intentions, if the TOS receiver is from Brazil or Egypt, such emphasis on logic and detail is likely to be decoded as somewhat inappropriate. (Emphasis on concepts, grace, and beauty would have been a better starting point in these cultures.)

Such different perceptions between the sender and the receiver result in communications "noise." Sometimes this noise is so great that little, if any, of the communications gets through. Such noise is common in international negotiating and requires much awareness and effort on the parts of both the sender and the receiver to ensure clear communication. This noise can come from both verbal and nonverbal communication. Let's first consider verbal communication.

Verbal Communication: "Would Somebody Please Talk to Me in Terms That I Can Understand?"

Communication patterns can be understood in terms of *high-context* or *low-context* cultures. Some countries, such as those in the Pacific Rim, are consid-

Exhibit 2-1. Sending a message to a receiver.

ered high-context cultures, where the meaning of the message is embedded in the context of the communication. Individuals from these cultures tend to put more responsibility on the receiver than on the sender. It is the receiver's responsibility to determine the full intent of the message from the context in which the message was sent. In other words, the sender provides most of the pieces of the puzzle, but it is the responsibility of the receiver to provide the missing links.[3]

Other countries, such as the United States, Canada, and most of Western Europe, are considered to be low-context cultures. That is, the meaning of the message is in what is explicitly stated, not the context of what is stated. In the United States, there is generally an equal responsibility for both the sender and the receiver. The sender is to speak in a way that can be understood, and the receiver is to listen.

These differences in communication patterns influence the international negotiation process. U.S. negotiators, in particular, prize direct and open communication. ("Just lay it on the line." "Let's net it out." "What's the bottom line?") Individuals from high-context cultures may perceive this approach to be insensitive and aggressive. Tom Wilson, a British management consultant, notes, "American negotiators sometimes appear to delight in their bluntness—which doesn't work very well with the British." Americans, by contrast, may consider the indirect communication of those from high-context societies difficult to follow and even deceptive, thinking, "This person must be shifty since he won't give me a yes or no answer."

An important part of verbal communication is literally speaking the same language. You might wonder if you really have to learn a foreign language to talk to these people. The short answer to this question is, of course, *yes*. Communication is enhanced when both parties are working to share a common language. The degree to which this is necessary, however, depends on the individuals with whom you are negotiating, their language, their culture, and the amount of business you are doing with them. On the one hand, a one-week trip to Hong Kong to finalize a deal at Citibank would not merit a great effort on your part to learn Chinese. It would be impractical and would not be expected by TOS. On the other hand, protracted joint venture negotiations in Paris would probably justify your learning French. The French expect it, they're unlikely to go out of their way to speak English, it would help build amicable relationships, and it would certainly help you understand the content and context of discussions. Keep in mind that in many countries the chief spokesperson for TOS may in fact speak excellent English, but others on the negotiating team may not.

Nonverbal Communication: The Unspoken Language

Nonverbal communication, or body language, is important for two reasons: (1) to help determine the meaning of what TOS is saying; and (2) to help you get your own message across. Body language varies widely among cultures. Facial behaviors, hand gestures, eye contact, touching, and other nonverbals are culturally driven. Greetings and handshakes come in different forms. For example, U.S., German, and Russian negotiators have very firm handshakes compared with most others. This can cause some practical perceptual problems: TOS may view Americans as too abrupt and, literally and figuratively, heavy-handed, while Americans may view those with less firm handshakes as unassertive.

This perception has caused difficulty for many American negotiators who later learn that their foreign counterparts are indeed quite assertive, and maybe even aggressive when it comes to negotiating an agreement. "I thought the Chinese might be somewhat of a piece of cake because their handshakes seemed so wimpy," recalls a California importer of his first trip to Beijing. "I soon found out that they were quietly effective, and the weak handshakes had nothing to do with the firmness of their positions."

North Americans generally like a lot of physical space in their organizational lives. Many North American clichés point to this: "Give me some space," "Get out of my face," "Back off." This translates into a typical distance of about three feet when addressing others in business situations. Very little touching takes place. When it does occur, it is usually somewhat conspicuous and a source of sensitivity. Handshakes last only a second or so. If two passengers remain after a crowded elevator has emptied, they immediately take dancelike steps to their respective corners. In many cultures, the social and business distance is much closer than it is in the United States. It is customary in parts of Latin America and the Middle East for business associates to embrace each other, to kiss each other lightly on the cheek, and to put only one foot or so between them in a business discussion. Indeed, a distance of about a foot between business associates is customary in many cultures.

Nonverbal communication is critical in decoding rites, gestures, forms of politeness, the concept of "face," silence, and pauses. Decoding, like all ways of finding the real meaning, often proves difficult because it is done through our filters of domestic norms and habits. What constitutes extreme versus appropriate nonverbal behavior is a matter of cultural interpretation. For example, the Latins touch more than Americans or Canadians, who, in turn, touch more than the Swedes or British. In Muslim countries the left hand is not used in Muslim cultures to touch others, point, or pass objects. The left hand is usually

used for hygiene purposes. The language of gestures varies widely, too. Although Americans, Canadians, and most Europeans understand the "thumbs up" gesture to mean "all right," Greeks and Southern Italians decode this gesture in a way North Americans would normally reserve for the middle finger.

Observe one caution with nonverbal communication: Look for *clusters of behavior* rather than only one action. If, for example, you ask TOS, "Is this your best price?" and TOS folds his arms, this doesn't necessarily mean he's being defensive or lying. Maybe the room is cold, or he simply is comfortable sitting that way. If, however, he suddenly folds his arms, moves in his seat, clears his throat, and starts blinking rapidly, then probe this situation further.

International negotiators must continually ask what kind of verbal and nonverbal images their foreign counterparts grasp, and what kind of words and actions convey these images. *"Holy cow!"* might be an appropriate exclamation in Chicago, but not in India, where a literal translation would be likely—and, of course, offensive—in a culture where cows are sacred to many. A hearty pat on the back to Bubba in Houston might indicate friendship, but it would be perceived as overbearing pushiness to Suresh in New Delhi.

How Negotiations Differ from Region to Region

We have just examined four factors that differ among cultures. These cultural differences are manifested in many different ways—how family members and friends relate to each other, for example, or how different societies respond to mavericks and troublemakers. As illustrated in Exhibit 2-2, these cultural factors also influence the six specific factors of the international negotiating proc-

Exhibit 2-2. Cultural factors and the international negotiating process.

ess: (1) pace of the negotiations; (2) negotiating strategies; (3) emphasis on personal relationships; (4) emotional aspects; (5) decision making; and (6) contractual and administrative factors.

Let's now review each of these six negotiation factors. They lay the foundation for how you will specifically approach negotiations in various parts of the world.

Pace

The negotiating process is shorter in North America than in most other cultures. North American negotiators typically invest little time in orientation and fact-finding, as compared with their international counterparts. North American negotiators want to get down to business, while their international counterparts may take additional time to build relationships or to reduce the ambiguity associated with this stranger (i.e., you, the North American negotiator). North American negotiators tend to spend more of their time than TOS in the resistance stage: debating, posturing, and taking positions. Reformulation of strategies, hard bargaining and decision making, and agreement are often truncated by North American negotiators as a result of factors such as organizational time pressures and a desire to "get on with it." Agreement can languish, particularly in group-oriented cultures where the decision making process is often slower than in North America. Follow-up is not considered an integral part of the bargaining process, if at all, by many U.S. negotiators. This is more likely to be the case with TOS, particularly where strong personal and supplier relationships have been established.

Negotiating Strategies

The negotiating strategies you employ—which have to do with your overall approach to the negotiation and include such issues as opening offers, the formality of your approach, how you deal with differences, and concession making—also differ from region to region.

The opening offer tends to be very close to the final settlement in some countries, such as Australia and Sweden, where haggling back and forth is not part of everyday business. Your opening offer in Sydney need not normally be as high (as a seller) or low (as a buyer) as in some other locations. In other countries, such as Russia, Egypt, and China, the opening offer tends to be far away from the final settlement. It would be wise to leave yourself a lot of room to negotiate in Cairo, where haggling is a way of life.

Another difference in strategy lies with the degree of formality in your negotiating approach. Specific, well-organized, data-oriented presentations are ex-

pected in Germany, the United Kingdom, Switzerland, and Japan. It would probably be a good idea to use color slides rather than transparencies in a formal presentation in these countries. An emphasis on broad concepts would be much more effective in other countries, such as those in Latin America or the Middle East.

Cultures also vary in the way they deal with differences. On one end of the spectrum is the expressive, demonstrative approach that one encounters in the Middle East. Beryl York, a New York–based management consultant who deals regularly with Egyptian companies, notes, "A disagreement with Middle Easterners can be quite an event. The individual might almost scream, wave his arms, sigh loudly in amazement at your intransigence—you name it. This is really nothing to take personally, however. Overstatement and emotion are their normal forms of expression when they want to make a point." By contrast, in other cultures one finds an understated, unexpressive approach to dealing with differences. Just getting TOS to tell you no directly would take a Herculean effort in Pacific Rim cultures, where surface harmony is of paramount importance. In this latter case, don't let the placid approach to dealing with differences fool you: TOS may be every bit as tough or resilient as another negotiator with a more direct style.

Meeting the needs of one's counterpart is critical to any successful negotiation, yet not all domestic or international negotiators look for win-win solutions to the negotiation. Some negotiators use negotiating games, or unfair tactics, where a hidden agenda or subterfuge is at work in order to "win" at your expense. Dealing with negotiating games is more complex internationally than it is domestically. The same behavior can have varied meanings in different cultures. In the case of dubious intentions already mentioned, *how* one goes about asking for details could be critical. In New York, you might say, "Jason, let's review your numbers again. I'm having trouble making them add up to mine." Such directness would almost surely create new obstacles in Osaka or Jakarta, where "loss of face" would be a big issue.

Effective international negotiators must also be careful not to misread behavior from TOS. In Rio de Janeiro, TOS may be forthcoming with few details as to their proposed financial responsibility in a joint venture. This might be perceived as a dubious intention by a Vancouver-based negotiator, who wonders, "Why are these people so secretive? What are they trying to hide?" To the Brazilian negotiators, a detailed level of financial involvement might seem less important than other issues. No attempt at a cover-up is intended. Understanding the different patterns of communication is important in determining which behav-

iors are intended games and which are unintended expressions of a culture's normal behavior patterns.

There are four ways for you to counteract negotiating games or unfair tactics:

1. Don't use them yourself.
2. Recognize them when TOS uses them, explicitly point them out, and negotiate about their use (i.e., establish the "rules of the game").
3. Know the cost of walking out if the other party refuses to negotiate fairly.
4. Recognize that tactics that may appear fair to you may be unacceptable to people from another culture.[4]

> *"A tactic perceived is no longer a tactic."*
> —HERB COHEN, AUTHOR OF *YOU CAN NEGOTIATE ANYTHING*

Emphasis on Personal Relationships

A key aspect of building any relationship is trust, and international negotiating is no exception. In fact, in order to be a masterful negotiator, you must build trust with TOS.

This is not an easy task. The lack of trust and credibility is greater in international business negotiations, largely because of stereotypes, biases, and uncertainty about TOS. Think of how you would feel in this situation. You've been in Taipei for negotiations on your new joint venture. Your first meeting has been in progress for two hours and seems to be proceeding quite well—if slowly—in English. Your Taiwanese counterparts have been friendly, but pretty much expressionless. Then suddenly, the five members of the Taiwanese bargaining team begin talking to each other in animated Chinese, with jovial, approving expressions on their faces. This goes on for five minutes. You might begin thinking, "What are they talking about? What's the big secret? I don't want to be paranoid, but I wonder if I'm about to get hosed and don't even know it." This might be a normal reaction, yet expressing these feelings to TOS would almost surely damage the relationship. The Taiwanese team may be merely engaging in a dialogue among themselves to understand your position better. Patience on your part is probably justified.

Building a good relationship is critical even if you are dealing with negotiators from cultures that are relatively standoffish, such as those from Switzerland, Germany, or Great Britain. The best way to build a relationship with a German negotiator is to respect the emotional distance and get down to business before too long. As for Great Britain, a British management consultant

notes, "My idea of a good negotiating relationship is one where the other party is friendly, doesn't get extremely personal, and knows his business." With these people, you are still building relationships—but relationships that are geared to their cultures.

Emotional Aspects

Emotional aspects deal with sensitivity, the degree of emotions, and loyalty. Sensitivity, too, is culturally defined. In the United States, it is normally associated with the female gender. Empathy for others' feelings, for example, is more often attributed to women, while displays of emotion such as crying are often considered unmanly. In Latin America, such behavior is viewed as more appropriate for men than it is in the United States. In other cultures, such as the Swiss and German, emotions are more subdued than among American males.

Loyalty differs among cultures according to allegiance to organizations as a whole and to whom that allegiance is given within the organization. The loyalty factor influences where you as a negotiator want to base your appeals: to the individual or to the whole company group. American negotiators complain that little loyalty exists in the United States from either organizations or their employees. Loyalty is often to oneself first, then to the organization. In other cultures, such as in Japan, Brazil, and Mexico, there is strong loyalty to organizations. This organizational loyalty may be directed to owners (such as in Brazil) or to the group as a whole (as in Japan). Bob Coshland, an international manager for a California company that sells high-performance lubricants, sees this concept at work in Pacific Rim negotiations: "When I'm in South Korea, I try to remember to emphasize how the sale will be really good for Hyundai as a whole. They are proud of their company, and this means a lot to them. Try this approach in Boston or Minneapolis and I don't think you'd get very far."

Decision Making

The way negotiators make decisions also differs from culture to culture. As a result, before you begin a negotiation it is important for you to determine the way your negotiating counterpart makes decisions. North Americans evaluate decisions in terms of their overall objective (good of the group versus the individual) and overall method (spontaneous versus planned). In Western European countries such as Germany and Switzerland, for example, decision making is planned and organized. No decision is made in Germany without a thorough analysis of all of the facts. In Eastern Europe, decisions are made in a somewhat more spontaneous manner, and in Latin America, decisions are often made impulsively.

We also evaluate decisions based on the emphasis on the group or team. In

a Latin American country such as Argentina, where there is a low emphasis on the team, you need to find a contact who will introduce you to the top person in the organization with which you are negotiating. Negotiating with middle managers is a waste of time since all decisions are made from the top. In Asia, however, there is a strong emphasis on the group or team, which slows down negotiations considerably. Be prepared to take your time in Japan, for example, as the group decision-making system, or *ringi*, will involve all the levels of the organization.

We also evaluate decision making in different cultures based on the emphasis on face saving, and the emphasis of special interest groups that influence decisions. In Japan, avoid abrupt statements or questions that might embarrass your counterpart. They do not want to embarrass you either, which leads them to avoid giving you a direct no. The French, by contrast, will be direct and open, sometimes being argumentative for the sake of a good discussion.

The influence of special interest groups will also differ from region to region. In Korea or Japan, special interest groups can openly influence key decisions; in the United States or Canada, there is very little involvement of special interest groups.

There are two main intercultural approaches to decision making, which are described by Nancy J. Adler in *International Dimensions of Organizational Behavior* (Fourth Edition).[5] Let's begin with the one typified by North American negotiators. First, if a problem arises in the negotiation, this is usually perceived as a situation where something should probably be changed. In fact, change is accepted as the norm. For instance, a typical approach would be to modify a contract if it is not meeting the needs of one or both of the two parties. Second, one gathers facts to help determine what decision should be made to resolve the problem. Third, alternatives are then determined based on these facts and are future-oriented. For example, let's say there is a delivery problem with one's supplier. Facts would be gathered based on the nature and extent of the problem, and then alternatives would be determined to make a logical decision that could be used in the future. Fourth, decisions are usually made by individuals rather than by the group. For instance, while a U.S. decision maker may consult with her team, group consensus is not required. As a result, these decisions are typically made quickly. The decision must then face the decision rule "Is it true or false?" based on objective facts. Finally, once the decision is made, the implementation of the decision is likely to be somewhat slow. This is often because getting "buy-in" from other groups in the organization is now key. Let's say that the sales team agrees to a particular price for a product or service in a negotiation with TOS and a contract is signed. Everybody is happy! Or so it would seem.

More likely, a whole new set of negotiations will be generated. For example, the sales team may meet resistance from those responsible for delivery of the product. They may also have to face the financial people or the legal staff or those from other parts of the organization.

Now let's review the second approach Adler describes, typified by Indonesian and Malaysian negotiators. First, in this approach, a problem is more often seen as something that should be accepted and not changed. Second, in searching for information, ideas and possibilities are explored, rather than the accumulation of facts. Third, alternatives are then established with a focus that includes past, present, and future options. Fourth, there is an emphasis on group decisions rather than individual decisions. The result is that decisions are often made slowly compared to the first approach. The main guideline for the decision is whether it is good or bad. Last, implementation of the decisions that were made is usually fast even though it involves participation of all levels. This is because many of the time-consuming dynamics of making the decision have already been addressed during step four. It is now the responsibility of the group rather than one person to implement the decision.

Knowing how your counterpart makes decisions is vital to help gauge the approach you should take to persuade TOS. On the one hand, cornering an individual Indonesian negotiator to convince him to make a quick decision by showing him detailed data would almost surely lead to disarray in the negotiation. A German or Swiss negotiator, on the other hand, might thank you for the interest you have shown in carefully detailing your data and the attention you are giving to the time constraints involved.

Special interest groups play a routine part in decision making in many cultures. In Latin America, for example, the influence from special interest groups such as government agencies is expected and condoned. Michael Kane, a New Orleans–based management consultant who works extensively in Latin America, puts it this way: "There is a system of reciprocity at work in much of Latin America. It is seen as proper and ethical for government parties to exercise influence on behalf of their party members. Special access to government ministries, for example, is likely only for a businessperson who is aligned with the party in power." Ted Cline, an engineering and construction executive who deals regularly with Saudi Arabian firms, sees a similar situation there: "Unless you do your homework, negotiations can be quite complicated because you're not always sure whom you're dealing with. Somebody's brother-in-law at one of the government ministries can really help or hurt a deal. Be aware that you are dealing with factions that may help or hurt your cause."

A Discussion of Japanese Decision Making

Japanese manager: Why do Americans make decisions so quickly? I cannot. Proper decisions take time. I want to know everything my boss knows about a negotiation or project, and I want my boss to know everything I know.
Acuff: What about people on your work team?
Japanese manager: I want everybody to be informed.
Acuff: Is this process slow?
Japanese manager: Oh yes. Very slow, but very effective. Everybody knows what to do.

Source: Discussion between the author and a Japanese manager on a two and one-half year assignment to the United States

Contractual and Administrative Factors

Finally, negotiations differ from region to region according to contractual and administrative factors. These differences express themselves in the need for an agent, degree of contract specificity, degree of bureaucracy, and need for an agenda at meetings.

The need for agents or local representatives differs from country to country. Agents in Japan can be helpful in such areas as making introductions to key people, providing translations, and resolving sensitive areas of the negotiation.[6] Some areas, such as Canada or the United Kingdom, where information on local business is more readily available, justify only a more limited role of an agent. Here are ten specific ways you may want to use an agent or local representative:

1. To introduce you to key people

2. For information on local negotiation practices

3. To translate the dialogue during the negotiation

4. As a go-between during sensitive areas of the negotiation

5. For special knowledge about products or services in the host country

6. To assist in developing market strategies

7. For government, customer, and public relations

8. To resolve problems with import regulations or permits

9. To assist in arranging financing

10. For collections

A technical dimension of international business negotiations lies with contractual considerations. There are significant differences in various families of

law: Roman-based law, case-based law, socialist law, and Islamic law. You needn't be an expert in all these different legal approaches. It is important, however, that you are aware that key differences do exist between U.S. case-based law and other legal systems. Regardless of the legal approach involved, international agreements are more likely to be committed to paper than are domestic agreements. This is due to differences in expectations and language—even after an agreement has been reached—and to a low degree of trust between the parties. Furthermore, you will be required to write contracts in the local languages of countries such as Germany, Belgium, Spain, India, and Pakistan.[7]

Misters Lo and Mo

Many feel that having a contract with the Chinese is a joke because, when you get right down to it, the Chinese do not view the contract as binding. I have even heard them say, "So what are you going to do, sue the Chinese government?" Even if a contract were negotiated in good faith with Mr. Lo, when Mr. Mo comes in to replace Mr. Lo, he might say, "Well, you signed the contract with Mr. Lo, not me. So to me this contract is void." I have seen this even if the contract was supposed to be binding for another five years.

SOURCE: Manager of contracts administration for a global payment services franchise

Your ability to get information is also influenced by the country involved. North American managers are accustomed to getting the information they need when they need it. Not so in many other cultures. If you are in countries such as Thailand, Nigeria, Poland, or Indonesia, you must do some real scrambling to get profile information on customers, competitors, the economy, suppliers, distributors, agents, import/export laws, and other routine data that North American negotiators take for granted.

The amount of bureaucracy in organizations also differs considerably from country to country. American managers sometimes complain about the red tape in their organizations. But whatever obstacles may be encountered in North America are relatively manageable compared with countries such as India or Russia, where even the most basic decisions can get bogged down for months in paperwork and confusing lines of authority. An American project manager notes her frustration related to an India-based project: "Prior to my trip I had requested a few critical items to follow through with a major contract. My Indian contact talked big about how well connected he was and how obtaining various governmental permits would be no problem. However, when I got to India, no permits were obtained. Of course, there were plenty of excuses. This is very typical when doing business in India."

Agendas are considered good business in the United States—a courtesy that provides participants a preview of key topics and focus for the discussion. In some countries, such as Mexico, Venezuela, and Saudi Arabia, an agenda is viewed as overly structured and restrictive.

Exhibit 2-3 summarizes the aspects of international negotiating that we have just discussed.

Gender Issues in Global Business Negotiations

Workplace gender issues are increasingly sensitive in North America and are even more complicated in other parts of the world. There are many countries where customs, attitudes, and religion are hostile to women in business, and there is no question that international business negotiations are still dominated by men. Resistance to international businesswomen comes from American firms as well as from foreign counterparts.

The laws of a country are not always clear indications of how women are treated in actual practice. In Russia, for example, businesswomen are legally

Exhibit 2-3. A summary of factors affecting international business.

1. Pace of Negotiations
2. Negotiating Strategies
 - Opening offers vis-à-vis final settlement
 - Presentation of issues (e.g., one at a time versus in a group)
 - Presentations (e.g., formality, level of detail)
 - Dealing with differences (e.g., argumentative, conciliatory)
 - Concession behavior
3. Emphasis on Personal Relationships
4. Emotional Aspects
 - Sensitivity
 - Degree of emotions
 - Loyalty (e.g., degree and to whom)
5. Decision Making
 - Overall method (e.g., amount of authority)
 - Areas of emphasis (e.g., logic, concepts)
 - Emphasis on group/team
 - Emphasis on face-saving
 - Influence of special interests on decision makers
6. Contractual and Administrative Factors
 - Need for an agent
 - Degree of contract specificity
 - Degree of paperwork/bureaucracy
 - Need for an agenda

equal to men, but there is less parity among the genders in decision-making positions. In Sweden, by contrast, where women make up almost half the work-force (48 percent), there is equal rights legislation and men share home and work responsibilities—a situation that is reflected in the business world. A man-ager for the Swedish company Ewos Aquaculture illustrates this point: "Remem-ber that your male counterpart might have to get the children from the day care center at 5:00 p.m. If the meeting is supposed to end promptly at 4:30 p.m., this could be the reason." Generally, the genders are less equal in less developed countries.

Although it is important to consider the sexist attitudes of the host country, remember that what may be an unacceptable business role for local women in the host country may differ for women negotiators from one's own country. An American businesswoman is likely to be seen first as a "foreign executive" and as an "American," and then as a "woman," who may have a restricted role in the local society. In Spain, Venezuela, India, and Japan, for example, the glass ceiling for businesswomen is quite low: Few women are able to penetrate key professional or managerial jobs. An American woman can be an effective negoti-ator in these countries, although the challenges may be formidable. Some women have adopted the slogan "Think like a man, act like a lady, and work like a dog" as their guiding principle for international business conduct.

Here are practical tips for international businesswomen offered by Marlene L. Rossman, an international marketing consultant:

- Especially in developing countries, the fact that you look different from the locals helps your clients to see you as an executive rather than a woman.

- If you are negotiating in a country where women are quite repressed, have a local male who is trusted and respected introduce you to the other party: "This is Linda Smith, our vice-president of finance. She will be handling the financing for our joint venture."

- If such a local person isn't available, ask a senior person from your home office to introduce you by telephone or in a letter: "Please give Joyce Trautman your usual cooperation. She will be responsible for Acme's in-terest in her discussions with you."

- When you enter a meeting room, stand tall even if you're only five feet high. Your height is unimportant; it's your posture that gives clues about your expertise and your general feeling about yourself.

Rossman also suggests that a woman take advantage of the fact that, as a professional businesswoman, you are an unknown quantity in many countries.

She relates the story of a client in Milan, Italy, who "lit up like a Christmas tree when he saw that M. Rossman was a woman who spoke some Italian. He said he was expecting a tall man in a baggy suit and heavy oxfords who couldn't pronounce his name, wore a college ring, and shook his hand so hard that the crest of the ring imprinted on his finger."[8]

Many international businesswomen have found that they were able to overcome initial barriers by ably demonstrating their expertise. Susan Cherion, a manager who negotiates communications contracts in many parts of the world, relates her experience in Argentina: "I have found that Argentine businessmen prefer to do business with other men, but once they realize that I am competent and I have some authority to make decisions, we are able to establish excellent working relationships."

Global business negotiations are indeed different from domestic negotiations. For all the many challenges, however, there are also opportunities for you to achieve your goals when you follow some key guidelines. In Chapter 3, we will review more skills that will make you a masterful negotiator.

Notes

1. S. G. Redding, "Results-Orientation and the Orient: Individualism as a Cultural Determinant of Western Managerial Techniques," *International HRD Annual* 1 (February 1985): 45–60.

2. William B. Gudykunst and Young Yun Kim, *Communicating with Strangers: An Approach to Intercultural Communication* (New York: Random House, 1984), p. 131.

3. Ibid, pp. 12–13.

4. Nancy J. Adler, *International Dimensions of Organizational Behavior*, 4th ed. (Cincinnati: South-Western, 2002), p. 241.

5. Nancy J. Adler, *International Dimensions of Organizational Behavior*, 4th ed. (Cincinnati: South-Western, 2002), p. 184.

6. Jeffrey Z. Rubin, "The Actors in Negotiation," in Victor A. Kremenyck, ed., *International Negotiation* (San Francisco: Jossey-Bass, 1991), pp. 93–94.

7. Lennie Copeland and Lewis Griggs, *Going International* (New York: Random House, 1985), p. 100.

8. Based on discussions with Marlene L. Rossman. See also Marlene L. Rossman, *International Business of the '90s: A Guide to Success in the Global Market* (New York: Praeger, 1990), pp. 133–141.

・ CHAPTER 3 ・

Ten Powerful Strategies for Negotiating Around the World

"If I listen, I have the advantage: if I speak, others have it."
—From the Arabic

- Strategy 1: Plan Your Negotiation
- Strategy 2: Adopt a Win-Win, Interest-Based Approach
- Strategy 3: Maintain High Aspirations
- Strategy 4: Use Language That Is Simple and Accessible
- Strategy 5: Ask Lots of Questions, Then Listen with Your Eyes and Ears
- Strategy 6: Build Solid Relationships
- Strategy 7: Maintain Personal Integrity
- Strategy 8: Conserve Concessions
- Strategy 9: Make Patience an Obsession
- Strategy 10: Be Culturally Literate and Adapt Negotiating Strategies to the Host Country Environment

There are many negotiating strategies that tend to work very well in one culture but are ineffective in other cultures. A case in point is the Miami-based project manager who put together a very detailed, thorough, research-oriented proposal and presentation for his Brazilian client. "I felt good that we had done our homework," he later noted. "I was very disappointed, however, to find that the Brazilian representatives were flatly uninterested in the details I was prepared to explain. A similar approach worked extremely well in Germany only four months earlier."

39

In spite of the many different negotiating approaches required among cultures, ten strategies tend to be effective anywhere in the world. While there may be local variations in how these strategies are applied, their basic premises remain viable. The ten strategies that tend to be effective in negotiations throughout the world are as follows:

1. Plan your negotiation.

2. Adopt a win-win, interest-based approach.

3. Maintain high aspirations.

4. Use language that is simple and accessible.

5. Ask lots of questions, then listen with your eyes and ears.

6. Build solid relationships.

7. Maintain personal integrity.

8. Conserve concessions.

9. Make patience an obsession.

10. Be culturally literate and adapt negotiating strategies to the host country environment.

Strategy 1: Plan Your Negotiation

Everybody wants to get a good deal, to get a sizable share of the pie, and to feel good about the negotiation. Everybody wants to be a winner. Yet not everyone is willing to do the homework necessary to achieve these ends. In Chapter 1, we discussed the essential steps necessary to plan your negotiation: (1) Identify all the issues; (2) prioritize the issues; (3) establish a settlement range; and (4) develop strategies and tactics. Make this preparation a habit, and you will set the stage for getting what you want.

There are other factors to consider prior to global negotiations. You can use the Tune-up Checklist to ensure that you put yourself in the strongest possible position before the negotiation.

The Tune-Up Checklist: Prior to the Negotiation

This is the data-gathering stage where you should get background information related to TOS (The Other Side), to TOS's culture and its effects on the negotiating process, to TOS's organization and other potential players in the negotiation, and to the history of any past negotiations. What do you know about:

TOS

- ❑ Family status (e.g., married, single, children)?
- ❑ Leisure or recreational activities?
- ❑ Work habits (e.g., long hours, early to work)?
- ❑ Behavior style (e.g., perfectionist, "big picture"–oriented, task-oriented, people-oriented)?
- ❑ Number of years with current organization?
- ❑ Stability in current position?
- ❑ Overall reputation as a negotiator?
- ❑ Special interest groups that might affect the negotiator?

TOS's Culture and Its Effects on Negotiations

- ❑ Are meetings likely to be punctual?
- ❑ What can you expect the pace of the negotiations to be?
- ❑ How important is saving face likely to be?
- ❑ Are differences of opinion likely to be emotional or argumentative?
- ❑ Will TOS bring a large team?
- ❑ Will you need an agent or interpreter?
- ❑ Should you prepare a formal agenda?

TOS's Organization

- ❑ What is the organization's main product or service?
- ❑ What is its past, present, and projected financial status?
- ❑ What organizational problems exist (e.g., downsizing, tough competition)?
- ❑ Who is TOS's boss, and what do you know about him or her?
- ❑ Is the organization under any time pressures?

Past Negotiations

- ❑ What were the subjects of past negotiations?
- ❑ What were the main obstacles and outcomes of the negotiations?
- ❑ What objections were raised?
- ❑ What strategies and tactics were used by TOS?
- ❑ How high were the initial offers compared with the eventual settlement?
- ❑ How was the outcome achieved, and over what period of time?

There are many ways to plan negotiations. One study identified five approaches skilled negotiators share when planning their negotiations:

1. They consider twice as wide a range of action options and outcomes as do less-skilled negotiators.

2. They spend over three times as much attention on trying to find common ground with TOS.

3. They spend more than twice as much time on long-term issues.

4. They set range objectives (such as a target price of $50 to $60 per unit), rather than single-point objectives (e.g., $55). Ranges give negotiators flexibility.

5. They use *issue planning* rather than *sequence planning*. That is, skilled negotiators discuss each issue independently rather than in a predetermined sequence or order of issues.[1]

Strategy 2: Adopt a Win-Win, Interest-Based Approach

We don't adopt the win-win approach simply because we are wonderful human beings. It helps us get what we want. There is a difference between how skilled and unskilled negotiators prepare for the win-win approach. Skilled negotiators, for example, tend to spend less time on defense/attack behavior and in disagreement. They also tend to give more information about their feelings and have fewer arguments to back up their position.[2] This last point may seem odd. It might seem that the more arguments one has for one's position, the better. Skilled negotiators know, however, that having only a few strong arguments is more effective than having too many arguments. With too many arguments, weak arguments tend to dilute strong arguments, and TOS often feels pressured or manipulated into settlement.

To achieve a win-win situation, you must tune in to the frequency with which TOS can identify: WIIFT (what's in it for them). This means different things in different cultures. For example, in Saudi Arabia, a certain amount of haggling back and forth on terms may indicate your sincerity about striking a deal. To refuse a somewhat expressive give-and-take would be an insult to many Saudi negotiators. A Dallas-based commercial building contractor now experienced in Saudi Arabia discovered this on his first trip there. "I really got off-base in our early discussions in Riyadh. I felt we were being extremely polite as we patiently explained the reasonableness of our proposal. We fell flat on our faces. The Saudis felt we were inflexible and not serious about doing business. The next project we bid had a lot of fat built into it. We haggled back and forth for four meetings, and they ended up loving us. That's what they wanted—someone to bargain with back and forth. It showed them we cared." This negotiator adds,

"I still get a knot in my stomach sometimes when I go through a Saudi negotiation, but at least I know what works now."

Fortunately for this negotiator, he quickly learned the win-win approach for his Saudi client. Yet the very idea of haggling would be a sure win-lose proposition in many parts of the world. In England, for example, it would be hard to come up with a worse idea than to engage TOS in an emotional afternoon of haggling back and forth. The British idea of win-win is a somewhat formal, procedural, and detailed discussion of the facts.

Achieving a win-win result also requires careful scrutiny of both parties' overall goals. You may be seeking short-term profit and cash flow, while your Japanese counterparts may be more interested in long-term viability. In many cases, different goals can lead to overall win-win results. Consider the company president negotiating a joint venture in Hungary in order to take advantage of a skilled, inexpensive workforce, while her TOS is motivated to find business linkages outside Eastern Europe.

Wherever you negotiate, focusing on win-win results sharply increases your chances for success, particularly in the long term.

Strategy 3: Maintain High Aspirations

Early in my career, the International Air Transport Association (IATA) discontinued its policy of airline ticket price compliance. IATA had been for many years a powerful enforcer that had maintained a firm grip on the airline ticket prices of the world's domestic and international airlines. Immediately after this announcement was made, Leroy Black, my boss, suggested that I contact the airlines to determine what, if any, ticket price concessions we might extract as a result of this policy change. The Middle East Division where we worked was located in Dubai, United Arab Emirates, a small oil sheikdom adjoining Saudi Arabia. Our 3,500 workers and many of their family members collectively logged millions of air miles per year.

"That's a good idea," I remember telling Leroy. Shaving 5 or 10 percent—perhaps even 15 percent—would amount to substantial savings on our $4 million annual airline expenses. I was stunned, though, when Leroy suggested we ask for a 50 percent price decrease in ticket costs.

"Are you kidding?" I asked, quite shocked.

"I think that 50 percent is about right," Leroy said serenely.

Our first appointment was with representatives from British Airways. They told us, in a reserved, nice kind of way, to take a hike.

Then KLM, in a not particularly nice kind of way, suggested the same re-

course as British Airways. The same with Lufthansa. "We really are being a bit chintzy on this thing," I thought to myself.

"Leroy, let's try asking for a little less and see what happens," I suggested.

"I don't know. Let's hang in there awhile longer," Leroy insisted.

Next was Alitalia, the Italian airline. As in our appointments with the other airlines, I went through a short prologue explaining the company's position, and assertively put forth that we would like to see a 50 percent reduction in future fares. This caused quite a commotion with the Alitalia representatives, who waved their arms and with great conviction gave us several reasons why this was not possible.

"This is really a little embarrassing," I thought.

They then asked if they could privately telephone their regional headquarters staff. They returned in about ten minutes in a solemn mood.

"Mr. Acuff," one of the representatives said with a grave look on his face. "What you ask is quite impossible. The very most we can offer you is a 40 percent reduction," he said apologetically.

"Excuse me?" I asked. He repeated his offer.

"Unbelievable," I thought to myself. "Give us some time to think about it," I replied.

As soon as they were out of earshot, Leroy and I almost jumped for joy. As it turned out, this was the first of several key concessions we received from the various airlines, ranging from 15 to 45 percent discounts. British Airways, KLM, Sabena, and Lufthansa all soon after reduced their rates well beyond my initial expectations.

This situation was a valuable lesson with regard to aspiration levels in negotiations. What at first seemed like a brash, overbearing approach to business turned out to be very positive. "But was it win-win?" you ask. "Didn't you just bleed the airlines at a time when they were vulnerable?" Not at all. We later found out that the airlines were quite pleased with the new arrangements. They thought discounts might be greater than they were, and, of course, some of the airlines were delighted that they had negotiated better terms than their competitors.

We have all kinds of negative fantasies about high initial demands (HIDs):

"They won't like me anymore. I'll make them really mad and it will hurt the relationship."

"I'll price myself out of the market."

"Maybe we aren't being reasonable."

"This is embarrassing."

In spite of these concerns, there are compelling reasons to go for it, which are summarized in the following key tips.

Key Worldwide Negotiating Tips:
Seven Reasons Why You Should Have High Initial Demands

1. Don't take away your own power. TOS may do it to you, but don't do it to yourself.
2. HIDs teach people how to treat you.
3. They lower the expectations of TOS.
4. HIDs demonstrate your persistence and conviction.
5. You can always reduce your asking offer or demand. HIDs give you room to make concessions.
6. Remember that time is on your side. Making HIDs gives you more time to learn about your counterpart, and time heals many wounds.
7. There is an emotional imperative for TOS to beat you down. It's important for TOS to feel that they've "won."[3]

Key Worldwide Negotiating Tip 7 is especially important. Many negotiators find it hard to accept that there is an emotional imperative for TOS to beat you down. To illustrate this point, let's get in the other person's shoes to see how TOS might feel. You are in Germany to negotiate the purchase of the Drillenzebit, a precision tool-making machine from a Munich-based firm. You say to yourself, "This time won't be like the other times. This time I'm going to do my homework—I will read appropriate industry periodicals and talk to consultants, clients, suppliers, and others who know a lot about the Germans, the German business environment, and the competitive market for precision tool-making machines." So you do your homework and begin to negotiate with the Germans for the Drillenzebit machine. When the subject of price arises, you are ready. You've got the facts, figures, and some savoir-faire about German negotiating practices. So you say, "Mr. Dietrich, today I'm going to offer you one price and one price only for this fine Drillenzebit machine. That final price is $74,000—that's U.S. dollars.

Dietrich looks at you for a moment and says, "Let me see if I have this right. That's $74,000—in U.S. dollars?"

"That's right," you repeat, proud that you're sticking by your guns.

"Seventy-four thousand dollars. You've got it. The machine is yours!" he beams.

How would you feel in this situation? Wonderful? Exuberant? If you are like

most people, you would have a morbid, sinking feeling that you had just been taken. Your first thought would probably be, "Damn. I should have offered less." Is this reaction logical? No. You did, after all, get what you asked for. You reacted as you did because only part of your needs were met—the logical part—while the emotional part was not.

There are cultural differences as to how high our aspiration level should be with our foreign counterparts, but as a rule of thumb, go for it! If you really want $30,000 for your widget machine, don't ask for $30,500. Ask for $60,000. Put TOS in the position of saying to his or her boss, "You know, this woman came in asking $60,000. This price was completely off-the-wall. Excellent negotiator that I am, I got her down to $38,000. I saved us $22,000." And if you are in a competitive bidding situation, stress the quality, service, and other aspects that make your price an excellent value.

Strategy 4: Use Language That Is Simple and Accessible

American English is filled with thousands of clichés and colloquialisms that make it very hard for others to understand. Phrases such as "getting down to brass tacks," "getting down to the nitty gritty," wanting to "zero in on problems," or "finding out where the rubber meets the road" only clog communication channels.

Don't assume that because your foreign counterpart speaks English, he or she fully understands it. This individual might know English as it was taught in school but might not be able to speak it or understand it in conversation with an American. An American executive who regularly travels to Taiwan makes this point. "When I first asked my Taiwanese client if he spoke English, he told me yes. I found out the hard way that his understanding was very elementary and that I used way too many slang expressions. We still do business together, but now I speak more slowly and simply, and I'm learning some Chinese."

This doesn't apply only to slang. Make sure you use the simplest, most basic words possible. Exhibit 3-1 provides examples of simplified words and terms you should use, even if you're both speaking English.

Strategy 5: Ask Lots of Questions, Then Listen with Your Eyes and Ears

Asking good questions is vital throughout the negotiation, but particularly in the early stages. Your main goal is receiving information. Making a brilliant speech to TOS about your proposal may make you feel good, but it does far less

Exhibit 3-1. Simplifying English words and terms.

Don't use this . . .	when this will do
annual premium	annual payment
accrued interest	unpaid interest
maturity date	final payment date
commence	start
utilize	use
acquaint	tell
demonstrate	show
endeavor	try
modification	change
proceed	go
per diem	daily

in helping you achieve your ends than asking questions that give you data about content and the emotional needs of TOS.

Skilled negotiators ask more questions than unskilled negotiators. They also engage in much more active listening than those who are less skilled.

There is one important consideration when asking questions: Don't do anything that would embarrass your international counterpart. Questions can be much more direct and open in cultures such as the United States, Canada, Australia, Switzerland, Sweden, and Germany than in Japan, Taiwan, Brazil, or Colombia, where indirectness is prized.

> *Judge a man by his questions rather than by his answers.*
>
> —Voltaire

Effective listening is especially challenging when different cultures are involved. This can be the case even when English is the first language of TOS. Mike Apple, an American engineering and construction executive, found this to be the case in England and Scotland. Apple notes that even though English is spoken, one must listen very carefully to English and Scottish negotiators because of their dialects. "When I first got to Scotland, I wondered if some kind of challenge was in the making when a union negotiator told me he was going to 'mark my card.' I asked a colleague about it. As it turned out, the term is one used by Scottish golfers to explain the best approach to the course for those who haven't played there before. The union negotiator was only trying to be helpful," Apple notes. "The lesson learned here? When in doubt, ask for clarification."

If the communication pattern is from low-context countries, such as Japan,

China, Saudi Arabia, Greece, or Spain, listening is even more challenging for Americans. In these cultures, the message is embedded in the context of what is being said. Mike McMahon, a former managing director for National Semiconductor's Singapore plant, found Singaporeans reluctant to respond directly to questions. He notes, "I had to listen very carefully to figure out what was really on their minds."[4]

Here are some additional tips for effective listening:

- Limit your own talking.
- Concentrate on what TOS is saying.
- Maintain eye contact (but don't stare).
- Paraphrase and summarize TOS's remarks.
- Avoid jumping to conclusions. Be postjudicial, not prejudicial, regarding what TOS is saying.
- Watch for nonverbal cues.
- Listen for emotions.
- Ask for clarification: Assume differences, not similarities, if you are unsure of meaning.
- Don't interrupt.
- Pause for understanding; don't immediately fill the voids of silence.

Some of the rituals of international negotiating serve dual purposes of entertainment and information gathering. Foster Lin, director of the Taiwanese Far East Trade Service Office in Chicago, considers formal Taiwanese banquets and other entertainment as a prime opportunity to gain information on one's negotiating counterpart. Says Lin, "Entertainment demonstrates courtesy toward our foreign guests. It also helps us find out more about the individual person. Is this someone we can trust and want to do business with?" Such occasions can help you as well. Careful listening in this "offstage" time, away from the formal negotiating sessions, can give you another side to the negotiators. Use this time to gather additional data on your counterpart.

A key part of listening relates to body language. TOS may encode messages, making sophisticated, cogent arguments. However, one thing almost always happens during a moment of insecurity or deception: Body movements change (e.g., the person literally squirms in his or her seat or blinks more rapidly). Also, be aware of the impact of your own nonverbal behavior. For example, if your gestures are quite expressive and TOS is from Sweden and quite reserved, tone

it down a bit. Alternatively, if your facial and arm gestures are unexpressive and you are meeting a Brazilian who is very expressive, loosen up a bit—smile and use expressive hand and arm gestures.

Key Worldwide Negotiating Tips:
Four Positive Things You Can Do Without Saying a Word

1. *Smile!* It's a universal lubricant that can help you open the content of the negotiation. A genuine smile says very loudly, "I'd appreciate doing business with you."

2. *Dress appropriately and groom well.* Shined shoes, combed hair, clean nails, and clothes appropriate for the occasion show that you respect yourself and your counterpart. It also communicates that you are worthy of your counterpart's business.

3. *Lean forward.* This communicates interest and attention in almost every culture.

4. *Use open gestures.* Crossed arms in front of your chest may be viewed as disinterest or resistance on your part. More open gestures send a signal that you are open to your counterpart's ideas.

Strategy 6: Build Solid Relationships

Stay away from value issues, which are full of potential landmines. When is the last time you won an argument on politics? On religion? That's right; you never have, and you never will. Discussion of subjects such as politics, religion, race, and the role of women in the workplace will not help build a relationship with your negotiating counterpart, even if the other person brings up the subject or there is potential agreement. No matter what our particular view on these subjects, we tend to think that we have God, truth, and light on our side.

The personal relationship you develop with your counterpart provides the basis, or context, for the content portion of the negotiation. In many cultures it is the quality of the relationship more than the work accomplished that counts. There is more emphasis on building a solid personal relationship in some cultures than others. In Brazil, Japan, Greece, Spain, and Czechoslovakia, for example, a strong personal relationship almost surely precedes any deal. In other countries, such as Germany and Switzerland, the content portion of the negotiation usually precedes any substantial relationship building. In most cases, a strong relationship is critical to even short-term success. In all cases, it is critical to long-term success.

Be a pleasure to do business with. Even if you don't agree on the content

part of the negotiation, you want TOS to have a positive view of you when they see you coming.

Key Worldwide Negotiating Tips:
Fifteen Statements That Will Help Build Solid Relationships
(Or at Least Keep You out of Deep Soup)

1. "I'm very pleased to meet you."
2. "Could you tell me more about your proposal?"
3. "I have a few more questions I'd like to ask you."
4. "We might be able to consider X if you could consider Y."
5. "Let me try to summarize where we stand now in our discussion."
6. "I'm very happy to see you again."
7. "Could you tell me more about your concerns?"
8. "Let me tell you where I have a concern."
9. "I feel disappointed that we haven't made more progress."
10. "I really appreciate the progress that we've made."
11. "Thank you."
12. "Can I answer any more questions about our organization or proposal?"
13. "What would it take for us to close this deal?"
14. "I've enjoyed doing business with you."
15. "I haven't talked to you since we signed the agreement. I just wanted to follow up with you to see how things are working out."

Even when you mean well, there are some terms and phrases that carry negative overtones. One study found that skilled negotiators used only 2.3 irritating words and phrases per hour in face-to-face negotiations, compared with 10.8 irritators per hour for average negotiators. Irritators included such phrases as "generous offer," "fair price," and "reasonable arrangement."[5] Exhibit 3-2 is a "dirty word list" that details other phrases that tend to upset others, regardless of the culture involved.

There's another word that should be taken out of your business vocabulary: *negotiate*. Yes, we use it when discussing the subject, but in real-life situations, all kinds of images come to mind when you tell someone, "Let's negotiate this deal." There's the feeling that something manipulative is about to happen. Instead, say something like, "Let's work out something that is good for both of us" or, "Let's discuss the concerns you have."

Exhibit 3-2. Words and phrases to avoid.

These words:	May provoke these reactions:
You always/You never . . .	I always, I never? Perhaps I often or seldom behave that way, but not always or never.
What you need to understand . . .	I'll let you know if I need to understand it.
Be reasonable . . .	I didn't think I was being unreasonable. (Have you ever met anyone in your whole life who told you, "I don't tend to be very reasonable, and I just thought I'd let you know"?)
Calm down!	If they were calm, they won't be after you tell them this!
Needless to say . . .	Then why are you saying it?
Obviously . . .	You've somehow cornered the market on what is and is not obvious?
The fact of the matter is . . .	You know what is factual and I don't?
You can't tell me . . .	You bet I can tell you—that is, if you'll just listen!
Listen . . .	I may choose to listen, but I don't want to be directed to do so.
We all know . . .	Maybe I do and maybe I don't.
Any thinking person . . .	I'm not exactly a potted plant here.

Reaching a deadlock or impasse is a common and often frustrating experience. This can happen even when both parties are bargaining in good faith and are trying hard to reach an agreement. When you reach an impasse with TOS, take steps to break the deadlock and yet keep the relationship strong. The following list of key tips provides some helpful methods.

Key Worldwide Negotiating Tips:
Seventeen Ways to Break Deadlocks and Yet Keep the Relationships

1. Recap the discussion to ensure there really is a deadlock.
2. Emphasize mutual interests.
3. Stress the cost of not agreeing and situations you want to avoid.
4. Reach an agreement in principle, postponing difficult parts of the agreement.
5. Try to find out if the problem is based on something TOS isn't telling you.

6. Change the type of contract.

7. Change contract specifications or terms.

8. Add options to the contract.

9. Hold informal discussions in a different setting.

10. Make concessions that are contingent upon settling all of the issues.

11. Form a joint study committee.

12. Change a team member or team leader.

13. Discuss how both you and TOS might respond to a hypothetical solution, without committing either party to a course of action.

14. Tell a funny story.

15. Take a recess.

16. Consider setting a deadline for resolution. Deadlines create a sense of urgency and encourage action.

17. Be patient.

Keep in mind that both the tone and the content of the current negotiation will affect future negotiations with TOS. This is true even if you don't successfully conclude the current negotiation; sometimes you are really setting the stage for the next one. It's like arguing with the umpire in baseball. Why do baseball managers do it? They never prevail. Aside from pleasing the crowd, the manager argues with the umpire for one simple reason—not for this call, but for the *next* call! So, too, in *your* negotiations, put markers in TOS's mind for the next time you sit down to do business. Leave TOS with two thoughts: (1) you're a good person to do business with; and (2) here are some expectations to keep in mind.

Strategy 7: Maintain Personal Integrity

A few years ago a businessman came up to me before I was about to make a speech on negotiations. He said that he was a good Christian and, as such, didn't know if he should stay for the speech since he assumed I'd be talking about scheming ways to manipulate other people. I told him that while I didn't know whether or not he should stay, negotiators who use manipulative, scheming, hidden agendas do not do very well in negotiations. He seemed somewhat shocked but relieved by my response.

Personal integrity is absolutely critical for your effectiveness as a worldwide negotiator. My conviction on this point is not related to religion but to pragmatism. There are two reasons why personal integrity and trust are vital. The first

reason has to do with information. No one tells you anything of importance if he or she doesn't trust you. If you are not viewed as trustworthy, people will tell you only what they must tell you because of your position or title. For example, if you are trusted, after a negotiating session TOS may ask for some confidential "whisper time." She may confide in you as follows:

TOS: Look, I know we've been pressing for A, B, C, and D in there. But, off the record, what we're really interested in is only C and D.

You: But you've been really pushing hard for A and B.

TOS: I know. But if you can find a way to give us C and D, we've got a deal.

This is a rich disclosure. This is the stuff that will make you successful, not because you are technically brilliant, but because you are trusted. Risky, key data are shared with you only if your personal integrity is unquestioned.

Personal integrity is vital to building your negotiating strength for a second reason: *Issues of trust are the most difficult relationship problems to repair.* In fact, these are often irreparable. With some hard work, some skill, and a little luck, other types of relationship problems can be healed, but the trust issue hardly ever gets fixed. Think of the people you really don't trust in your professional or personal life. Is there *anything* they can do to repair the relationship and get back in your good graces? If you are like most people, the answer is no.

American negotiators sometimes try to resolve issues of trust by formalizing the intent of the parties in an ironclad contract. We then hold TOS to the contract, regardless of how much we trust them. In many cultures, however, it is the person or the relationship that your counterpart trusts, not a piece of paper. Making and keeping contractual commitments is not a high priority for many of your international counterparts. Much of this view relates to the relative uncertainty felt by those from other cultures compared with Americans. Malaysians, for example, prefer to have exit clauses in their contracts in case things don't work out. They feel little control over future business events or even their country as a whole and want provisions for a respectable withdrawal should future circumstances make their compliance impossible.[6] In much of the Arab world, negotiators stress mutual trust and see themselves doing business with the person, rather than a company or a contract.[7] In Britain, there are strong legal precedents but less reliance on formalized contracts than in the United States. Tom Wilson, a British management consultant, observes, "Detailed legal contracts are seldom the order of the day. The British feel aggrieved when outsmarted by clever contract language. Besides," he adds, "a legal decision will not enforce that for which there is no will to perform."

Building trust can be a long process, particularly in global negotiating, and it can be harmed in subtle ways. This is why you should avoid excessive use of phrases such as "to be honest with you . . ." (are you not normally honest?), "to tell you the truth . . ." (are you not normally truthful?), and "frankly . . ." (are you not usually candid?). Although TOS may not be conscious of why he or she doesn't trust you, too many of these phrases lead to a conclusion that you are not trustworthy, even if you are honest.

If you are viewed as trustworthy by TOS, protect this aspect of the negotiation at all costs. Remember, lose the deal if you must, but keep the trust. This will be vital for your next negotiation with TOS.

Strategy 8: Conserve Concessions

Concessions give valuable information about you, your style, and your resolve. How you use them sets the tone, not only for a current negotiation, but for future negotiations as well. Your current concession pattern teaches TOS how to treat you in the future.

Let's say you're in Budapest, involved in a tough negotiation with the Hungarians. You have traded data with them and made logical defenses of your negotiating position for five long meetings. The negotiation seems to be going nowhere. This particular negotiation is price-sensitive, and in the first meeting, you quoted $80 per unit for your product. The Hungarians have offered you $20. You know that building a good relationship is important in any negotiation. They haven't budged from the $20 since the first meeting.

In order to break the logjam, you show your good faith in working out this negotiation by making a counteroffer of $45. This, you think, shows that you mean business in resolving this issue and that you are acting in good faith. Besides, your *really asking* price is $40, and you will certainly have gone more than halfway. The Hungarians will surely do the same, and you can all conclude the session, have some vodka, and go home.

It may not work out this way. In fact, in the case just related, you can bet you are about to get clobbered. Like many negotiators, you might feel that making a concession will create goodwill or soften up TOS. Unfortunately, a much more likely scenario is that such a concession will suggest weakness on your part, make your counterpart greedy, or even make your counterpart suspicious. You must therefore be extremely careful in making concessions.

Key Worldwide Negotiating Tips:
Ten Guidelines on Making Concessions

1. Don't be the first to make a concession on an important issue.
2. Never accept the first offer.

3. Make TOS reduce a high initial demand; don't honor a high demand by making a counteroffer.

4. Make small concessions. Lower the expectation of TOS.

5. When you make concessions, make them slowly (like a fine red wine, they improve with time).

6. Make TOS feel good by making concessions of low value to you but of perceived high value to TOS.

7. Defer concessions on matters that are important to you.

8. Make contingent concessions (i.e., get something in return, or concede only on the condition that all issues be settled).

9. Celebrate (inwardly) the concessions you get. Don't feel guilty.

10. Don't feel that you must reciprocate every concession made to you.

The number of initial concessions differs among cultures. One study found that Japanese negotiators made fewer initial concessions per half-hour bargaining session (6.5) than did negotiators from the United States (7.1) or Brazil (9.4).[8] As a rule, the fewer the concessions, the better.

Also, beware when TOS asks for concessions on the grounds of "fairness." Whenever your counterparts tell you that they want you to make a concession because their offer to you has been very "fair" or "reasonable," don't believe them. More often than not, this is a manipulative tactic to make you feel guilty.

Strategy 9: Make Patience an Obsession

Since almost every stage of a global negotiation tends to take longer than the domestic version, patience is not only a virtue, but a necessity. Patience serves three vital functions: (1) It facilitates getting information from TOS; (2) it builds the relationship by sending out signals of courtesy; and (3) it increases your chances of effective concession making. Patience is linked to concession behavior because impatient negotiators tend to make both more counterproposals and more concessions. Skilled negotiators make fewer counterproposals than do less-skilled negotiators.[9]

Just-in-Time Management

I was in the small Central American country of Belize to address a management conference. I was scheduled to speak at 9:00 a.m., so I was ready to go about 8:00 a.m., waiting for my hosts in the hotel lobby. They weren't there. 8:15—no one. 8:30—nobody. 8:45—nope. I checked with

the front desk to make sure I had set my watch to the correct time zone. 9:00, 9:15—still no one. Now I'm getting out my letter of invitation, thinking, "Could this be my worst nightmare? Could I be in the wrong country on the wrong date?" At about 9:20 my host showed up, and we drove to the hotel where the conference was being held. After a short discussion about my flight, the weather, and related items, I said, "It's about 9:30. Wasn't I on the agenda for 9:00 a.m.?"

No response.

"I'm just curious, but if it's about 9:35, aren't we late for the conference?" I persisted.

"Oh no, Mr. Acuff," one of my hosts said jovially. "Nothing here in Belize starts at the time on the agenda. We'll be quite early. The conference won't start for another hour or so."

"Thank you," I said, relieved. My life was good again.

Patience may also be one of TOS's negotiating tactics, since TOS tries to wear you down with their patience. They are counting on your becoming anxious and making concessions that you otherwise wouldn't make. Don't be a victim. Take these countermeasures:

- Give yourself plenty of time.
- Relax and make yourself comfortable.
- Prepare your own people back home for a long negotiation.
- Recognize that it might be tougher on TOS than on you.
- Consider setting a deadline.

Patience, as important as it is, can be hard work. One manager from an American oil company illustrates this point in the Pacific Rim: "Negotiating in Indonesia is like drinking a thousand cups of tea—very challenging and very slow." Ted Cline, who has negotiated many large contracts in the Middle East, stresses the importance of persistence. "I tell my people: If you beat your head on the wall, it will get bloody. But if you keep constant pressure on the wall, someday it will fall down."

Strategy 10: Be Culturally Literate and Adapt Negotiating Strategies to the Host Country Environment

By acquiring insight into the culture of TOS, as well as into your own cultural predispositions, you can bridge the cultural gap to become a more effective negotiator. You can be empathetic with TOS only if you understand the culture

and environment in which TOS operates. Every step of the negotiating process must be seen through the lens of the host-country culture. Increasing your cultural IQ pays off in every step of the negotiating process, from the initial planning and greeting TOS right down to setting the stage for future business.

Cultural savvy takes many forms. Witness, for example, a supplier of oilfield technology that sent a program administrator to resolve the snags associated with a Russian joint venture. Despite the progress on technical details, the Russians continued to be very standoffish. Only later did the firm learn that sending a mid-level manager with the title of program administrator was an insult to the Russians, who felt that anyone with such a lowly title was unlikely to have the authority to negotiate a substantial deal, and that sending a midlevel manager was disrespectful of them. Such title and rank considerations are important to Russian negotiators. In this particular case, the firm's vice president of international projects relates that now, when the program administrator travels to Russia, his title is revised to "managing director of special projects." The vice president notes, "The title change makes the Russians feel like they are dealing with the right level of person, and all it costs us are new business cards."

Moira Crean, manager of contracts administration for MasterCard International, finds that cultural savvy takes the form of sensitivity to age in mainland China. "Age," she explains, "can be a key aspect in a big negotiation. Our Chinese partners have been known to dismiss a young person—let's say, a 35-year-old vice president—and say, 'Send over the old guy.'"

Even concession making must be seen through a cultural perspective. Exhibit 3-3 illustrates different perceptions of your good intentions. The reaction to a large concession may range from pleasure (a U.S. negotiator) to dismay (a Swiss negotiator).

Two guidelines will help you to be not only culturally literate, but also a superb global negotiator: Adopt the Platinum Rule, and conduct yourself as an effective foreigner.

Exhibit 3-3. How a large concession from you might be perceived by negotiators from different countries.

TOS Negotiators	Likely Reaction
United States	"I gotcha."
Netherlands	"I cannot trust you."
Japan	"This has hurt the harmony."
Switzerland	"This person did not prepare well."
Saudi Arabia	"This is how business is done."

Adopt the Platinum Rule

Most of us grew up with the Golden Rule or something similar: "Do unto others as you would that they do unto you." This works well when we are surrounded by people like us—whoever "us" might be. We know how to treat the other person because of shared backgrounds and traits. With our international counterparts, the Golden Rule is no longer very helpful, because how you want to be treated may indeed be very different from how Chin, Suresh, Ivan, Miguel, Mohammed, Isobella, or Isa wants to be treated. Instead, adopt what I call the Platinum Rule: "Do unto others as they would have done unto them." You might be comfortable with a firm handshake, with being direct and open, and with getting right down to business. But if the culture of TOS encourages other behaviors and your cultural savvy enables you to engage in them, you will be ahead of the competition. As you increase your comfort zone with others, so too will you increase your negotiating effectiveness.

Is there a place for common courtesy? You bet, as long as such courtesy isn't defined only on your terms. If common courtesy means a smile upon greeting or not interrupting others, this works almost anywhere. If it means inviting TOS to lunch, picking up the tab, complimenting TOS about his or her office, extending a firm handshake, or providing a gift as a token of your appreciation, then your courtesy may be another person's idea of irritating behavior. Tact has been called intelligence of the heart. In global business affairs, tact includes knowledge of the host-country culture.

Conduct Yourself as an Effective Foreigner

The idea is not to go native, but to be culturally savvy while remaining a foreigner.[10] Don't worry about minor gaffes in the many rituals and customs associated with every culture. If your handshake is a little too firm in Rio de Janeiro, or you can't remember that phrase you learned in Polish, it is not the end of the world. TOS will normally give you an A for effort, even if the details of the execution need a little work.

Be culturally savvy, but also be authentic. If the sight of fish eyes makes you squeamish in Singapore, don't eat the fish eyes if it means you're going to spend an hour being sick in the bathroom. However, in almost every country outside of the United States, it is considered polite to keep both hands (but not your elbows) above the table during a meal. If you put one hand on your lap, TOS might assume that you never learned basic table manners. Another general rule of thumb is not to joke about the lifestyle of TOS's home country. This is not only a lack of cultural savvy—it is rude in any culture unless you've become very good friends with TOS.

Middle East Business Practices 101: When Compliments Are Costly

The labor minister for the United Arab Emirates was in my office to help negotiate an end to a work stoppage by the local Dubai construction workers. The meeting went well until we finished our discussions. While walking with His Highness to the door of my office, I mentioned that he had a beautiful briefcase (mine was in a general state of disrepair). As I reached the door I noticed that he was no longer walking with me. I turned around to see His Highness emptying the contents of his briefcase on my desk.

"Did you lose something?" I asked, trying to be helpful.

"No, no," he replied. "I want you to have," he added as he presented his briefcase to me. "This is for you. You are my friend."

After profusely apologizing, I convinced him that I really couldn't accept the briefcase.

The lesson learned? In that part of the world, don't go around complimenting people on their possessions. You just might end up with them.

Now that we have examined some negotiating strategies, let's turn in Chapter 4 to some of the toughest challenges you can expect to face as a global negotiator and explore strategies to deal with them.

Notes

1. Neil Rackham, *The Behavior of Successful Negotiators* (Reston, Va.: Huthwaite Research Group, 1976), as reported in Ellen Raider International, Inc. (Brooklyn, N.Y.) and Situation Management Systems, Inc. (Plymouth, Mass.), International Negotiations: A Training Program for Corporate Executives and Diplomats (1982).

2. Ibid.

3. See Phil Sperber, *Fail-Safe Business Negotiating: Strategies and Tactics for Success* (Englewood Cliffs, N.J.: Prentice-Hall, 1983), pp. 40–41; and Roy J. Lewicki and Joseph A. Litterer, *Negotiation* (Homewood, Ill.: Richard D. Irwin, 1985), pp. 75–79.

4. Frank L. Acuff, "What It Takes to Succeed in Overseas Assignment," *National Business Employment Weekly* (August 25, 1991): 17–18.

5. Rackham, *The Behavior of Successful Negotiators*.

6. Nancy J. Adler, *International Dimensions of Organizational Behavior*, 4th ed. (Cincinnati: South-Western, 2002), pp. 179–180.

7. Robert T. Moran, Phillip R. Harris, and Sarah V. Moran. *Managing Cultural Differences*, 7th ed. (Butterworth-Heinemann, 2007).

8. John Graham, "The Influence of Culture on Negotiations," *Journal of International Business Studies* 16 (1) (Spring 1985): 81–96.

9. Rackham, *The Behavior of Successful Negotiators*, p. 180.

10. Adler, *International Dimensions*, p. 187.

The Four Most Difficult Challenges Faced by Global Negotiators (and How to Deal with Them)

"Remember not only to say the right thing at the right time in the right place, but far more difficult still, to leave unsaid the wrong thing at the wrong moment."

—BENJAMIN FRANKLIN

- Challenge 1: Overcoming Culture Shock
- Challenge 2: Negotiating with Your Boss and Headquarters Staff Back Home
- Challenge 3: Resolving Bribery and Questionable Payment Issues
- Challenge 4: Dealing with International Virtual and Remote Teams

Any negotiation presents challenges, but there are unique challenges in international business negotiations. It is important that you learn about these challenges before they occur, and then take preventive measures. Specifically, there are four key challenges that are most likely to affect you as an international negotiator. Some of these challenges are unique to international business negotiations (such as dealing with international virtual and remote teams), while others can occur domestically but are magnified internationally (such as dealing with a bribe). Let's review the impact of these problems and examine the action steps you must take to overcome them.

Challenge 1: Overcoming Culture Shock

Culture shock occurs when we do not have the familiar signposts of how to conduct ourselves. These signposts involve both our professional and personal lives, and often guide us in activities that we normally take for granted. In international business negotiations, these might include how to shake hands; what forms of address to use; to whom your comments should be addressed; how direct to be with TOS (The Other Side); determining if the meaning is really no when TOS says yes; and what should be discussed over dinner.

Most individuals who work internationally go through four phases of adjustment to other cultures and negotiating situations. These phases of growth can be very troublesome and perplexing, but they are a normal and expected part of the intercultural journey.

Four Phases of Growth

Each phase has its own unique characteristics and challenges. Let's review the four phases.

1. *Predeparture anticipation and enchantment at the new location.* The first phase is a time of great excitement and anxiety. There is excitement about the new opportunity to work in a foreign culture, coupled with anxiety about adjusting to the new situation. There is a desire to plunge in and enjoy every aspect of the host culture. You read about the surroundings, history, and architecture and maybe take a tour as you celebrate differences between the host culture and the United States. You have a somewhat naive acceptance of the host culture without much critical analysis of its shortcomings. You feel buoyed by optimism about doing business with TOS. You begin thinking, "People all over are basically the same."

2. *Awakening.* This is known as the *wake-up phase*, when you begin slowly realizing that people from different cultures are more substantially different from those in one's own culture than originally thought. Annoyances begin to grind emotionally. For example, in South America it seems that your negotiating counterparts are never on time for meetings. They are overly friendly, always grabbing you and hugging you like you were their best friend. They seem more interested in talking about their brandy than about the negotiating issues; they won't give you straight answers to your questions; and four of them talk at once. In this phase, you come face-to-face with your own ethnocentrism. Initial culture shock can become permanent unless acknowledged and resolved.

3. *Disillusionment.* In this phase, you become very specific about what is wrong with the host culture and with the individuals with whom you must deal. You begin thinking that if only you could extricate yourself gracefully from the negotiation, you would happily board an airplane in the morning and go home.

4. *Realization and productivity.* The final phase is characterized by serenity and a realization of what can and cannot be accomplished in the host culture. You realize that the host culture has existed, in certain cases, for centuries before your arrival—and will likely continue after your departure—and you begin to work creatively and enjoyably among its challenges and opportunities.

The time frame of these phases differs from person to person and may endure from one extended trip to the host country to several trips.

Action Steps for Dealing with Culture Shock

• *Find a cultural mentor.* Ask for advice from others who have negotiating experience in the areas of the world where you will be doing business. Talk with both people who have had successful negotiating experiences there and those who have had bad experiences there. In this way, you can get a balanced view of the host country and its negotiators. The sooner you get this type of information, the better prepared you will be when it comes to the later phases of adjustment.

• *Be flexible and patient with yourself and with those in the host culture.* Events, services, issues, mechanical devices—in short, practically all aspects of your life—are not going to flow as smoothly and predictably as they do back home.

• *Withhold judgment about the new culture and its people.* Rather than being prejudicial about your new environment, be postjudicial. Try not to go overboard with either positive or negative reactions.

• *Recognize that the negative feelings you may have at the "awakening" and "disillusionment" stages are normal and appropriate for these phases of adjustment.* Annoyances, irritations, and letdowns are to be expected. After all, you have spent little or no time in the host-country environment.

• *Keep a sense of humor about yourself and your situation.* This doesn't mean joke telling, but rather, keeping a sense of proportion and a positive attitude about whatever culturally irritating situation you find yourself in.

• *Reduce stress by being as self-sufficient as possible with regard to business services.* "Routine business services" is an oxymoron in some countries. In a developing country, for example, there are often no computers, copiers, faxes, and other business fundamentals. There may also be a confidentiality issue in many host-country business settings, so don't depend on TOS to type your bar-

gaining position or other similar material. Take along a personal computer (with appropriate electrical adapters) for your notes, strategies, and other uses, or arrange for service at a hotel or other professional services provider where possible.

• *Process what has happened, and draw lessons for growth from your experience.* Learn from your cultural experiences, both good and bad ones. When you make mistakes, try to smile and learn from them. Continue to ask, "What is working well, and not well? And why is this the case?"

Challenge 2: Negotiating with Your Boss and Headquarters Staff Back Home

Negotiating with your international counterpart can be challenging, but experienced negotiators can tell you that negotiating with your own boss, legal staff, and others back in the home office can be brutal.

If you recognize what could go wrong, you are on your way to taking the steps to preventing problems. Here's a likely scenario: You've been in Japan for two weeks, and the tally is seven formal dinners with your counterpart, about two hundred toasts, forty-seven sakes, and one less-than-impressed boss back home at headquarters.

"So what exactly is the status?" he asks you.

"Things seem to be on schedule. I feel we're building a good relationship with their negotiating team."

"Say what?"

"You know, building trust and all."

"Gosh, you don't know how happy that makes me. But let me remind you that I sent you over there to build a refinery."

From there the discussion goes directly downhill. Moreover, the boss is so concerned about how things are going that he asks you to run everything through the legal department. Now you are likely to run into difficulties negotiating with your own legal staff or counsel, in addition to the real work of negotiating with TOS.

In many cases, you may get a lot more "help" with the negotiation than you want. Your legal counsel is likely to want more detail than will be acceptable to your foreign counterpart. Expect the legal staff to challenge, correct, and attempt to overrule portions of or even the entire agreement you are negotiating with TOS. They are only trying to keep you and the organization out of trouble.

Action Steps for Preparing Your Boss and Headquarters Staff for the International Negotiation

• *Stress the protracted nature of international negotiations in most parts of the world.* Lower expectations as to the chances of a speedy agreement. Stretch out their time horizons.

• *Be clear as to who has the authority to negotiate on the organization's behalf.* The negotiation process will be undermined if TOS feels concessions can be gained from the home office that you wouldn't agree to.

• *Take time to educate the boss and others on the key cultural factors that influence the negotiation.* Contrast and compare specific instances overseas with how they would have been handled domestically (for example, the degree of emphasis put on the relationship aspects of the negotiation).

• *Cue the boss and legal staff to differences in contract length, specificity, and other matters early on in the negotiation.* Try to determine the absolute necessities of protecting your side versus what would be in the nice-to-have category.

• *Keep your own attorneys away from the negotiating table in most other countries.* Their presence would be perceived as overly rigid and would show a lack of good faith.

• *Don't ask the corporate legal staff dozens of questions as to whether you can put various legal items in the agreement.* The lawyers will tell you no. It's their job to tell you no. It's your job to combine the necessary legal protections with the practicalities of achieving an agreement that is good for both parties.

• *Don't surprise the technocrats with a big problem.* If you see that there is a potential legal, financial, or other problem, give ample notice to the appropriate person. By getting them involved early in the process, you have a chance to make your case to the technocrats before a final decision is made, and also to save yourself some potential problems with TOS.

• *Give your boss or other headquarters staff a lesson in International Negotiating 101.* If the boss or others make a trip with you, ensure that they are educated in detail regarding the status of the negotiations and the expectations associated with the culture of TOS.

Challenge 3: Resolving Bribery and Questionable Payment Issues

What constitutes a bribe or payoff in the United States may be considered day-to-day business in many foreign countries. This point was brought home to me

during negotiations for contract labor in the Philippines. I negotiated with Chito, a Filipino labor supplier, to contract for several hundred Filipinos to work mainly as welders, fitters, and other craftspeople on various projects throughout the Middle East. Chito delivered qualified people in remarkably short time frames, cutting through a labyrinth of Filipino administrative rules and regulations. Exactly what he had to do with governmental officials I didn't know then, and I don't know now. I did know, however, that he had repeatedly asked for a fee increase because his "government overhead" was increasing. (Yes, we gave him the increase.)

As always on my trips to Manila, Chito was engaging and gracious. One evening, as we walked a short distance from the restaurant where we had had dinner back to the hotel where I was staying, I briefly paused at an art show window to admire an oil painting of an old shack in an open field. Back at the hotel, Chito and I shook hands and said good-bye.

Four hours later, about midnight, the phone rang.

"Hello."

"Hello, Frank. This is Chito. How are you?"

"Fine," I lied. I had been asleep about an hour.

"Can I come up to your room?"

"Right now?" I asked, incredulously.

Chito came up to my room all right—with the painting about which I had remarked earlier that evening and the artist who painted it. I was certainly awake by now. As the engaging and gracious Chito and the proud, smiling artist stood there, clear thoughts rushed through my head about the Foreign Corrupt Practices Act and several internal company policies dealing with gifts. My awkward protestations that I really couldn't accept the gift fell on deaf ears, and I eventually took the painting, thanking both of them.

After they left, I sat there for quite some time staring at the painting. Was I going to be sitting in some federal court two years from now, explaining why I had accepted a bribe from a company agent connected with a foreign government? Although I enjoyed a good working relationship with my boss, I was sure he would be singularly unimpressed with my new painting. As it turned out, our corporate legal staff approved of me keeping the painting, and to this day I have it hanging in my office.

If you are an American and are put in the same situation of accepting a gift that might be construed by the American legal system as a bribe, don't take a chance. Get your corporate legal staff's opinion on any ambiguous gift to avoid serious problems later.

What's in a Name? International Names for Bribes

Backsheesh	Middle East
La busterella ("envelope left on bureaucrat's desk")	Italy
Dash	West Africa
Grease	United States
La morbida ("bite")	Latin America
Kumshaw	Southeast Asia
Pot du vin ("jug of wine")	France

Is It a Bribe or a Gift?

It has been acknowledged in the international business community for many years that gifts or money payments are necessary to obtain positive action from government officials, whether to secure a large order or to gain favorable treatment from customs officials, taxing authorities, and so on. Although U.S. negotiators tend to bargain over issues such as price, quality, and service and are not normally comfortable with considerations such as gifts or payoffs, such gifts or payoffs are an important tradition in some countries.

Members of the inner circle in communal cultures, such as those in many parts of Latin America and Asia, maintain their relationships through a system of favors. It is assumed in these systems that any person who is obligated to another person or group has the duty to repay the favor at some time in the future. A lifetime cycle of obligations has thus been formed. Another factor is that to non-Westerners, Americans and other Westerners seem to be preoccupied with the business aspects of the negotiation rather than the important relationship aspects. Therefore, non-Westerners see gift giving as an appropriate way to increase social ties and to create a sense of obligation by the Western negotiator. Small gifts—such as pens, cups, and key rings engraved with your company logo—are not only acceptable, but also virtually essential in global business. Home and office decorations and books and magazines are also popular.

You should be concerned about the legal issues concerning gifts, payments, or bribes from the perspectives of both the United States and the host country. Tips, commissions, and finder's fees may be legal abroad, but they are a legal nightmare within Uncle Sam's long arms of the law. During the 1970s, revelations of dubious or questionable payments made by U.S. companies to foreign officials rocked governments in the Netherlands and Japan. The U.S. Congress,

considering corporate bribery "bad business" and "unnecessary," then passed the Foreign Corrupt Practices Act. The FCPA prohibits any U.S.–based company from "corruptly" offering or giving money or "anything of value to a foreign political official" for the purpose of obtaining or retaining business. However, the law allows "facilitating payments"—that is, payments made to expedite solely nondiscretionary official actions such as customs. This usually means routine promotional gifts, reimbursement of reasonable expenses for promotional meals or travel, and payments that are legal under the laws of the foreign country.

It is not always clear, however, where illegal bribes end and facilitating payments begin. There are also uncertainties as to how far management must go in order to learn whether an employee has violated the FCPA. Also, while there are probably less stringent rules about bribes in the host country you are dealing with, it is vital that you know its laws in this respect.

Action Steps for Resolving Bribery and Questionable Payment Issues

• *Above all, check with your legal staff about any vague areas of home or host-country laws*. Here's a time when you want the legal staff's involvement. It may be necessary to get legal counsel in the host country as well.

• *Keep your boss informed.* This is no time to be the Lone Ranger. Be sure he or she is aware of any concerns you have.

• *If you must make a payment, find out how to do it.* Rather than make a direct money payment, it may be feasible for you to invest in community projects, such as building a school for the children of customs officials.

• *If a monetary payment must be made, don't make the payment yourself.* Use a go-between such as a consultant or someone's relative in the host country.

Challenge 4: Dealing with International Virtual and Remote Teams

Negotiations within your own organization can sometimes be the toughest negotiations that you will face. In today's global business environment, your international negotiations may be taking place with people within your own organization who are spread around the world. It is hard enough for people to work well together in the same building, but there are additional challenges when they're in different global locations. Getting your team in Toronto to deal effectively with your teams in India, China, or Mexico will likely come with some substantial challenges. You must establish the team, build the team's culture, address

organizational barriers and individual concerns, build trust, and address the team's inevitable successes and failures.

The increase in international virtual teams is attributable to several reasons. Sourcing workers globally is often seen as a way to use less expensive labor compared to that of the home country. Too, the substantial improvements in communications and common database technology have facilitated this change, along with global mergers and acquisitions. A *remote team* exists when members of the team are located in a different location from the manager or leader. A *virtual team* is one where the team members are spread across different time zones, spaces, cultures, and/or organizations.

Challenges of International Teams

There are four main challenges in dealing with international virtual and remote teams:

1. The team is located away from you.
2. The people with whom you are dealing are in different time zones.
3. The teams are from different cultures.
4. Communication is seldom face to face; most communication is by telephone or e-mail.

Does Anybody Really Know What Time It Is?

Here's a typical situation. Jessica is a manager working out of Los Angeles and is responsible for a 24/7 shift operation based in Manila. Jessica hosts a group call once a month to keep everyone well informed about individual roles and collective responsibilities. This month, Jessica is going to host a Webinar because the team will be launching a new product that she will demonstrate online.

Suddenly, Jessica is facing several challenges. Only one of the Manila shifts will be working when the call is scheduled. So, how can it be scheduled in a way that's fair to everyone? Too, all of the Webinar participants need to log on and call in. Those not in the office can't do so from home because it is cost-prohibitive, and many employees don't have the right hardware and software at home. Then there's the overtime issue for those joining the call that are not officially on the clock.

Jessica's now thinking, "I've suddenly got a bunch of negotiations on my hands. The Manila team is great, but life was sure a lot simpler when the whole team was right there in LA."

Action Steps for Dealing with International Virtual and Remote Teams

• *Familiarize yourself with the cultural differences discussed in this book.* This is particularly important as to how these differences relate to communication and how employees and bosses relate to each other in each location.

• *Make extra efforts to keep lines of communication open.* All parties should be kept informed as to the teams' successes, failures, and concerns.

• *Use e-mail for the orientation and fact-finding stage of the negotiation (for example, for providing information or an agenda), and to summarize the discussion or agreement, but not for hard bargaining.* Negotiating with your team about project metrics, deadlines, dealing with setbacks and so on should preferably be done in person, or—when that isn't feasible—by telephone. The same can be said for blunt statements, challenges, or criticism—don't do it by e-mail.

• *Use clear language that is unlikely to be misconstrued by your international team members.* Slang has no place here. Even attempts at humor can go terribly wrong in an e-mail to someone from another culture.

• *Resolve time-zone differences in a way that is acceptable to all the parties concerned.* Getting a telephone call at 3 o'clock in the morning is not welcomed by you and is not going to be welcomed by your international counterpart, either.

• *Periodically, do an assessment as to how well the teams are working.* This assessment should be completed by those in both the manager's location and those in the host country.[1]

Notes

1. American Management Association's seminar, *Leading Virtual and Remote Teams*, 2001.

Negotiating Around the World

In Part Three, we examine the specific skills required for effective business negotiations throughout the world. In Chapters 5 through 11, you will learn the how, what, when, and where of international negotiating on a regional and country-by-country basis. Seven regions of the world are profiled, with key information on the business environment, the specific cultural factors that affect negotiating, and practical dos and don'ts.

The discussion of each of the seven regions is divided into four sections:

1. The business environment
2. Cultural factors that affect negotiating
3. How negotiations work
4. Your negotiating primer

These sections consist of a great deal of practical, relevant information that will help you become a masterful negotiator. Keep in mind that the guidelines throughout these sections are primarily from a North American perspective and that such guidelines are relative. For example, when we say that the pace of negotiations in Western Europe is moderate; this is from a North American viewpoint. The Japanese might consider these negotiations to be quite fast-paced.

The "Cultural Factors" section in each chapter encompasses the four factors discussed in Chapter 3: (1) use of time; (2) individualism versus collectivism; (3) role orderliness and conformity; and (4) patterns of communication. The section "How Negotiations Work" is patterned after the six aspects of global negotiations also outlined in

Chapter 3: (1) pace of negotiations; (2) negotiating strategies; (3) emphasis on personal relationships; (4) emotional aspects; (5) decision making; and (6) contractual and administrative factors.

A "negotiating primer" has been prepared for sixty-three countries, divided into regions:

Western Europe (Chapter 5)

Austria	France	Italy	Spain
Belgium	Germany	The Netherlands	Sweden
Denmark	Greece	Norway	Switzerland
Finland	Ireland	Portugal	United Kingdom

Eastern Europe (Chapter 6)

Czech Republic	Kazakhstan	Romania	Turkey
Hungary	Poland	Russia	Ukraine

Latin America (Chapter 7)

Argentina	Colombia	Ecuador	Peru
Brazil	Costa Rica	Guatemala	Venezuela
Chile	Cuba	Mexico	

North America (Chapter 8)

Canada	United States

The Middle East and North Africa (Chapter 9)

Algeria	Israel	Morocco	The United Arab
Egypt	Kuwait	Saudi Arabia	Emirates

Asia and the Pacific Rim (Chapter 10)

Australia	Indonesia	Pakistan	Sri Lanka
China	Japan	Philippines	Taiwan
Hong Kong, China	Malaysia	Singapore	Thailand
India	New Zealand	South Korea	Vietnam

Sub-Saharan Africa (Chapter 11)

Nigeria	South Africa	Zimbabwe

The primers consist of practical dos and don'ts and other important day-to-day information. The focus for each country is on five areas:

1. *Fast facts*: trading partners, key imports and exports, and other profile information on the country. This is based on 1990 data unless otherwise noted, and monetary figures are given in U.S. dollars.
2. *Reducing communication noise*: techniques for getting your message through.
3. *Key negotiating pointers*: country-specific negotiating guidelines.
4. *Day-to-day pointers*: business entertainment and related matters.
5. *Gender issues*: sensitivities and guidelines.

In addition, there is a section at the end of each primer called "Also Remember This . . . ," which provides further important background information to help you negotiate in that country.

The points that are emphasized within each of these categories differ from country to country. For example, a particular tactic is highlighted only if it seems of consequence in a particular country. Similarly, the ritual of toasts is mentioned under "Day-to-Day Pointers" only when this behavior is a key part of business entertainment. In some cases, a particular point is included because the information was available for that country and not for others.

Some issues are mentioned in almost all the primers. For example, the importance of being punctual is highlighted almost everywhere, even if TOS (The Other Side) keeps you waiting. This is because there is usually an expectation from TOS that you be on time, even if TOS is not. Popular sports are mentioned under "Conversation" in most primers because many individuals find it easy to discuss such matters. In all cases, use your own judgment on how to use this information. For example, many Canadians are rabid ice hockey fans, but if you sense that TOS has no interest in the subject, or if you clearly feel like a phony discussing it, then leave it alone. ("Conversation" also covers such topics as personal space and touching.) Some guidelines, such

as the avoidance of political or religious discussions, can generally be followed anywhere, but are emphasized in those countries where these can be especially sensitive topics.

Let's continue our intercultural journey by stopping in Western Europe.

Negotiating in Western Europe

The Business Environment of Western Europe

Remember that negotiating in Western Europe can sometimes be quite challenging and that negotiating styles differ from country to country. If your experience in Western Europe is limited to vacations, you will probably find that behavior in business situations is quite different from what you have experienced.

The most important business development in Western Europe in the last few decades is the emergence of the European Union (EU). The European Union currently consists principally of Western European countries: Belgium, Denmark, France, Germany, Greece, Ireland, Italy, Luxembourg, the Netherlands, Portugal, Spain, and the United Kingdom. Eastern European countries are also members, such as the Czech Republic, Hungary, and Poland. It is likely that other countries will join the EU, mainly from Eastern Europe. The EU is a powerful economic and political force whose goals are to reregulate a Europe that is a single market—a Europe without frontiers, where there will be an unrestricted movement of money, products, services, and people.

Europeans see the EU as a critical step in regaining their competitive position with the United States, Japan, China, and other parts of the world. The biggest opportunities for member countries may lie in the ability to exploit economies that are available in the widely expanded "home" market.

The most likely impact of the EU on your business activities is in the area

of common standards, deregulation, economic research and development, fiscal harmony, open government procurement, and taxation and tariff reforms.

What all this means in practical terms is that, among many other things, workers from member countries will be able to work anywhere in the EU, sales taxes and value-added taxes (VATs) will be made more uniform, foreign exchange controls will be discontinued, and property laws will be standardized. Products will be sold anywhere in the EU as long as they meet home-country standards. Flexible manufacturing will produce standard products (regarding packages and sizes) that will cater to local markets. But, again, realize that member countries will almost certainly retain key national differences when it comes to negotiations.

Cultural Factors That Affect Negotiating in Western Europe

Use of Time

The Western Europeans, more than any of the other cultures that we examine, share common views of time with North Americans. Business life is generally quite fast-paced, and meetings almost always start and end on time. Expect negotiations to move crisply in most of Western Europe.

Individualism vs. Collectivism

Western Europeans are generally quite individualistic. There is generally a distinction between one's core of intimate associates and those outside that core. Status and class consciousness are prevalent. One joins groups that are within one's class status. Friendships usually take a long time to develop. As with other high-individualism parts of the world, the individual is emotionally independent from the work organization. The emphasis is on individual initiative and achievement.

Role Orderliness and Conformity

Order, discipline, and responsibility are highly valued in the family and at work. The path to the corporate world is a mixture of education and connections. Leisure time with the family is extremely important, and month-long summer holidays (vacations) are typical.

Power in organizations flows from the top down, and the hierarchy is important. Top managers usually have a great deal of technical expertise and tend to dislike power sharing and delegation of responsibility. In addition, top managers do not communicate regularly with lower management. Consequently,

lower-level managers may not have much information about the corporate goals or mission. An exception is Scandinavia, where top management communicates regularly with middle management, and substantial power is delegated for key decisions.

Though Western Europeans have high occupational mobility, long tenures exist within the same organization. Job hopping tends to be viewed with disfavor, and loyalty and hard work are rewarded.

Patterns of Communication

Verbal Communication

Articulate speakers are valued. Many Western Europeans have a low tolerance for ambiguity. The communication is generally formal, understated, and subtle. It is expected that there will be face-to-face communication on initial contact. Emotional outbursts are looked upon very unfavorably.

Nonverbal Communication

Western Europeans are typically more reserved in their body language than North Americans, and much more so than Latin Americans or Middle Easterners. Wide, rapid gestures are almost always inappropriate in either a business or social setting.

Expect most Western Europeans to have about the same personal space as do North Americans in business settings—usually about three feet. Physical contact is usually limited to a brief handshake in business situations.

HOW NEGOTIATIONS WORK IN WESTERN EUROPE

Negotiating Factors

1. *Pace of Negotiations* — Moderate

2. *Negotiating Strategies*
 Opening Offers vis-à-vis Settlement — Moderate initial demands
 Presentation of Issues — One at a time
 Presentations — Formal
 Dealing with Differences — Polite, direct
 Concessions — Fairly slow

3. *Emphasis on Personal Relationships* — Low

4. *Emotional Aspects*
 Sensitivity — Moderate
 Degree of Emotions — Moderate

5. *Decision Making*

Overall Method	Planned, organized
Emphasize	Logic
Emphasis on Group/Team	Moderate: Decisions from top management
Emphasis on Face Saving	Moderate
Influence of Special Interests on Decision Makers	Moderate

6. *Contractual and Administrative Factors*

Need for an Agent	Average
Degree of Contract Specificity	High
Degree of Paperwork/Bureaucracy	Moderate
Need for an Agenda	High

AUSTRIA

Fast Facts

Monetary Unit: euro

Major Industries: foods, iron, steel, machinery

Primary Trading Partners

　　　Exports: Germany, Italy, Switzerland, United States, United Kingdom

　　　Imports: Germany, Italy, United States, France, Switzerland

Key Exports: machinery and equipment, paper and cardboard, metal goods

Key Imports: vehicles, machinery and equipment, apparel, metal goods

Major Cities: Vienna (cap.) (1.5 mil.), Graz (232,200), Linz (203,900), Salzburg (144,000)

Ethnic Groups: Germans (97%), Other (3%)

Primary Religions: Roman Catholic (78%), Protestant (5%), Muslim and Other (17%)

Languages: German is the official language; English is required in high schools and is spoken by many people.

Reducing Communication Noise

Greetings

- Common greetings are *Gruß Gott* (May God bless you) (pronounced "Gruss Gott"), *Guten Morgen* (Good morning), *Guten Tag* (Good day), and *Guten*

Abend (Good evening). Casual greetings include *Servus* (used as Hi) and *Gruß Dich!* (Greetings to you!). Austrians do not ask, *Wie geht es Ihnen?* (How are you?) unless they want to hear a lot of details.

- Dress well, wearing a business suit for business meetings.
- Shake hands when meeting and parting.
- In Vienna, a man may occasionally still kiss a woman's hand when meeting.
- Use professional titles when they are known. Otherwise, titles such as *Herr* (Mr.) and *Frau* (Mrs. or Ms.) are combined with family names in business meetings. First names are reserved for close friends.
- Limit hand gestures.

Conversation

- Austrians love to engage in conversation.
- Austrians are known for their excellence in winter sports. Soccer is also a favorite sport.
- Taking a walk is a national pastime. Hiking, skiing, swimming, and boating are also popular.
- Austrians enjoy modern art and music, but traditional music is also extremely important. The opera and orchestral concerts are well attended. Haydn, Mozart, Strauss, Beethoven, and Brahms all lived in Vienna. Folk music is important in Austria. Nearly every village has a band (usually brass).
- Austrians value their professionals, academics, and artists.
- Be respectful of Austria's environment. They take pride in their country's beautiful landscape.

Sensitivities

- Although Austrians and Germans both speak German (of different dialects), refer to Austrians only as Austrians, not Germans. The two cultures have a different political heritage and different customs, values, and attitudes.
- Austria was annexed by Nazi Germany in 1938 and joined Axis powers in World War II. The republic was restored in 1955 after ten years of Allied occupation.

Key Negotiating Pointers

- Austrians are used to international dealings and have a lot of business savvy.
- Be punctual for meetings. Punctuality is prized.
- Be friendly, but get to the point in your discussions. The personal relationship generally follows the business relationship.
- Be reserved and respect formalities.

- Make your presentations matter-of-fact, detailed, and subdued.
- Translate as much of your information into German as possible.

Day-to-Day Pointers

Business Entertainment Guidelines

- Business entertainment may be in a restaurant or an Austrian's home.
- If invited to an Austrian's home, bring flowers, candy, or a small gift. Flowers are given only in odd numbers, since even numbers are considered bad luck. Red roses are given only as a sign of romantic love.
- Most Austrians round up the bill to the nearest schilling (Austrian) as a tip.

Table Manners and Food

- Austrians love good food. Specialties include *Wienerschnitzel* (breaded veal cutlet), *Sachertorte* (a rich chocolate cake with apricot jam and chocolate icing), and *Knodel* (moist potato dumplings).
- Austrians enjoy beer, wine, herbal teas, fruit juices, and soft drinks.
- Keep your hands above the table during the meal. Avoid placing your elbows on the table when eating.
- Austrian men will typically stand when a woman enters the room or when talking to a woman who is standing. Gifts are normally given to the wife, not the husband, even if the gift is for the family.
- Austrians eat in the continental style, with the fork in the left hand and the knife in the right.

Gender Issues

- International businesswomen can expect to be treated well in Austria.
- Women make up almost 40 percent of the workforce. Austrian families are usually small, and married couples tend to share household duties, giving Austrian women the opportunity to be full partners in work outside the home.

Also Remember This . . .

- Austria is often considered a model of political, economic, and social stability. It has a mixed free-market/social welfare economy.
- Because of Austria's neutrality, Vienna has become a key United Nations city where nations meet to discuss issues.
- Austrians are hardworking, yet are known for their relaxed and happy approach to life.

BELGIUM

Fast Facts

Monetary Unit: euro

Major Industries: engineering, motor vehicle assembly, metal products, processed food, beverages, chemicals

Primary Trading Partners: Germany, France, Netherlands, United Kingdom, United States, Italy, Ireland

Key Exports: machinery and equipment, chemicals, diamonds, metals and metal products

Key Imports: machinery and equipment, chemicals, diamonds, pharmaceuticals, foodstuffs

Major Cities: Brussels (Bruxelles) (cap.) (1.8 mil. metro area), Antwerp (952,600 metro area), Ghent (250,000), Charleroi (206,900)

Ethnic Groups: Flemish (Dutch) (58%), Walloon (31%), mixed or other (11%)

Primary Religions: Roman Catholic (75%), Protestant or other (25%)

Languages: Flemish (Dutch) (60%), French (40%), German (less than 1%); all three are official languages; many businesspeople speak English and French.

Reducing Communication Noise

Greetings

- Shake hands quickly with light pressure upon meeting. When leaving, shake hands again and bid farewell to each member of the group.
- *Goeiedag* (Good day) is a typical Dutch greeting, or *Bonjour* in French. English greetings would be acceptable in Brussels and the larger cities.
- First names are not used in business settings, unless there is an established relationship. Address French-speaking as *Monsieur, Madame*, or *Mademoiselle*. For Dutch-speaking people, use *Mr., Mrs.*, or *Miss*.

Conversation

- Belgians enjoy talking about their fine food, art, and architecture. Artistic masters such as Van Eyck, Rubens, and Van Gogh lived in Belgium.
- Participant sports are very popular. Cycling and soccer are the most prominent.
- Delicate Belgian chocolates, beer, and lace are world famous.
- Dutch is more prominent in the north, and French is more widely used in the capital and southern areas.

Sensitivities

- Avoid personal questions about private lives. Belgians guard their privacy.
- Avoid discussing language, political, and cultural distinctions between the Flemish and Walloons in Belgium, and try not to confuse the two groups. The Flemish live in the northern part of Belgium (Flanders), while the Walloons live in the south (Wallonia). A Walloon is a member of the French-speaking minority living mainly in Wallonia and in neighboring parts of France.
- The Flemish sometimes tell jokes about people from the Netherlands (and vice versa). Stay out of this rivalry.
- Don't flaunt wealth.

Key Negotiating Pointers

- Belgians exhibit business savvy and are tough negotiators.
- Be punctual. Expect the regulation to proceed at a rapid pace. Be friendly but to the point in your discussions.
- Be reserved and respect formalities. The personal relationship generally follows the business relationship.
- Back up your information with lots of facts and figures.
- Have written materials translated into both French and Dutch.

Day-to-Day Pointers

Business Entertainment Guidelines

- Meals are a social and cultural event and are usually protracted. You may discuss business during a meal, but let your host initiate the subject.
- Dinner is usually 7:00 p.m. or 8:00 p.m.
- Do not send chrysanthemums as a thank you for an invitation, since they are a reminder of death.
- In restaurants, normally pay your bill at the table. Tips are included in the bill. You can leave a bit extra if you wish, but it isn't expected.

Table Manners and Food

- Finish your food. Belgians are thrifty and despise waste.
- Pork, game birds, fish, cheeses, fruits, vegetables, breads, and soups are favorite foods. Wine, beer, or mineral water is usually served with meals.
- Belgians prefer bottled water to tap water.

Gender Issues

- Although there is still a traditional view of female careers in business, Belgium is a good place for international businesswomen to do business.

Also Remember This . . .

- Belgium is sometimes considered the *de facto* capital of Europe.
- Belgium's strong foreign trade is aided by Antwerp, one of the largest seaports in the world, and its central location among EU countries.
- Belgium is a key producer of automobiles for foreign companies.
- Belgians are very family-oriented, and in spite of their cosmopolitan orientation, often live close to the towns where they were raised.
- Belgium has one of the shortest workweeks in the world—an average of about thirty-six hours. Vacations are usually one month long.

DENMARK

Fast Facts

Monetary Unit: krone

Major Industries: iron, steel, nonferrous metals, chemicals, food processing, machinery and transportation equipment

Primary Trading Partners: Germany, Sweden, United Kingdom, United States, the Netherlands, Norway, France, Italy, China

Key Exports: machinery and instruments, meat and meat products, dairy products, fish, chemicals, furniture

Key Imports: machinery and equipment, raw materials for industry, chemicals, grain and foodstuffs

Major Cities: Copenhagen (cap.) (1.9 mil.), Arhus (220,700), Odense (144,600), Alborg (120,600)

Ethnic Groups: Danish (99%); Inuit, Faeroese

Primary Religions: Evangelical Lutheran (95%), other Protestant and Roman Catholic (3%), Muslim (2%)

Languages: Danish (official), Faeroese, Greenlandic, German; English is widely used and is part of the curriculum after the fifth grade.

Reducing Communication Noise

Greetings

- Shake hands with both men and women upon meeting and leaving. Handshakes are firm and brief.
- A typical greeting upon meeting and leaving is *Heij* (Hello), pronounced "Hi." *Goddag* is the term used for "Good day."

- Though Danes are informal and friendly, use a person's last name accompanied by a title (Mr., Mrs., Ms.) unless invited to use a first name.

Conversation

- Maintain direct eye contract during conversation.
- Expect few hand gestures from your Danish counterpart.
- Soccer (called football by most soccer nations) is Denmark's favorite sport. Handball, badminton, swimming, sailing, rowing, and jogging are also popular. Watching television and reading are favorite family pastimes.
- Denmark has a high standard of living and is respected for its science, art, literature, and architecture.
- Danish furniture design is known worldwide.
- Many Danes attend cultural events.
- About 65 percent of the Danes have last names than end in -sen (for instance, Andersen, Christensen, Hansen).

Sensitivities

- Avoid questions or comments that might be taken as too personal, such as those related to one's family, appearance, or status.
- Don't criticize others' beliefs, or political or social systems. The Danes are quite tolerant of others.
- Danes are very proud of their country's achievements and institutions, so a foreigner's criticism of the state church, royal house, or system of government would probably be taken personally.

Key Negotiating Pointers

- Be punctual for meetings.
- Be friendly, but minimize small talk. The Danes tend to get down to business right away.
- Make your presentations factual, detailed, and subdued.
- Use a soft sell. The Danes' approach is one of understatement, so avoid any approach that might be construed as exaggeration.
- Emphasize practicality. Danes don't tend to be entrepreneurial because they are somewhat risk averse and face bureaucratic roadblocks.
- Expect candor from your Danish counterpart. The Danes have a somewhat dry sense of humor by some standards.
- Remember that summer is the time for leisure. Little business gets done during July or August.

Day-to-Day Pointers

Business Entertainment Guidelines

- Top Danish executives often host black-tie dinners. Conservative dress is important.
- Dinner is the main meal. Dinner typically consists of meat or fish, potatoes and gravy, vegetables, salad, and dessert.
- Although the service charge is included in the bill, some people also leave a small tip.
- Gifts are not necessary in order to do business.

Table Manners and Food

- Let your host suggest where you sit.
- Danes eat in the continental style, with the fork in the left hand and knife in the right.
- The *frokostbord*, a cold buffet of many different foods, and *bof*, a hamburger steak with a brown sauce and fried onions, are very popular.
- Lunch often consists of *smorrebrod* (open-faced sandwiches) and a drink.
- You might say *Voer sa god* and *Tak* (Thank you) when passing and receiving food.
- If having dinner in a private home, thank your hosts by saying *Tak for mad!* (Thanks for the meal!).

Gender Issues

- International businesswomen can expect good treatment in Denmark.
- Both father and mother work in a typical Danish home. Husbands and wives share household and childcare responsibilities.

Also Remember This . . .

- Denmark consists of several small islands in the North and Baltic Seas. Jutland, the largest, connects to the European continent. Copenhagen is located on Sjaelland, commonly called Zealand.
- The Danes have an elaborate social welfare scheme, supported by heavy individual taxes. Danes generally try to minimize social differences. Denmark has some of the world's toughest environmental legislation.
- Though autonomous, Greenland and the Faroe Islands are part of the Danish Kingdom.
- Denmark has one of the shortest workweeks in the European Union (EU)—averaging thirty-two hours. Employers and employee organizations jointly determine wages and working conditions for a two-year period.

FINLAND

Fast Facts

Monetary Unit: euro

Major Industries: metal manufacturing, shipbuilding, forestry and wood processing, copper refining

Primary Trading Partners: Sweden, Germany, Russia, United Kingdom, United States, Netherlands, Denmark, France

Key Exports: machinery, chemicals, paper and pulp

Key Imports: foodstuffs, petroleum and petroleum products, chemicals, transport equipment

Major Cities: Helsinki (cap.) (525,000), Espoo (191,200), Tampere (182,700), Vantaa (166,500)

Ethnic Groups: Finnish (93%), Swede, Sami, Roma, Tatar, and other (7%)

Primary Religions: Evangelical Lutheran (89%), Russian Orthodox (1%), other or unknown (10%)

Languages: Finnish (93%), Swedish (6%); both are official languages; English is widely spoken.

Reducing Communication Noise

Greetings

- Terms for greeting include a nod of acknowledgment and a simple *Hei* (Hello), or *Hyvaa paivaa* (Good morning/afternoon) and *Hyvaa huomenta* (Good morning).

- Make eye contact when meeting, and shake hands with both men and women. Handshakes are firm. Finns occasionally use both hands. When greeting a group, shake hands with women first.

- Finns typically mention first and last names, or a title and last name, upon greeting. Using first names upon greeting is becoming more common, but wait until invited to do so.

- Bring plenty of business cards.

Conversation

- Maintain direct eye contract.

- Finns put an emphasis on recreation and physical fitness. Favorite hobbies include fishing, hunting, camping, and other sporting activities. Ice fishing is

popular during the winter. Other popular sports include skiing, track and field, basketball, Finnish baseball (*Pesapallo*), ice hockey, cycling, and boating.

- Finns take great pride in their health programs. Finland ranks among the world's best in doctor-patient and nurse-patient ratios.
- Spending time in the sauna is a national pastime. Part of the sauna ceremony is relaxing afterward with a cold beer.

Sensitivities

- Avoid criticizing others' beliefs or political or social systems. The Finns tend to be quite tolerant to others.
- Don't ask personal questions of your host.
- Men should remove their hats when entering a building or when talking with another person.
- It is considered bad manners to talk with one's hands. Avoid folding your arms; this is viewed to be a sign of arrogance or pride.
- Although it is proper to cross one's legs with one knee over the other, it is inappropriate to sit with one ankle over the other knee.

Key Negotiating Pointers

- Make prior appointments, and be punctual for meetings.
- Be friendly, but minimize small talk. The Finns tend to get down to business right away.
- Mean what you say. Finns tend to take promises and agreements seriously.
- Expect the decision maker to be at a high level in the organization. Try to deal with the managing director (the top person).
- Make presentations factual, detailed, and subdued.
- Don't be surprised by periods of silence from your Finnish counterpart.
- Address your Finnish counterpart with a title and last name in written communication.
- Remember that summer is a time of leisure. Little business is conducted in July. Most Finns also take a one-week winter holiday in February.

Day-to-Day Pointers

Business Entertainment Guidelines

- Finnish men wear suits for both business and social events. Tuxedos are not uncommon for social events. Women should wear a dress or suit, or a cocktail dress for business entertaining.
- Meals are considered a social event and business is seldom discussed.
- Business entertainment is usually confined to restaurants.

- Dress can be from casual to formal, depending on the restaurant.
- A 15 percent tip is usually included in the bill. A further tip is not usually expected. Porters, doormen, and coat checkers do receive tips. Taxi drivers usually take credit cards, and the tip is included in the fare.

Table Manners and Food

- Expect a toast at the beginning of the meal.
- Finnish food has been heavily influenced by the French, Russians, and other cultures and includes a number of Finnish specialties using fish and seafood, wild game, and vegetables. Also popular are potatoes, cheeses, and a Finnish buffet, such as a *smorgasbord*. Reindeer steak and salmon are specialties. Wild berries are popular in desserts and liquors.
- The Finnish appreciate fine wines, beer, and vodka. There can be heavy drinking, so pace yourself.
- Wait until the host takes the first sip before you drink your beverage, and until the host begins eating before you eat.
- Finns eat in the continental style, with the fork in the left hand and the knife in the right.
- Most offices and public places are smoke-free.

Gender Issues

- Both parents usually work outside the home.
- Finland is a leader in women's rights. Finnish women expect to be involved in careers, politics, social issues, and motherhood. Many women keep their original last name upon marriage.
- Women typically hold a substantial number of parliament seats.

Also Remember This . . .

- Finland is a Scandinavian or Nordic country that borders Russia and is known as the Land of 10,000 Lakes (actually it has almost 188,000 lakes). Finnish environmental laws are tough.
- Finland declared its independence from Russia in 1917. A 1992 treaty with Russia recognized Finland's equality, sovereignty, and economic relations.
- Finns enjoy a high standard of living. Finland has a large free-market economy that is highly industrialized and relies heavily on imports for many raw materials and important goods.
- Finland's skilled and well-educated workforce contributes to its global competitiveness.

FRANCE

Fast Facts

Monetary Unit: euro

Major Industries: steel, machinery, chemicals, automobiles

Primary Trading Partners: Germany, Spain, United Kingdom, Italy, Belgium, United States, the Netherlands

Key Exports: machinery and transport equipment, chemicals, foodstuffs, agricultural products, iron and steel products

Key Imports: crude petroleum, machinery and equipment, vehicles, aircraft, chemicals, iron and steel products

Major Cities: Paris (cap.) (2.2 mil.), Marseille (820,700), Lyon (443,900), Toulouse (411,800), Nice (332,000)

Ethnic Groups: Celtic and Latin with Teutonic, Slavic, North African, Indochinese, and Basque minorities

Primary Religions: Roman Catholic (83–88%), Muslim (5–10%), Protestant (2%), Jewish (1%)

Language: French

Reducing Communication Noise

Greetings

- Shake hands with a single, quick shake and light pressure upon meeting. When leaving, shake hands again with all those to whom you were introduced.
- Women may not offer their hands to men; if so, men should initiate the greeting. Don't offer your hand to a person of superior authority.
- First names are used only among close friends. The use of first names is initiated by the person who is older and superior in rank.
- Until told to do otherwise, it is best to address everyone as *Monsieur, Madame,* or *Mademoiselle* without adding the surname.
- Common greetings include *Bonjour* (Hello), *Comment-allez-vous?* (How are you?), *Ca va?* (a casual How are you?).

Conversation

- The French value politeness. *S'il vous plait* (Please) is a commonly used expression.
- Try talking about French art, architecture, food, and history.

- Soccer and rugby are popular spectator sports. Fishing, bicycling, tennis, hiking, skiing, and sailing are popular individual sports. The annual Tour de France is a major international cycling event.

- The business language in France is most certainly French. Though knowledge of English is commonplace, your counterpart may or may not want to accommodate you. If you speak little or no French, your best bet is to speak English (except for greetings or toasts), or have a French-speaking representative.

- Don't take it personally if you sense that your French counterpart is shocked by your inept French (they are also often shocked by the way other French people speak French). The French are as ethnocentric as are Americans—extremely proud and self-centered about their culture.

- There tends to be a lot of touching compared to many other Western European countries.

Sensitivities

- Avoid talking about politics, money, and personal matters.

- Prepare yourself for graceful responses to challenges on French wines and those from other countries.

- The American *okay* sign (with the thumb and index finger forming a circle) means "zero" to the French. The French gesture for *okay* is the thumbs-up sign.

Key Negotiating Pointers

- Avoid a hard sell. The French are rather formal and conservative in business.

- Make prior appointments and be punctual.

- After a brief exchange of pleasantries, expect to get to the point of your discussions. Let your host take the lead in this. The personal relationship is normally solidified after the business relationship has been formed.

- New ideas should be well-researched and conceptually strong. The French apply reason and logic to negotiations.

- Presentations should be formal, informative, rational, and subdued.

- Allow plenty of time; decisions are made after much deliberation.

- Be aware that although the French are often reserved, the team may be argumentative, disagreeing for the sake of discussion. Expect them normally to state their intentions directly and openly.

- An agreement may be reached orally, with written contracts to follow.

- A local representative or agent is advised. Joint ventures or branch offices, or even a network of distributors throughout France, may be needed for success.

Day-to-Day Pointers

Business Entertainment Guidelines

- Most entertaining is done in restaurants. You are generally invited to someone's home only if you become very good friends as well as business associates.
- Business lunches and dinners may last over two hours, with more than ten courses.
- Cultural conversation is as important as fine food. Avoid talking about business over a meal until your host gives a signal.
- Eat something light before a formal dinner since your guests are likely to arrive late.
- Lunch (*dejeuner*) is the main meal of the day, eaten at noon.
- Whether you are entertained at home or in a restaurant, telephone the next day or write a brief note to express your thanks.
- When a key negotiation is completed, the heads of the two negotiating groups usually toast each other and wish each other a long, fruitful relationship.
- Logo gifts with your company name should be reserved and unobtrusive.

Table Manners and Food

- Etiquette in eating is important.
- Keep your hands (but not your elbows) above the table.
- French restaurants are often very expensive. Avoid ordering the most expensive item on the menu, overeating, and overdrinking.
- Be sure to compliment the fine cuisine.
- You should always ask permission before you smoke. Smoking in public places is frowned upon.
- French cuisine is world-famous, with French standards often the gauge of fine cooking. Expect large multicourse meals and *nouvelle cuisine* (lighter foods).
- Have only one helping of cheese. Lettuce is folded into small pieces, but do not cut it.

Gender Issues

- France is generally a good place for international businesswomen to do business, though they should expect to be treated with some gallantry and flirtatiousness.
- Women increasingly occupy professional and management positions in such areas as retail, service, media, advertising, law, finance, and human resources.
- Women make up about 40 percent of the French workforce.

Also Remember This . . .

- The French are very proud of their culture, heritage, and way of life.

- The French generally enjoy economic prosperity through their large industrial economy and welfare-style government. High unemployment and budget deficits are ongoing challenges, however.

- Though the French are quite formal in their on-stage business dealings, they usually have an off-the-record web of informal networks that help them get what they want done in their organizations.

- Most French workers take five weeks of vacation: four in the summer, and one during Christmas.

- France is the number one destination of tourists in the world.

GERMANY

Fast Facts

Monetary Unit: euro

Major Industries: iron, steel, coal, cement, chemicals, machinery, vehicles, machine tools

Primary Trading Partners: France, United States, United Kingdom, the Netherlands, Belgium, Austria, Spain, China

Key Exports: machinery, vehicles, chemicals

Key Imports: machinery, vehicles, chemicals, foodstuffs

Major Cities: Berlin (cap.) (3.9 mil.), Hamburg (1.7 mil.), Munich (1.3 mil.), Cologne (965,300), Frankfort (656,200)

Ethnic Groups: German (92%), Turkish, Slavic, and Danish (8%)

Primary Religions: Protestant (34%), Roman Catholic (34%), Muslim (4%), unaffiliated or other (28%)

Language: German

Reducing Communication Noise

Greetings

- Shake hands firmly upon meeting and leaving.

- Don't use first names unless invited to do so. Address people as *Herr* or *Frau* with the last name. Anyone with a doctorate (such as a lawyer) is addressed Herr or Frau Doktor X, and professor is Herr or Frau Professor X. It is important to know a person's proper title.

- Common greetings are *Guten Morgen* (Good morning), *Guten Tag* (Good day), and *Guten Abend* (Good evening).

Conversation

- Try talking about the weather, your trip over, hobbies (many Germans have one or more), or travel (many Germans like to vacation to other countries). German wines and beers are world-famous and are good topics of conversation.
- Soccer, hiking, and bicycling are popular sports.
- Germans tend to be formal and reserved at first meetings and may seem unfriendly. It takes time to get on a first-name basis.

Sensitivities

- Avoid personal questions other than general, polite inquiries about one's family. The German sense of privacy is very strong.
- Avoid discussing politics and World War II.
- It is considered impolite to keep your hands in your pocket while talking with someone.

Key Negotiating Pointers

- Germans have a reputation as hard bargainers.
- Make appointments well in advance at the highest possible level. Be punctual.
- Prepare an agenda for the meeting. Germans conduct business with great attention to order and planning, and tend to be uneasy with ambiguity. The tone of the negotiations is formal.
- Dress neatly and maintain a formal decorum. Practice restraint. Remain silent rather than offer an uninformed opinion.
- Do not try to establish personal relationships beyond normal courtesies. Germans tend to remain aloof until business is completed, though younger Germans are a bit more informal. Avoid joke telling to break the ice.
- Try to arrange smaller meetings if you can, where the atmosphere tends to be less formal.
- Avoid surprises and a hard sell. Don't spring a startling new proposal on your counterpart at a formal meeting.
- Be well prepared. Proposals and presentations should be detailed, logical, and filled with appropriate technical data. Be thoroughly knowledgeable in product and contract details.
- Negotiating proposals should be concrete and realistic, presented in a clear, orderly, and authoritative manner.
- Decision making in Germany involves a thorough analysis of all the facts and

may take longer than in the United States. A top manager may make even minor decisions.

- Follow up with an e-mail or letter that summarizes discussions. Germans like to have things in writing.
- Be aware of last-second demands. If you must make the concession, do it conditionally.
- This is one of the few places in the world where contracts tend to be more specific than those in the United States. German contracts spell out what U.S. contracts might leave to standard trade practice. There are two kinds of signing authority. The marks *p.p.* or *ppa* (*per procura*) indicate someone with restricted authority, while *i.V.* (*in Vertretung*) indicates a manager with full authority.
- Participate in German trade fairs and contact the chambers of commerce. Both are prestigious institutions in Germany.

Day-to-Day Pointers

Business Entertainment Guidelines
- A customer should be invited for a business lunch or dinner. But if your customer insists on being the host, readily accept the invitation.
- Lunch is normally the main meal of the day. The evening meal is generally simple, except on special occasions.
- A gift of flowers should be brought if invited to a private home for an evening meal or party. The visitor is expected to make the first move to terminate the visit, and should never stay too late.
- Germans have a great respect for social formalities. Much handshaking takes place on social occasions.

Table Manners and Food
- It is customary to say *Guten appetit* before eating and not to start drinking before the host has toasted the guest with *Prost*, *Prosit*, or *zum Wohle*. If someone raises the glass to you personally, reciprocate sometime during the meal.
- Keep your hands on the table.
- Do not smoke during a meal until after the last person has finished eating and coffee or brandy is being served.
- Potatoes, noodles, dumplings, sauces, vegetables, and pastries are common foods. Germans also enjoy sausages, pork, chicken, and other meats.

Gender Issues
- Germany is one of the hardest places for international businesswomen to do business in Europe. Chauvinism is alive and well.

- Germans are more resistant to women working than those in some other European countries. Women who do work are unlikely to obtain key professional or management positions. Almost no sex discrimination laws exist.

Also Remember This . . .

- Germany is one of the world's top economic powers.
- The Eastern states have made substantial progress toward shifting to a market economy but still rely heavily on subsidies from the Western states.
- Germany's generous social benefits, high labor costs, and rigid work rules are seen by some as impediments to its global competitiveness.
- Germany is one of the world's largest exporters of cars, televisions, and other manufactured goods.

GREECE

Fast Facts

Monetary Unit: euro

Major Industries: tourism, food, tobacco, textiles, chemicals, metal products, mining

Primary Trading Partners: Germany, Italy, United Kingdom, Bulgaria, United States, Cyprus, Turkey, France, Netherlands

Key Exports: food and beverages, manufactured goods, petroleum products, chemicals, textiles

Key Imports: machinery, transport equipment, fuels, chemicals

Major Cities: Athens (cap.) (3.2 mil. metro area), Thessaloniki (361,200), Piraeus (179,300)

Ethnic Groups: Greek (98%), other (2%)

Primary Religions: Greek Orthodox (98%), Muslim (1%), other (1%)

Languages: Greek is the official language; English and French are widely understood.

Reducing Communication Noise

Greetings

- Greeks are usually expressive in their greetings. Shake hands upon meeting and leaving.
- The Greek custom is to embrace and kiss each other on the cheek. As a visitor, you are not expected to do so.

- Upon first meeting, use the title *Kyrie* (Mr.) or *Kyria* (Mrs.) with the last name.
- The Greeks are generally formal with names but use first names with colleagues of similar age and status. Do not use first names until you are invited to do so.
- Common greetings are *Kalimera sas* (Good morning) and *Kalispera sas* (Good evening).

Conversation

- Greeks enjoy talking about their history, culture, families, and sports. Many Greeks are movie and theater fans. Men often spend their leisure time talking with friends in coffeehouses.
- Soccer, basketball, swimming, windsurfing, and sailing are popular sports.
- Don't be surprised if you are asked personal questions about your family.
- Don't praise an object too much. Your Greek host may insist on giving it to you.
- Be aware that a head nod can mean *no* as well as *yes*. Tilting (not shaking) one's head to either side usually means *yes* or *of course*.
- Greeks may smile to express happiness or anger and are likely to use their hands a lot in conversation.

Sensitivities

- Avoid discussing Cyprus and other political issues.
- Older Greeks value family, religion, and tradition, though status and friends are also very important to the younger generation.

Key Negotiating Pointers

- In Greece, connections with the right people are critical. The *xorio*, or close network of family alliances, extends into business considerations.
- Prior appointments are not necessary but are appreciated. Be punctual, though your meetings probably won't start on time. Meetings are also not likely to have a specified ending time. Greeks are generally casual about time.
- Don't expect a formal agenda to be followed.
- Build a solid relationship. Trust is more important than expertise. Any suspicion that you are trying to exploit or dominate a relationship could cost you the deal.
- Expect discussions to be spirited. Greeks like to debate, usually with expressive words and body language. What might seem like a major confrontation is really just a normal exchange of views. Be more concerned if your counterpart becomes silent and withdrawn rather than about a somewhat boisterous exchange.
- Be firm and persistent, yet patient and courteous.

- Try to do your negotiating in person, the preferred method of communication in Greece. If possible, avoid the telephone and written communication.
- Keep contracts simple. They are generally distrusted.

Day-to-Day Pointers

Business Entertainment Guidelines
- Don't discuss business during meals. Meals are a social occasion.
- Lunch is usually the main meal of the day, served between noon and 2:00 p.m. Dinner is usually a small meal, usually around 7:00 p.m. to 9:00 p.m.
- The Greeks are very generous and sincere hosts. You may be invited home for dinner. If so, take flowers or a cake to the hostess.
- In restaurants, a service charge is usually included in the bill for the server; a tip may be left for the busperson.

Table Manners and Food
- The elderly, who are given an unusual amount of respect in Greece, are served first.
- It is typical for a group to order several dishes that everyone shares.
- Having a second helping is considered a compliment to your host.
- Lamb, chicken, seafood, olives, cheese, potatoes, rice, beans, fruit, and vegetables are common foods. Many foods are cooked in olive oil. Spices are popular.
- Salads are usually eaten with the main meal. A popular dish is *souvlaki*, a shish kebab with cakes of meat (usually lamb) and vegetables.

Gender Issues

- Greece is a good place for international businesswomen to do business.
- Although Greek society is generally male-dominated, women are in leadership roles in business, civil service, and politics.
- Business success depends more on one's connections than on one's gender.

Also Remember This . . .

- Although the industrial sector is growing, Greece has a strong agricultural base. About 20 percent of the labor force is employed in agriculture.
- The key unit in Greek business has traditionally been large conglomerates run by dynastic families, closely affiliated with the banks. Many large conglomerates have been socialized, with family managers replaced by political appointees.
- Greece has strong partnerships with European Union members and is continuing to develop ties with Eastern European and Black Sea countries.

- A typical workday extends from 8:00 a.m. to 1:30 p.m., and then from 5:00 to 8:00 p.m.

IRELAND
(Eire)

Fast Facts

Monetary Unit: euro

Major Industries: food products, brewing, textiles, clothing

Primary Trading Partners: United States, United Kingdom, Belgium, Germany, France, the Netherlands, Italy

Key Exports: chemicals, computers, industrial machinery

Key Imports: data processing equipment, chemicals, petroleum and petroleum products

Major Cities: Dublin (cap.) (916,000), Cork (174,00), Limerick (76,000), Galway (51,000)

Ethnic Groups: Celtic, with English minority

Primary Religions: Roman Catholic (92%), Church of Ireland (2%), other (6%)

Languages: Irish (Gaelic) and English are both official languages. English is widely spoken; Gaelic is spoken by about a quarter of the population, though often not on a daily basis.

Reducing Communication Noise

Greetings

- The Irish shake hands and greet one another with phrases such as *Hello,* and *How are you?* The most typical Irish-language greeting is *Dia Dhuit* (God to you), to which one responds *Dia is Muire duit!* (God and Mary to you).

- Use a title (Mr., Ms., Mrs., Miss, or Doctor) and last name unless invited to use a first name by your Irish counterpart.

- Use *Slan*, meaning "safe," for goodbye.

Conversation

- Some say that conversation is a national pastime among the Irish.

- The Irish are sports oriented. The two national pastimes are Gaelic football and hurling. Hurling is played on a field, with wooden sticks and a small leather ball. Other favorite sports include soccer, rugby, sailing, cycling, golf, and horse racing. Trout and salmon fishing are common pastimes.

- The Irish are proud of their beaches, scenic sunsets, green valleys, and towering cliffs.
- Many literary giants are from Ireland, such as Jonathan Swift, George Bernard Shaw, W. B. Yeats, Oscar Wilde, and James Joyce.
- The music of "The Emerald Isle" is known worldwide.
- St. Patrick's Day (March 17) is a major holiday throughout Ireland, with street parades in every city. St. Patrick is Ireland's patron saint.
- Expect mild hand gestures from your Irish counterpart during conversation.

Sensitivities

- Avoid discussions associated with the status of Ireland (that is, the Republic of Ireland) and Northern Ireland. Their differences are rooted in centuries-old conflicts.

Key Negotiating Pointers

- Make appointments in advance.
- Engage in small talk before getting down to business.
- Be on time for meetings, though the Irish are often not very time-conscious.
- The Irish tend to be easy-going, good-natured, and polite. Mirror this behavior.
- Be aware that the Irish tend to avoid personal confrontation, and will rarely say no directly. If embarrassed, however, they can have very long memories.
- Presentations should be informative and subdued.
- Remember that religion pervades virtually all aspects of life.
- Agreements can be reached orally, with a contract to follow.

Day-to-Day Pointers

Business Entertainment Guidelines

- Business entertainment usually takes place in restaurants, or perhaps a pub.
- Tea is served with most meals.
- If invited to an Irish home for dinner, bring a gift such as flowers, chocolates, wine, or cheese. Other business gift giving is not a common practice in Ireland.
- Tipping is not typical but is becoming more common in more expensive restaurants.

Table Manners and Food

- Traditional Irish cuisine is hearty and simple. Ireland produces many fresh vegetables. Potatoes are a staple. Apples, oranges, and pears are a key part of the Irish diet. Chicken, pork, beef, and mutton are the main meats.

- Smoked salmon, Irish stew, and Irish lamb are Irish specialties. Farmhouse restaurants feature traditional Irish recipes.
- Keep your hands, though not your elbows, above the table.
- The Irish use the continental style, with the fork in the left hand and the knife in the right.

Gender Issues

- International businesswomen can expect chauvinistic behavior from Irishmen. For all the chivalry, the international businesswoman may not be taken as seriously as she would like in getting the deal done.
- A woman should not expect to feel welcome in what appears to be a male preserve, such as a pub, where a lot of drinking is done.
- Women compose about one-third of the Irish workforce.

Also Remember This . . .

- The Anglo-Irish Treaty of 1921 established an Irish Free State as a British dominion and the six northern counties to remain in the United Kingdom as Northern Ireland. The Irish Free State changed its name to Eire (Ireland) in 1937, and withdrew from the British Commonwealth in 1949.
- Ireland's economy relies heavily on trade, especially with countries belonging to the European Union (EU).
- Ireland's economy is small but rapidly growing. It is in the process of expanding its economy beyond agriculture to rely more heavily on the services and technology sectors.

ITALY

Fast Facts

Monetary Unit: euro
Major Industries: tourism, machinery and transport equipment, iron, steel, chemicals
Primary Trading Partners: Germany, France, United States, Spain, United Kingdom, Switzerland, Netherlands, China
Key Exports: engineering equipment, textiles and clothing, production machinery, motor vehicles
Key Imports: engineering products, chemicals, transport equipment, energy products

Major Cities: Rome (cap.) (2.8 mil.), Milan (1.4 mil.), Naples (1.2 mil.), Turin (1.0 mil.), Palermo (695,000)

Ethnic Groups: primarily Italian, but includes small clusters of German-, French-, and Slovene-Italians in north, and Albanian-Italians in south; Sicilians

Primary Religions: almost all nominally Roman Catholic

Languages: Italian; French and English are spoken by some businesspeople in the large cities.

Reducing Communication Noise

Greetings

- Shake hands upon meeting and leaving. Guests are introduced first.
- Address people by their formal titles. Use *Dottore* if you are unsure of your counterpart's title. First names are reserved for close friends.
- Common greetings are *Ciao* (Hi or Goodbye), *Buongiorno* (Good morning and Good afternoon), and *Buona Sera* (Good evening).
- Bring plenty of business cards.

Conversation

- Italians enjoy talking about international events, their fine food and wine, and their many museums, art galleries, and historical sites. Italy has been the center of the arts for centuries.
- Italians are avid sports fans, particularly when it comes to soccer. (Italy has won the World Cup several times.) Bicycling, horse racing, skiing, tennis, boxing, and swimming are other popular sports. Basketball and American football have recently attracted an Italian following, but most Italians remain partial to soccer and other traditional sports.
- Italians are very family oriented, and general discussions about one's family are common.
- Don't be surprised if you see persons of the same gender walking arm-in-arm in public.

Sensitivities

- Italians like discussing politics. Do more listening than talking.
- Italians often refer to one another by their city origin (for example, Roman, Milanese, Florentine) and some regional attitudes remain.

Key Negotiating Pointers

- Make appointments well in advance. Punctuality is not a preoccupation for Italian businesspeople, so you may occasionally be kept waiting.

- Avoid making a cold call. Announce yourself by sending a letter or e-mail first. This helps make you a known quantity.
- Take every opportunity before, during, and after the negotiating session to build a relationship with your Italian counterpart. Italians like to deal with people they know well.
- Expect to get down to business after a few minutes of small talk. Let your host take the lead on this.
- Italy's negotiating style gets more informal as you move south.
- Make your presentations factual and relevant to local applications.
- Avoid any sense of urgency. The Italians often exhibit a calculated nonchalance. For example, a common tactic is to unexpectedly close a negotiating session, pretending the whole thing is of minor importance. Conversely, the deal can come together quickly when all seems lost. Urgency on your part may send a signal that you are desperate to do the deal.
- Get a local agent and consider getting an attorney.

Day-to-Day Pointers

Business Entertainment Guidelines

- Except in Milan, there is not a lot of business entertainment in Italy.
- Business entertainment is usually done in a restaurant.
- Don't discuss business during meals or social events.
- Lunch is the main meal of the day, usually served around 1:00 p.m. A light dinner is eaten in the evening, usually around 8:00 or 9:00 p.m.
- If you are invited to a private home, take wine, flowers (not chrysanthemums, used only for funerals), or chocolates.
- Gift-giving among business associates is common.
- In restaurants, a service charge is usually included in the bill. A small tip for the waiter is also appropriate.

Table Manners and Food

- Keep your hands above the table, not in your lap.
- Compliment your host on the fine cuisine.
- When finished eating, place the utensils parallel to each other on the plate.
- Lunch usually consists of three courses: pasta, fish, or meat with vegetables, and fruit.
- Take your time during meals. They may last from one to four hours.
- Wine is a common drink at meals.

Gender Issues

- Italy has a male-dominated business environment, but other international businesswomen can successfully do business.

- International businesswomen should expect some gallant behavior from their Italian male counterparts—for example, having doors opened for them with some flair. Such actions should be accepted graciously.

- A woman traveling with a male colleague should define clearly what her role is. If the male is her superior, the male should define her role.

- Women make up about one-third of the Italian workforce, among the lowest percentages in Western Europe. With the exception of the fashion industry, there are few Italian women in professional positions and decision-making positions.

- There is little equal employment opportunity legislation for working women, though there are generous maternity benefits and a well-developed system of free day care.

Also Remember This . . .

- The Italian economy is based on agriculture in the south and industry in the north.

- Italy is one of the world's largest wine producers. Tourism is another major source of revenue.

- Milan is the leading business city.

- Italy has a history of political instability, with about sixty successive governments since World War II.

- Italy includes the islands of Sicily and Sardinia. Italy also surrounds two independent nations: San Marino and Vatican City (Holy See).

THE NETHERLANDS

Fast Facts

Monetary Unit: euro

Major Industries: agro-industries, metal and engineering products, electrical machinery and equipment

Primary Trading Partners: Germany, Belgium, United Kingdom, France, United States, China

Key Exports: machinery and equipment, chemicals, fuels, food, tobacco

Key Imports: machinery and transport equipment, chemicals, foodstuffs, fuels, clothing
Major Cities: Amsterdam (cap.) (737,900), The Hague (admin. cap.) (465,900), Rotterdam (600,700), Utrecht (263,900)
Ethnic Groups: Dutch (83%), other (17%; 9% of which are Moroccans, Turks, Antilleans, Surinamese, and Indonesian)
Primary Religions: Roman Catholic (31%), Protestant (21%) (mainly Dutch Reformed), Muslim (4%), other (4%), unaffiliated (40%)
Languages: Dutch; English is widely spoken in business.

Reducing Communication Noise

Greetings

- Shake hands with everyone present, including women and children, upon meeting and leaving. Women are insulted if men do not shake hands with them.
- The Dutch are fairly informal. First names are common, but do not use them until you are invited to do so. Until that time, address people as *Mr.*, *Mrs.*, or *Miss*. If the other person is much older or very senior in position, be careful about using first names even if invited to do so; this invitation may be out of courtesy and will be perceived as being overly familiar if you accept it.

Conversation

- The Dutch enjoy talking about their art, music, museums, beautiful country, and international affairs. Many famous artists are from Holland, such as Rembrandt, Vermeer, and Van Gogh. The Dutch also appreciate compliments on their homes and their flowers, and like to talk about traveling.
- The Dutch are sports-minded. Soccer is the most popular sport, followed by tennis, bicycling, field hockey, swimming, sailing, and ice skating.
- Maintain eye contact during conversation. Personal space is about the same as in North America (about three feet).

Sensitivities

- Avoid discussing religion.
- If you discuss politics, do more listening than talking. The Dutch see their politics as very plain and down-to-earth compared with the relative glamour of U.S. or British politics.

Key Negotiating Pointers

- Make prior appointments and be punctual.
- The pace of negotiations is fast.

- Make your proposals conceptually strong as well as quantitatively correct. The Dutch pay attention to the bottom line but are not obsessed by numbers.

- Presentations should be professional looking, practical, and factual. Consider using charts and graphs. Sloppiness would be hard to overcome.

- Leave yourself some room to negotiate, but make your first offer fairly close to your *really asking* price. The Dutch are not hagglers. You may lose points if you start making large concessions.

- Be straightforward and downplay humor. Even informal business discussions tend to remain serious. The Dutch prize plain speaking.

- Comply with the details of your promises. Failure to do so will hurt your credibility. The Dutch are practical and efficient and expect results.

Day-to-Day Pointers

Business Entertainment Guidelines

- Business entertaining is not common, but when done, usually takes place in restaurants.

- It is appropriate to discuss business during a business lunch. (Most Dutch feel somewhat guilty if they have fun during working hours.)

- The main meal of the day is dinner.

- If invited to a Dutch home, shake hands with everyone, including children. Leave after coffee is served, usually before 10:00 p.m.

- In restaurants, tips are usually included in the bill, but leave a small additional tip if the service is good.

Table Manners and Food

- The Dutch tend to pay attention to table manners.

- Men usually wait until all the women are seated before sitting down.

- Before eating, the host or hostess will usually says *Eet smakelijk* (ATE-smaahk-AY-lick), meaning "Eat deliciously."

- Keep your hands (but not elbows) above the table.

- Dinner usually consists of meat or fish and potatoes and gravy, with vegetables of the season. Herring, smoked eel, oysters, pea soup, and *hutspot* (mashed potatoes mixed with various vegetables) are typical dishes.

Gender Issues

- International businesswomen can successfully conduct business with the Dutch. However, in spite of the social responsibility of the Netherlands as a nation, the Dutch are sometimes chauvinistic about women in business.

- There is a powerful Old Boy Network in industry and a male-dominated aristocracy within banking and the diplomatic service.
- Women seldom have professional careers, and married women tend to end their careers when they have children.
- Dutch women make up only about 35 percent of the workforce, somewhat low by Western standards.

Also Remember This . . .

- The Dutch welcome foreigners and are generally open to new ideas, yet have some of the toughest immigration policies in Europe.
- The Netherlands has a strong economy that is based on commerce, industry, and agriculture. Banking and tourism are also key sectors of the economy.
- The distribution of income in the Netherlands is among the most equitable in Europe.
- The Netherlands produces food for export and is responsible for more than half of the world's flower exports.
- The Dutch are quite liberal in terms of using marijuana, and have legalized prostitution and euthanasia.

NORWAY

Fast Facts

Monetary Unit: Norwegian krone

Major Industries: petroleum and gas, food processing, shipbuilding, pulp and paper products, metals

Primary Trading Partners: United Kingdom, Germany, the Netherlands, France, United States, Sweden, Denmark, China

Key Exports: petroleum and petroleum products, machinery and equipment, metals, chemicals, ships, fish

Key Imports: machinery and equipment, chemicals, metals, foodstuffs

Major Cities: Oslo (cap.) (791,500), Bergen (211,200), Stavanger (168,600), Trondheim (144,000)

Ethnic Groups: Nordic (Scandinavian), and small Sami (or Laplander) minority

Primary Religions: Evangelical Lutheran (state church) (86%), other Protestant and Roman Catholic (4%); other or unknown (10%)

Languages: Norwegian (official), small Lapp- and Finnish-speaking minorities; English is widely spoken.

Reducing Communication Noise

Greetings

- A common greeting is *God dag* (Good day). Slightly less formal greetings are *Morn* (literally Morning), regardless of the time of day, and *Hei* (Hi).
- Handshakes should be firm and short. Shake hands with both men and women.
- Use formal titles, followed by the last name. When being introduced for the first time, address your counterpart by both the first and last names.

Conversation

- Norwegians are very involved in sports activities. Participation is stressed more than winning.
- Norwegian children learn to ski at an early age. Alpine (downhill) and Nordic (cross-country) skiing are very popular, as is ice skating.
- Fishing is excellent in Norway. There are many boating enthusiasts when the frozen lakes (fjords) thaw.
- Theater, concerts, or other cultural events are also popular.
- The Norwegian themes of peace and progress are symbolized by the Nobel Peace Prize.
- Dressing well is important and usually follows conservative, European fashions. Unkempt appearance is seen as a sign of disrespect. The Norwegians are less formal than their Scandinavian counterparts, but a suit is recommended for men, particularly for the first meeting. A sports jacket is usually acceptable for follow-up meetings.
- Maintain direct eye contact.
- Hand gestures are held to a minimum during conversations.

Sensitivities

- Avoid criticizing others' beliefs, or political or social systems. The Norwegians are quite tolerant of others.
- Avoid discussions about whale hunting.
- Don't generalize about Scandinavians. Norwegians will appreciate your knowledge of distinctions between them and their Danish, Finnish, and Swedish counterparts.
- Don't discuss personal issues, such as employment, salary, or social status.

Key Negotiating Pointers

- Norwegians are generally informal in their approach to business.
- Make prior appointments through your Norwegian counterpart's secretary. Begin and end meetings on time. Punctuality is stressed.

- Avoid interruptions, loud speech, or other behavior that would be considered aggressive. Courtesy is prized.
- Make presentations factual, detailed, and subdued.
- Try to avoid or reduce the use of lawyers. Norwegians do not like a legalistic approach to business.
- Remember that summer is a time of leisure. Little business gets done during Easter time, or July or early August.

Day-to-Day Pointers

Business Entertainment Guidelines
- Business can be discussed during meals.
- Business lunches are common. Dinner is the main meal, usually about 5:00 p.m.
- A service fee is usually included in the bill, but a 5 to 10 percent tip is also customary.
- If invited to a Norwegian home, expect dinner to consist of several courses and last two or three hours. Bring a small gift such as flowers or chocolates.

Table Manners and Food
- A typical dinner consists of meat or fish, vegetables, soup, and dessert. A favorite meal consists of meatballs with potatoes and gravy.
- Norwegian specialties include fish balls in a sauce, smoked salmon, *lutefisk* (cod or codfish, soaked in a potash lye), and *smalahode* (sheep head).
- Wait until you are invited to sit down, and begin eating only after your host invites you to do so.
- Keep your hands above the table.
- The continental style of eating is used, with the fork in the left hand and the knife in the right.

Gender Issues

- International businesswomen can expect good treatment from the Norwegians. Equality for women is quite advanced in Norway.
- Women make up about 40 percent of the labor force and typically about one-third of parliament.
- Husbands and wives generally feel that they both have equal authority.

Also Remember This . . .

- Norway, one of the four Scandinavian countries, is mountainous, with many natural resources, including crude oil (in the North Sea), minerals, and timber.

- Norway is characterized by political stability and economic progress.

- Norwegians are very patriotic, and are proud of their social system and high standard of living.

PORTUGAL

Fast Facts

Monetary Unit: euro

Major Industries: textiles and footwear, wood pulp and paper, metals and metal-working, oil refining

Primary Trading Partners: Spain, France, Germany, United Kingdom, United States, Italy, Netherlands

Key Exports: clothing and footwear, machinery, chemicals, cork and paper products, hides

Key Imports: machinery and transport equipment, chemicals, petroleum, textiles, agricultural products

Major Cities: Lisbon (cap.) (2.6 mil. metro area), Oporto (264,200), Amadora (176,100), Setubal (103,200)

Ethnic Groups: homogeneous Mediterranean stock; small minority of black African descent

Primary Religions: Roman Catholic (94%), Protestant and other (6%)

Languages: Portuguese (official), Mirandese (official, but locally used); English, French, and German are widely understood; French is often spoken in business.

Reducing Communication Noise

Greetings

- Shake hands upon meeting and leaving. Expect a warm, rather firm handshake. *Ola* (Hello), *Bom dia* (Good day), and *Boa noite* (Good evening) are common greetings. Other typical phrases are *Adeus* (Good-bye), *Por favor* (Please), and *Obrigado* (Thank you).

- Men who are friends often greet each other with an embrace. Women usually kiss each other lightly on the cheek when greeting.

- Titles are usually used with the last name in business, though occasionally the title is used with the first name.

- Although a senior person may address you by your first name, don't reciprocate unless asked to do so. Touching or hugs are reserved for friends.

Conversation

- The Portuguese are proud of their cultural heritage, sense of nation, and economic progress.
- Soccer is the most popular national sport. Roller skating, hockey, and sailing are also popular. Portugal is also known for its tradition with horses. Bullfighting is a popular spectator sport; the bull is not killed, and the participants are amateurs, not professionals.
- Going to Portugal's beautiful beaches is a favorite pastime.
- There tends to be a lot of touching compared to most other Western European countries.
- Expect a lot of gestures during conversation.
- The Portuguese tend to be conservative in dress. Men, for example, are more likely to wear suits than a sports coat.

Sensitivities

- The Portuguese like to discuss politics but, as always, be careful. Do more listening than talking.

Key Negotiating Pointers

- Remember that the Portuguese are generally traditional and conservative, and that people and relationships are more important than time.
- Make prior appointments. Be punctual for meetings, though you may be kept waiting. Business meetings in Lisbon and other urban centers will be more punctual than in smaller towns.
- Be patient. Expect negotiations to be extensive with concessions coming slowly.
- Establish a strong personal rapport. The Portuguese believe that friendships should last a lifetime.
- Remember that personal relationships and patronage are considered more important than technical expertise.
- Stress the personal benefits to your Portuguese counterpart when making presentations. Limit an excessive amount of facts.
- Don't expect strict adherence to a written agreement. Personal relationships are considered more important than rules or laws.
- Dress well, ensuring that your clothes are well pressed. Appearances are important.

Day-to-Day Pointers

Business Entertainment Guidelines

- Business lunches are common, and lunch is the main meal of the day.
- Business entertainment is likely to be done in a restaurant. Emphasize building friendships rather than business during the meal.

- Large lunches are typical, usually about 1:00 p.m. Dinner is usually eaten between 8:00 and 9:00 p.m.

- Be sure to reciprocate if invited out for lunch or dinner. However, it would be considered impolite for you to say you "owed" your Portuguese counterpart a meal.

- A service charge is usually not included in the bill; there is sometimes a tip if the service is good.

Table Manners and Food

- A typical main meal might consist of two main dishes (meat and fish), a soup, vegetables, and more than one dessert. *Bacalhau* (dried cod) is a national dish. *Bica*, a strong espresso-type coffee, is often served after the meal. Wine is inexpensive and accompanies almost every lunch and dinner.

- If rabbit, pig, or fish is eaten, it is not unusual for the guest of honor to receive the head.

- The continental style of eating is followed, with the fork in the left hand and the knife in the right. The knife is used to push food onto the fork. Don't use other food or fingers to push food onto the fork.

- Keep your hands (not elbows) above the table.

- Try to finish your meal at the same time as your Portuguese host.

Gender Issues

- International businesswomen can expect *macho* and chauvinistic attitudes toward women in business from many Portuguese male counterparts.

- Women often work outside the home in urban areas. Women make up more than one-third of the workforce.

Also Remember This . . .

- The Portuguese Republic includes the mainland and the Azores and Madeira Islands.

- Portugal is much less secularized than other European countries. The Catholic Church traditions play an influential role in the personal lives of the Portuguese (for example, weddings, funerals, and religious holidays), even though many consider themselves nonpracticing.

- Though Portugal lags behind its European neighbors in economic development, significant progress has been made since joining the European Union (EU) in 1986.

SPAIN

Fast Facts

Monetary Unit: euro

Major Industries: textiles and apparel (including footwear), food and beverages, metals, chemicals

Primary Trading Partners: France, Germany, Portugal, Italy, United Kingdom, the Netherlands

Key Exports: machinery, motor vehicles, foodstuffs, pharmaceuticals, medicines

Key Imports: machinery and equipment, fuels, chemicals, unfinished goods, food-stuffs

Major Cities: Madrid (cap.) (5.1 mil. metro area), Barcelona (1.7 mil.), Valencia (741,100), Seville (679,100)

Ethnic Groups: composite of Mediterranean and Nordic backgrounds

Primary Religions: Roman Catholic (94%), other (6%)

Languages: Castilian Spanish (official nationally), and is the main language of business and government; second languages include Catalan (17%), Galician (7%), Basque (2%), each official regionally; English and French are also spoken in business.

Reducing Communication Noise

Greetings

- Shake hands upon meeting and leaving. Men should wait for women to extend their hands first.
- *Abrazos*, or hugs, are reserved for friends.
- Typical greetings are *Buenos días!* (Good day), *Buenas tardes!* (Good after-noon), *Buenas noches!* (Good evening) or the more casual *Hola!* (Hi).
- Titles—*Señor* (Mr.), *Señora* (Mrs.), or *Señorita* (Miss)—are usually used with the last name in business. *Don* and *doña* are used with the first name to show respect. The mother's family name is attached to a person's name in written communication (e.g., Sr. Franco Martinez Rodriquez).
- Although a senior person may address you by your first name, don't reciprocate unless you are invited to do so.

Conversation

- Spaniards enjoy discussing Spain's history, culture, and rapid economic growth and their families.

- Soccer is a very popular national sport. Many Spaniards are also involved in tennis, basketball, swimming, skiing, and hunting. Bullfighting is a popular spectator sport, and is seen as both an art and a sport.
- There tends to be a lot of touching compared to most other Western European countries.

Sensitivities
- Spaniards like to discuss politics. Do more listening than talking.
- Avoid comparisons with the United States.
- Don't be critical of bullfighting. The Spanish see it as an important part of their culture.

Key Negotiating Pointers

- Be punctual, though you may be kept waiting. Business meetings generally start within fifteen or so minutes after the designated time.
- Expect a relaxed pace of negotiations.
- Establish a solid relationship. Trust, rapport, and compatibility are essential in order to do business in Spain.
- Never embarrass your counterpart. Pride and honor are very important to Spanish negotiators.
- Leave yourself room for concessions. Though bargaining is part of everyday life in Spain, don't haggle so much that you jeopardize the relationship.
- Make your proposals detailed and practical. Grandiose schemes are not likely to be well accepted.
- Business is not conducted during the afternoon *siesta* (break), from about 1:30 to 4:30 p.m.
- Don't be put off by occasional advice giving or corrections. Spaniards often consider it their duty to correct perceived errors by others.
- Dress well and speak with as much flair and eloquence as you can. Appearances are important.

Day-to-Day Pointers

Business Entertainment Guidelines
- Business entertainment is usually done in a restaurant. Invitation to one's home may be extended only as a polite courtesy. Accept only if the host insists.
- *La comida*, or lunch, is eaten around 2:00 p.m. and is usually the main meal. A snack *(merienda)* is eaten about 5:00 or 6:00 p.m. Dinner, or *la cena*, is very late—normally around 9:00 or 10:00 p.m—and is not as substantial as lunch.

- Your host will indicate seating arrangements if the dinner is formal. Take a small gift if invited to a private home.

- The national toast is *Salud* (To your health), usually spoken before sipping a glass of *jerez* (sherry), the national drink.

- In restaurants, a 15 percent service charge is often added to the bill. If not, leave a 10 to 15 percent tip.

Table Manners and Food

- Compliments on meals are well received.

- Keep your hands (but not elbows) above the table.

- The continental style of eating is used, with the fork in the left hand and the knife in the right. The knife is used to push food onto the fork. (Don't use other food or fingers to do so.)

- Place the utensils side by side on the plate when you are finished eating. Leaving them any other way indicates that you want to eat more.

- Fresh vegetables, meat, eggs, chicken, and fish are typical foods. Most foods are cooked in olive oil.

- There are several regional Spanish dishes: *gazpacho* (a cold vegetable soup) from the southern province of Andalusia; *paello* (a stew of seafood, rice, and vegetables) from the eastern province of Valencia; *marmitako* (fisherman's stew) from the Basque region.

- Wine is usually served with meals.

Gender Issues

- International businesswomen can expect *macho* and chauvinistic attitudes toward women in business from many Spanish male counterparts.

- Although changes are taking place, there are few career-oriented Spanish women, and even fewer in management or key decision making positions. The Spanish business community is polarized as to the appropriate role of women in business.

Also Remember This . . .

- Spain is one of the poorest countries in Western Europe, though its economy has been steadily improving.

- Industry has been expanding, though agriculture and the service sectors are key parts of the economy.

- Spain is a leading wine producer.

SWEDEN

Fast Facts

Monetary Unit: krona

Major Industries: iron and steel, precision equipment (bearings, radio and television parts, armaments), paper and pulp

Primary Trading Partners: United States, Germany, Norway, United Kingdom, Denmark, Finland, France, the Netherlands, Belgium

Key Exports: machinery, motor vehicles, paper products, pulp and wood, iron and steel products

Key Imports: machinery, petroleum and petroleum products, chemicals, motor vehicles, foodstuffs

Major Cities: Stockholm (cap.) (1.6 mil. metro area), Goteborg (506,600), Malmo (245,300), Uppsala (127,300)

Ethnic Groups: ethnic Swede (85%), Finnish (5%), foreign-born or first-generation immigrants (10%)

Primary Religions: Evangelical Lutheran (80%); other faiths include Roman Catholic, Protestant, Muslim, Jewish, Buddhist

Languages: Swedish; small Sami and Finnish-speaking minorities. English is widely spoken.

Reducing Communication Noise

Greetings

- Shake hands firmly upon meeting.

- First names are used quite quickly, but do not use them until you are invited do so. Titles and last names are usually reserved for very formal occasions.

- Typical greetings are *God dag* (Good day), *God morgon* (Good morning), and *Adjo* (Good-bye). A more casual greeting is *Hej* (meaning "Hi", and pronounced HEY). The most common way to say "Good-bye" is *Hej da*.

Conversation

- Swedes enjoy talking about Sweden's accomplishments, the theater, movies, and sports.

- Soccer, skiing, ice hockey, tennis, and golf are popular sports. Many Swedes are also involved in hiking, fishing, and bird watching.

- Sweden is the home of the Nobel Prize.

- Try to learn a few words of Swedish. This will be appreciated.
- Avoid very expressive hand gestures when speaking. Swedes tend to be very friendly, but reserved.
- Maintain eye contact during conversation.

Sensitivities

- Avoid discussing politics or personal matters.
- Don't praise one area of Sweden over the one you are visiting. Swedes have a strong regional loyalty.
- Swedes are very concerned about the environment and typically have strong opinions about the disappearing ozone layer, global warming, and pollution.
- Avoid lumping the cultural distinctions of Sweden with other Scandinavian countries (Norway, Denmark, and Finland).

Key Negotiating Pointers

- Swedes have a reputation as tough negotiators—not hagglers who enjoy the process, but methodical, detailed individuals who are slow to change positions. However, expect your Swedish counterpart to push for concessions.
- Make prior appointments. Punctuality is important.
- Negotiations are similar to those in North America in that they move crisply and are task-oriented.
- Make presentations factual, practical, precise, and reserved. Showy behavior is not rewarded.
- Be friendly, but get to the point of your discussions. Use a modest and direct communication style.
- Remember that strong personal relationships follow a solid business relationship.
- Look for decision makers to be at middle to lower levels of the organization. Swedish senior management often delegates key decisions. Expect to negotiate with middle managers most of the time.
- Expect decision making to be rather slow. Alternatives are often worked out with the middle management before a decision is made. This can be a time-consuming process, but once a decision is made, implementation is usually rapid.
- Dress well. As in other Scandinavian countries, public presentation is considered very important.
- Contracts are detailed.
- Try to avoid scheduling business during the summer. Swedish executives normally have six weeks' vacation. July is virtually closed for business.

Day-to-Day Pointers

Business Entertainment Guidelines

- Swedes do not usually combine business and entertainment, though business lunches are not unusual.
- Business may be discussed over meals.
- Toasting is quite formal. Don't toast your host or those who are senior in rank or age before they first toast you. Don't touch your glass until your host says *Skal.*
- Gift giving is not typical in business.

Table Manners and Food

- The main meal is lunch, or *middag*, usually eaten at midday. Be punctual for the meal—the meal is usually served right away.
- Keep your hands (not elbows) above the table.
- Try to eat everything on your plate.
- The continental style of eating is used, with the fork in the left hand and the knife in the right.
- Use a separate knife for the butter rather than your dinner knife.
- Place the utensils side by side on the plate when you are finished eating.
- The Swedish diet has traditionally been heavy on meat, fish, and cheese, but it now includes fresh vegetables and fruits as a result of Swedes' efforts to eat more healthfully. Potatoes are eaten a few times a week. A favorite meal is *Kottbullar med kokt potatis, brun sas och lingonsylt* (meatballs with brown sauce, boiled potatoes, and lingonberry jam).
- The *smorgasbord* (a large buffet) is not an everyday meal, but eaten at parties or during the Christmas season.

Gender Issues

- Sweden is a good place for international businesswomen to do business.
- Swedes' views toward women in the professions and management are somewhat more conservative than their sexually liberated reputation might indicate. Nevertheless, women are becoming accepted at higher levels of management.
- Women make up about half of the workforce—one of the highest portions in the world.

Also Remember This . . .

- Sweden has one of the world's most prosperous economies, and has a very high standard of living. The country is highly industrialized, has an excellent distribution system, and has an educated and skilled workforce.

- The economy has been somewhat sluggish in recent years. Various economic reforms have been introduced to stimulate it.

- Swedish income taxes are among the highest in the world. These taxes fund a comprehensive social welfare system. Most Swedes are quite supportive of it.

- Swedish trade unions are very strong. One or two trade union representatives are likely to be on the board of any large company.

- Swedes have one of the shortest workweeks in Western Europe (usually less than thirty-five hours).

SWITZERLAND

Fast Facts

Monetary Unit: Swiss franc
Major Industries: machinery, chemicals, watches, textiles, precision instruments
Primary Trading Partners: Germany, United States, France, Italy, United Kingdom, Spain, the Netherlands, Austria
Key Exports: machinery, chemicals, metals, watches, agricultural products
Key Imports: machinery, chemicals, vehicles, metals, agricultural products
Major Cities: Bern (cap.) (135,100), Zurich (971,800 metro area), Geneva (178,900), Basel (162,800)
Ethnic Groups: German (65%), French (18%), Italian (10%), Romansch (1%), other (6%)
Primary Religions: Catholic (49%), Protestant (48%)
Languages: German (64%), French (20%), Italian (7%), all official; Romansch (1%); English is widely spoken.

Reducing Communication Noise

Greetings
- Shake hands firmly with both men and women upon meeting and leaving.
- Address people by their title and last name. Address German-speaking people as *Herr* and *Frau;* French-speaking people as *Monsieur, Madame,* or *Mademoiselle*; and Italian-speaking people as *Signor, Signora,* or *Signorita.* First names are usually used only among close friends.
- For those of German or Italian backgrounds, use the person's surname, as in,

"Good morning, Herr (or Signor) Johnson." For the French a simple "Good morning, Monsieur" will do.

- Verbal greetings vary because Switzerland is a multilingual society. English greetings are usually acceptable, though the Swiss appreciate attempts to speak the language of the region you are visiting.
- Give your business card to the receptionist when visiting a company.

Conversation

- The Swiss enjoy discussing their country's nature and beauty and their travels.
- Soccer and bicycling are the most popular sports. Hiking, skiing, and other outdoor sports are also enjoyed.
- If you are fluent in only English, try to speak a few phrases in the language of the region you're visiting.

Sensitivities

- Avoid personal questions about one's job, salary, age, or family.
- The Swiss like discussing politics. Do more listening than talking.
- Do not flaunt wealth. Despite their high standard of living, the Swiss are conservative.

Key Negotiating Pointers

- The overall conduct of Swiss negotiating is similar to that in the United States, somewhat impersonal, brisk, orderly, planned, and task-oriented. Swiss negotiations tend to be a little more formal than in the United States, however.
- Make prior appointments and be punctual. This is particularly important to the Swiss.
- Pay attention to formalities and courtesies. Be conservative in your dress.
- Expect a brief amount of small talk before getting to the task at hand. The personal relationship tends to follow the development of a solid business relationship.
- Make proposals practical, detailed, precise, and reserved. The Swiss value hard work, sobriety, and thrift.
- Presentations should be orderly and well prepared. Consider the use of Power-Point, graphs, and charts. If you have a laser-jet printer, use it.
- Be thoroughly knowledgeable in product and contract details.
- Leave yourself some room to bargain, but keep your initial offer fairly close to your *really asking* position. The Swiss aren't hagglers.
- Be patient in both the negotiations and the project details that are discussed. The Swiss are often cautious and pessimistic about achieving project deadlines.

- Expect decision making to be methodical, with many questions and requests for information. Decisions are usually centralized and slow.
- Deemphasize deals that stress the Swiss production of labor-intensive items. Swiss manufacturers must overcome high wages and very low unemployment.
- Follow up with an e-mail or letter that summarizes discussions. The Swiss like to have things in writing.
- Contracts are detailed.

Day-to-Day Pointers

Business Entertainment Guidelines

- Lunch, the main meal of the day, is the most common business meal. Dinner is usually light and is served around 6:00 p.m. or 7:00 p.m.
- Business is often discussed over meals.
- If you are invited to a Swiss home, wipe your feet before entering. Candy and unwrapped flowers are appropriate gifts. Avoid red roses, however, since they imply romantic interest. Shake hands with all members of the family when leaving.
- Gift giving is not common for business acquaintances.
- In restaurants, the bill usually includes the service charge and is paid at the table.

Table Manners and Food

- Don't drink until a toast is made. Typical Swiss toasts are the Germanic *Prost*, the French *Sante*, and the Italian *Cincin*.
- Asking for salt and pepper is sometimes interpreted as an insult because it implies the food is improperly seasoned.
- Keep your hands (but not elbows) above the table.
- Asking for a second helping of food is a great compliment to your host.
- Place utensils side by side on the plate when you are finished eating. Leaving them any other way may indicate that you are still hungry.
- Lunch usually consists of meat and potatoes or pasta and salad. Dinners consist of an open-faced sandwich.
- Sausages, leek soup, cheeses, fish, and wines are regional specialties.

Gender Issues

- Switzerland is generally a good place for international businesswomen to do business.
- Although banking and finance are dominated by men, women get a fair hearing and are treated professionally.

Also Remember This . . .

- Switzerland has one of the world's strongest and most stable economies. The Swiss enjoy a high standard of living.
- Banking, finance, tourism, and industry are all strong segments of the economy.
- Switzerland has four distinct ethnic communities—German, French, Italian, and Romansch.
- Try to avoid doing business in Switzerland during July and August, when most Swiss are on vacation.

 # UNITED KINGDOM

Fast Facts

Monetary Unit: British pound

Major Industries: machinery and transportation equipment, metals, food processing

Primary Trading Partners: United States, Germany, France, Ireland, the Netherlands, Belgium, Spain

Key Exports: manufactured goods, machinery, fuels, chemicals, semi-finished goods, transport equipment

Key Imports: manufactured goods, machinery, fuels, foodstuffs

Major Cities: London (cap.) (7.6 mil. metro area), Glasgow (1.1 mil.), Birmingham (1.0 mil.), Leeds (724,400)

Ethnic Groups: English (83%), Scottish (8%), Welsh (4%), Northern Irish (3%), other (2%)

Primary Religions: Christian (Anglican, Roman Catholic, Presbyterian, Methodist) (71%), Muslim (3%), Hindu (1%), other (2%), unspecified or none (23%)

Languages: English, Welsh (26% of population of Wales), Scottish form of Gaelic (60,000 in Scotland)

Reducing Communication Noise

Greetings

- Shake hands with men upon meeting and leaving. Women don't have to shake hands, so wait for them to extend their hands first.
- When introduced, both parties say, "How do you do." As in the United States, it is also polite to add some form of expression of pleasure about getting to meet the other person.

- Address people as *Mr., Mrs.,* or *Miss*, until specifically invited to call them by their first name.

Conversation

- The British enjoy talking about their rich cultural heritage. They also love their animals and like to talk about them.
- Football (soccer), rugby, cricket, and tennis are very popular. Badminton, sailing, swimming, darts, and squash are also very popular sports. The British are proud of the Wimbledon tennis tournament, an international sporting event.
- Remember that many "English" words have a totally different meaning than they do in the United States—for example, *vet* (to check or appraise, such as "to vet a contract"), *lift* (elevator), *chemist* (druggist), *intercourse* (friendly conversation, such as, "I had intercourse with my negotiating team before the session began").

Sensitivities

- Avoid talking about politics or religion. Don't criticize the status, role, or wealth of the royal family.
- Avoid personal questions and demonstrative touching. Many British consider Americans pushy and aggressive.
- Be careful with humor. While the British enjoy a good joke, they often don't get American jokes, and vice versa.
- Avoid poking fun at the British affection for their dogs (it is not unusual to see dogs accompany British on visits to restaurants or pubs).
- Be conspicuously polite to older people.
- Tone down discussions on genealogy. If you are British by heritage, this is of less interest to your counterpart than it might be to you.
- Use the term *British* rather than *English*. Remember that while people may live in London, they may have Welsh, Irish, or Scottish backgrounds. Also, people from Scotland are called Scots or Scotsmen (or British). *Scotch* is what you drink.
- Avoid comparisons with the United States.
- Don't talk loudly or gesticulate wildly. Project your voice to reach only your conversation counterpart.

Key Negotiating Pointers

- Make connections with the traditional power brokers. The old class system still influences business, particularly in England. Traditions are important.
- Make prior appointments and be punctual.
- Most British negotiators will be less competitive in their style than American

negotiators. Bargaining is not a usual fact of everyday life for the British. Expect formalities and attention to protocol, especially in London. Northern England, Scotland, Wales, and Northern Ireland are less formal.

- Leave yourself room for movement, but you needn't build a large amount of fat into your proposal. The British tend to have moderate initial demands.

- Presentations should be matter-of-fact, detailed, and subdued.

- Be friendly, but keep your small talk impersonal and to a minimum.

- Expect the pace of negotiations to be crisp, but slower than in the United States.

- Try not to push for agreement or appear in a hurry. Avoid doing most of the talking.

- Delivery time may be a sticking point if you are the buyer. Be sure to include a contract clause that imposes hefty payment penalties for late deliveries.

- Financing and quality are lesser problems. Chances are the British will be helpful with financing, and generally their goods are of high quality.

- Be aware of the political and union context of the negotiation. Bureaucratic requirements can be cumbersome, political signals mixed, and unions powerful. Seek counsel on finding the "right" union if you are negotiating the start-up of a new facility that is likely to be unionized.

Day-to-Day Pointers

Business Entertainment Guidelines

- Most business entertainment is done in pubs and restaurants.

- The business lunch is an institution. It is customary to discuss business over the meal if there are no spouses present.

- A night at the theater or ballet are good entertainment options.

- Tea is often the main meal of the day and is eaten between 5:00 p.m. and 7:00 p.m.

- You are likely to be offered coffee or tea when calling on a business associate. The United Kingdom is one of the few places in the world where declining a beverage is not an offense.

- An invitation reading "black tie" or "smoking" means men must wear dinner jackets and women, long dresses.

- A small gift (flowers or chocolates) is appropriate if invited to a home and you are likely to be the only guest.

- Gift giving is prevalent. Logo gifts with your company name should be unobtrusive. Be careful not to leave an impression that you are trying to bribe your counterpart.

Table Manners and Food

- Do not smoke before a meal is finished and not without asking the permission of your host. Smoke only after the toast to Her Majesty's health, subsequent to the main course.
- Beef, mutton, potatoes, and vegetables are part of the traditional British diet, though cuisine in London and other major metro areas is cosmopolitan and multicultural. Tea and beer are popular drinks. Fish and chips (french fries) are as popular as the American hamburger.

Gender Issues

- Although international businesswomen find a very acceptable business climate in the United Kingdom, the Old Boy Network is still very much alive.
- Although women make up about 40 percent of the workforce, there are few British women in management positions.

Also Remember This . . .

- The United Kingdom has one of the largest economies in Europe, and continues to be a global economic power.
- Great Britain consists of England, Scotland, and Wales. When Northern Ireland is added, the correct name is United Kingdom.
- As with many other aspects of doing business in the United Kingdom, how one does things is important.
- London is a key financial center in the world.
- There is a trend to move from large cities to smaller towns to avoid big-city problems and to achieve the dream of a house and garden.

• CHAPTER 6 •

Negotiating in Eastern Europe

The Business Environment of Eastern Europe

Though definitions vary in the fast-changing European political and economic landscape, Eastern Europe consists of countries such as the Czech Republic, Hungary, Poland, Romania, and Turkey, as well as Russia, Kazakhstan, Ukraine, and other countries that formerly constituted the Soviet Union. Russia is the world's largest nation, spanning eleven time zones.

Eastern Europe can be a very tough part of the world for a negotiator. The business environment is characterized by fundamental changes in economic and political structures. There are, however, also great opportunities. An emphasis is likely to be put on the creation of an auto industry in Hungary, Poland, and the Czech Republic to meet projected domestic and international demand. Feeder industries will involve the mechanical engineering, electronics, electro-technical, chemicals, glass, and sheet metal subsectors.

You should give consideration to investing in Eastern Europe if your company is involved in selling to priority areas such as the auto industry, consumer goods, processed food, health, telecommunications, or computers. Investment viability will be enhanced by improvements in business conditions. From the perspective of a global procurement strategy, Eastern Europe offers major cost advantages, mainly because of inexpensive labor. The attractiveness of Eastern Europe is also enhanced by active involvement by the World Bank, United Nations, International Monetary Fund, and New European Bank for Reconstruction and Development.

127

The business arrangements favored in Eastern Europe in the twenty-first century by many multinational companies are joint ventures, direct investment, or start-ups. Joint ventures are popular because of their export and hard currency potential.

There are key obstacles to overcome in much of this part of the world. First, the concept of "profit" is still not fully understood in some parts of Eastern Europe. Another obstacle is that of currency. As a rule, Eastern currencies are considered of little value in other parts of the world. Alternative financial arrangements must therefore be found to circumvent this problem. Certainly, entrance into the European Union by the Czech Republic, Hungary, Poland, and other Eastern European countries should aid this process.

Cultural Factors That Affect Negotiating in Eastern Europe

Use of Time

Expect Eastern Europeans to be punctual or, at most, to begin meetings no more than ten to fifteen minutes past the appointed time.

Individualism vs. Collectivism

As one would expect given the strong influence of a communist political system over the past several decades, a "we" consciousness, or collectivist orientation, still predominates. Group ideals are prevalent in many business discussions.

The group emphasis may help explain the limited authority of most Eastern European negotiators. Checking with headquarters, even on minor points, is typical. In addition, one can almost always expect team negotiations. There is also often lack of clarity about the decision-making process, leaving questions as to who is in charge. These factors tend to make negotiations slow and tedious.

Role Orderliness and Conformity

There is, on the one hand, a predictability as to one's place and strict rules and regulations surrounding organizational behavior. On the other hand, it is not always clear who exactly is in charge. This is probably the result, in large part, of the cumbersome bureaucracies that generate duplication of effort and occasionally blurred lines of authority. Decisions generally flow from the top down.

Patterns of Communication

Verbal Communication

Eastern Europeans are generally direct in their communication, making straightforward, firm requests and demands. Once past any language barrier,

there is little guesswork regarding their point of view. Though they are very gracious as hosts, the communication styles of Eastern Europeans may sometimes seem abrupt and aggressive, even to Western Europeans and North Americans.

Nonverbal Communication

Personal space in Eastern Europe is generally closer than in North America or most of Western Europe. Hand and arm gestures are usually quite expressive. Handshakes are firm and brief. An exception is handshakes between men and women, which can be quite lengthy in countries such as Poland or the Czech Republic, with the man kissing the woman's hand.

HOW NEGOTIATIONS WORK IN EASTERN EUROPE

Negotiating Factors

1. *Pace of Negotiations* Slow

2. *Negotiating Strategies*
 Opening Offers vis-à-vis Settlement High initial demands
 Presentation of Issues Group of issues may be
 presented
 Presentations Fairly formal
 Dealing with Differences Argumentative
 Concessions Slow

3. *Emphasis on Personal Relationships* Very low

4. *Emotional Aspects*
 Sensitivity Not highly valued
 Degree of Emotions Moderate

5. *Decision Making*
 Overall Method Somewhat impulsive
 Emphasize Logic
 Emphasis on Group/Team Moderate: Decisions from
 top management
 Emphasis on Face Saving Fairly high
 Influence of Special Interests on Decision Usually not condoned
 Makers

6. *Contractual and Administrative Factors*
 Need for an Agent Average

Degree of Contract Specificity	Moderate
Degree of Paperwork/Bureaucracy	High
Need for an Agenda	Moderate

CZECH REPUBLIC

Fast Facts

Monetary Unit: koruna

Major Industries: metallurgy, machinery and equipment, motor vehicles, glass, armaments

Primary Trading Partners: Germany, Slovakia, Austria, Poland, United Kingdom, France, Italy, the Netherlands, China, Russia

Key Exports: machinery and transport equipment, chemicals, raw materials and fuels

Key Imports: machinery and transport equipment, raw materials and fuels, chemicals

Major Cities: Prague (cap.) (1.4 mil. metro area), Brno (376,400), Ostrava (317,700), Pizen (164,900)

Ethnic Groups: Czech (91%), Moravian (4%), Slovak (2%), Polish, German, and other (3%)

Primary Religions: Christians (nominally 60%); most Czechs are nonpracticing or unaffiliated

Languages: Czech is the official language; Slovak and Polish are also spoken.

Reducing Communication Noise

Greetings

- Shake hands when greeting. A man usually waits for a woman to extend her hand before shaking hands.

- Use a title (such as doctor, professor, director, Mr., Mrs., Miss) with the last name.

- First names are usually reserved for friends and relatives.

- A common greeting is *Dobry den* (Good day). Another greeting is *Tesi mne* (Pleased to meet you), pronounced Teh-shee-mnye. The word for "Thank you" is *Dekuji* (de-ksee).

- It is common to precede the title with *Pan* (sir) or *Pani* (madam) when greeting

the person: *Pani Doktorkova Cekan*. *Pan* or *Pani* are also used without professional titles.

Conversation

- Czechs like to discuss their cultural heritage. Czechs have a history of great composers and famous authors such as Dvorak, Kafka, and Capek. Czech gothic and baroque architecture are superb.
- Czechs spend a good deal of their leisure time in nature, spending their weekends visiting forests, mountains, and lakes.
- Czechs also like to discuss the many fine regional wines.
- Soccer is the most popular sport, followed by ice hockey and tennis. The Czech Republic's national hockey team has won several world titles.

Sensitivities

- Avoid discussing politics, religion, or social conditions.

Key Negotiating Pointers

- If you are negotiating the purchase of a business, don't expect many clues as to what the business is worth (asset valuations, cash flow analyses, or marketing plans).
- Make prior appointments far in advance. Be punctual.
- Take time to build a solid rapport with your Czech counterpart.
- Stress your firm's link to the global economy. Access to Western economies is key to Czech organizations.
- Be patient. Negotiations will probably be time consuming. Decision making is slow. Czech organizations are bureaucratic and cumbersome. Many executives will be reviewing the details of the negotiation.
- Use an interpreter unless you speak Czech or Slovak.
- Consider hiring a Czech lawyer to help you with the legal aspects of setting up a joint venture and related issues. There is a tangle of laws that your Czech counterpart probably will not fully understand.
- Emphasize your firm's ability to transfer business skills and technology know-how.

Day-to-Day Pointers

Business Entertainment Guidelines

- The main business meal is lunch, eaten about noon.
- Toasting is often part of both formal and informal meals.

- If you are invited to a Czech's home, bring an odd number of flowers (except for red roses, which signify romantic affection), wine, whiskey, or cognac.

Table Manners and Food
- Both hands are kept above the table during the meal, but don't rest your elbows on the table.
- Water is served in restaurants, though mineral water can be ordered.
- A popular meal is pork roast, dumplings, and sauerkraut. Prague specialties include roast goose and ham and sausages. Fruits and vegetables must be imported. Wine and beer are typical beverages.

Gender Issues

- International businesswomen must contend with almost exclusively male-dominated organizations at almost every decision-making level.

Also Remember This . . .

- For Eastern Europe, the Czech Republic has a high standard of living.
- Until 1990, the economy was centrally controlled and trade was conducted mainly with other communist countries. The private sector was virtually nonexistent before 1989.
- Czechoslovakia split into two separate countries in 1993—the Czech Republic and Slovakia.
- The Czech Republic became a member of the North Atlantic Treaty Organization (NATO) in 1999, and joined the European Union in 2004.

HUNGARY

Fast Facts

Monetary Unit: forint

Major Industries: mining, metallurgy, construction materials, processed foods, textiles, chemicals

Primary Trading Partners: Germany, Austria, France, Italy, United Kingdom, Russia, the Netherlands, China

Key Exports: machinery and equipment, other manufactures, food products, raw materials, fuels and electricity

Key Imports: machinery and equipment, other manufactures, fuels and electricity, food products, raw materials

Major Cities: Budapest (cap.) (2.6 mil., metro area), Debrecen (217,700), Miskolc (189,700)

Ethnic Groups: Hungarian (90%), Roma (4%), German (3%), Serbs and other (3%)

Primary Religions: Roman Catholic (57%), Calvinist (20%), Lutheran (5%), Greek Catholic (3%), unaffiliated (15%)

Languages: Hungarian (called Magyar in Hungary); English and other languages are spoken by few people.

Reducing Communication Noise

Greetings

- Shake hands upon meeting and parting. Men should wait for women to extend their hand first.
- Address people by a title (such as *Doctor, Professor, Director, Mr., Mrs.,* or *Miss*) with the last name. First names are usually used only among close friends.

Conversation

- Hungarians are proud of their artists, composers, folk music, food, and fine wines. Franz Liszt and Béla Bartók are two famous Hungarian composers.
- Hungary is called a "nation of horsemen." Hungarians were historically known for their horsemanship, and even today horses are a prominent part of recreation and tourist activities.
- Soccer is the most popular sport, along with swimming, tennis, fencing, and sailing.

Sensitivities

- Avoid discussing politics or religion.
- Avoid discussing social conditions.

Key Negotiating Pointers

- Make prior appointments and be punctual.
- Be patient. Negotiations are likely to be time consuming. Decision making is slow. Hungarian organizations are still bureaucratic and cumbersome.
- Stress your firm's links to the global economy.
- Emphasize your firm's ability to transfer business skills and technology know-how.
- If you are negotiating the purchase of a business, don't expect many clues as to what the business is worth (asset valuation, cash flow analyses, or marketing plans).

- Use an interpreter unless you speak Magyar (Hungarian). Few Hungarian businesspeople speak English.

Day-to-Day Pointers

Business Entertainment Guidelines

- Most business entertainment is done in restaurants.
- Lunch is the main meal of the day, usually eaten between noon and 2:00 p.m. Dinner is normally eaten after 7:00 p.m.
- In restaurants, a 10 to 15 percent tip is appropriate.

Table Manners and Food

- The continental style of eating is used, with the fork in the left hand and the knife in the right hand.
- Many ethnic cuisines are available because of Hungary's central European location. A famous Hungarian specialty is *goulash*, a stew of meat, potatoes, onions, and paprika.
- Pork and chicken are common meats. Popular side dishes are noodles, potatoes, and dumplings. Most dishes include spices and sauces. Other common dishes include *halaszle* (fish soup), stuffed paprika (sweet peppers), stuffed chicken, strudel, and pancakes.

Gender Issues

- International businesswomen must contend with almost exclusively male-dominated organizations at almost every decision-making level.
- Hungarian women make up almost 50 percent of the workforce, one of the highest percentages in the world, but few are in professional or management positions.

Also Remember This . . .

- Hungary is one of the most prosperous and politically open countries in Eastern Europe.
- Hungary is a member of NATO and the European Union.
- Key strengths are foreign investment, a stable government, and a hardworking labor force. The government continues to accelerate privatization of the larger Hungarian companies.
- The World Bank, International Monetary Fund, and other international organizations influence Hungary's business development. A large deficit remains a challenge.

KAZAKHSTAN

Fast Facts

Monetary Unit: tenge

Major Industries: oil, mining, tractors and other agricultural machinery, construction materials, chemicals, metallurgy

Primary Trading Partners: Russia, Bermuda, Germany, China, France, Italy, United Kingdom, Ukraine

Key Exports: oil, ferrous and nonferrous metals, chemicals, grain, wool, meat, coal

Key Imports: machinery, oil and gas, chemicals and chemical products, transport equipment

Major Cities: Astana (cap., since 1997)) (319,000), Almaty (1.5 mil.), Karaganda (436,000), Shymkent (360,000)

Ethnic Groups: Kazakh (53%), Russian (30%), Ukrainian (4%), Uzbek (3%), German (2%), other (8%)

Primary Religions: Islam (mostly Sunni) (47%), Russian Orthodox (44%), other, such as Protestant, Roman Catholic, and Jewish (9%)

Languages: Kazakh replaced Russian as the state language in 1989, but Russian is widely spoken. Russian commands equal status at state-owned organizations, local government bodies, and in everyday business.

Reducing Communication Noise

Greetings

- Men shake hands with other men by clasping both hands around one of the other hands.
- People use their first name and patronymic, and last name in formal introductions. The patronymic is based on one's father's first name and is modified with a male or female suffix. Last names may have a male or female variant, though they come from the father's side of the family.
- Only good friends of similar age address each other by first names.
- Common Kazak greetings include *Salemetisisba?* (How do you do?) or the more casual *Salem* (Hi). Russians use *Zdravstvuyte* (Hello) or the less formal *Privyet* (Hi).
- Guests to a Kazakh home are usually greeted with *Torge shygynyz* (a place above my place), derived from the nomadic tradition of placing one's guest in the warmest place.

Conversation
- Kazakhs tend to be kind and open, and there is strong respect for elders.
- Kazakhs are proud of their musical and poetic traditions. One example are *aitys*, where two people debate by spontaneously singing their arguments and rebuttals.
- Popular spectator sports include soccer, boxing, and hockey.
- Many Kazakhs also enjoy ballroom, modern, and traditional dancing.
- The larger cities will usually have a movie theater and a "Palace of Culture" for plays, concerts, and dance performances.

Sensitivities
- Avoid discussing politics and social conditions, or the negative aspects of Kazakhstan's history, such as conditions related to Stalinism and other Kazakh-Russian conflicts.
- Economic and social changes have left a gap between those who are positive about the future and those would like to return to a time when opportunities were more limited but life was more stable.

Key Negotiating Pointers

- Establishing a legal presence goes through the Ministry of Justice. Once all the required documents are gathered, registration usually takes about four weeks.
- Make prior appointments and be punctual.
- Expect Kazakhs and Russians to be open and hospitable.
- Wear Western-style clothes.
- A disheveled appearance is considered in poor taste.
- Business presentations should be detailed.
- Building a relationship will precede serious business deals, though no long-term personal relationship is necessarily desired or expected by your Kazakh counterpart.
- Personal connections are important here, so using an agent is key. Kazakh negotiators usually have limited authority, so be patient. Expect slow concessions.
- Make at least one trip to Kazakhstan before finalizing your negotiation.
- You can expect compliance with the spirit, if not always the letter, of the agreement.

Day-to-Day Pointers

Business Entertainment Guidelines
- There is normally a three-meal-a-day diet. Breakfast is called *tanertengi*, or *zavtrak* in Russian.

- Lunch is the midday meal and is called *tycki*, or *obed* in Russian. Supper is usually the biggest meal and is eaten around 7 p.m. and is known as *kyeshki as*, or *uzhyn* in Russian.

Table Manners and Food

- *Besbarmak* (five fingers) is a traditional dish and is named for how it was eaten in the past—with the hand. It consists of dough rolled into thin, wide noodles and cooked in a broth called *sorpa*. Meat and onions then cover the noodles.
- A boiled sheep's head is served with *besbarmak* for special occasions.
- Tap water is safe in many areas.
- Mutton and fish are popular in most households, and horsemeat is saved for special occasions.
- People drink hot tea all year around. A popular summer drink is the Kazakh *khumiss* (fermented mare's milk); another is the Russian *kvass*, which is a tangy juice made from dried bread. Cold drinks are not popular because they are thought to cause sore throats and other health problems.

Gender Issues

- Kazakh women legally have equal rights and access to professional positions, although there are usually male-dominated organizations at almost every decision-making level.

Also Remember This . . .

- Kazakhstan became independent from the collapsing Soviet Union in 1991. It is about twice the size of Alaska, or equal to the size of Western Europe.
- Kazakhstan is an economic leader of Central Asia. It has very large mineral and oil resources and encourages Western investment. Offshore oil was discovered in Kazakhstan's portion of the Caspian Sea in 2000, believed to be one of the largest offshore oil finds in several decades.
- Kazakhstan's growing economy has brought wealth to several parts of the population, and the movement from a planned to a market economy has been difficult for most people.
- It remains to be seen if democratic and civil reforms allowing for opposition political parties and a free press will be institutionalized.
- Kazakhs have historically identified with Islam, while people of Slavic and European descent are more aligned with Christianity.
- The United States has been the top foreign investor in the Kazakh economy in recent years, followed by the European Union.

POLAND

Fast Facts

Monetary Unit: zloti

Major Industries: machine building, iron and steel, coal mining, chemicals, ship-building, food processing

Primary Trading Partners: Germany, Italy, France, United Kingdom, Czech Republic, the Netherlands, Russia, China

Key Exports: machinery and transport equipment, manufactured goods, food and live animals

Key Imports: machinery and transport equipment, chemicals, minerals, fuels, metals, lubricants

Major Cities: Warsaw (cap.) (2.2 mil. metro area), Lodz (851,500), Krakow (743,700), Wroclaw (640,700)

Ethnic Groups: Polish (97%), German, Belorussian, Ukrainian (3%)

Primary Religions: Roman Catholic (90%) (about 75% practicing), other (5%); none or unknown (5%)

Languages: Polish (98%), other (2%)

Reducing Communication Noise

Greetings

- Shake hands upon meeting and parting. Poles will sometimes kiss the extended hand of a woman when meeting. First names are used only among close friends.

- Address men by the title *Pan* (pronounced pahn) with the last name. For women, the term is *Pahni* (pronounced pahn-ee). A professional person's title is used before one's last name.

- A common greeting is *Dzien dobry* (pronounced jean du-bree), meaning Hello or Good morning.

Conversation

- Try talking about Poland's great history in art, music, literature, and dancing. For example, romantic composer Frédéric Chopin is Poland's best known musician.

- Conversations about life in your home country and your family will also probably be welcomed.

- Soccer is a very popular sport. Bicycling, table tennis, skiing, and basketball are also popular. Bridge is a favorite card game.

Sensitivities
- Avoid discussing politics, social conditions, or German or Russian involvement in World War II.

Key Negotiating Pointers

- Poles are generally outgoing and outspoken.
- Make prior appointments and be punctual.
- You will meet mainly with representatives from state-owned and -operated businesses.
- Be patient. Negotiations are likely to be time consuming. Decision making is slow. Polish organizations are still bureaucratic and cumbersome.
- Stress your company's links to the global economy.
- Emphasize your company's ability to transfer business skills and technological know-how.
- If you are negotiating the purchase of a business, don't expect many clues as to what the business is worth (asset valuation, cash flow analyses, or marketing plans).
- Explore options with regard to a wide variety of business arrangements such as liquidations, joint ventures, and sales to foreigners.
- Focus on small and midsize enterprises as possibilities for joint ventures.
- Use an interpreter unless you speak Polish. If your counterpart speaks English and you conduct the negotiation in English, speak slowly and distinctively. Avoid jargon.

Day-to-Day Pointers

Business Entertainment Guidelines
- The main meal of the day is eaten after 3:00 p.m.
- You may be entertained in a *kawiarna* (café), where the local specialty and French pastries are usually available.
- Pace yourself with alcohol. The Poles tend to drink a lot of hard liquor. Toasting is often a part of both formal and informal dinners.
- If you are invited to a private home, bring flowers (except for red roses, which signify romantic affection).

Table Manners and Food
- Keep your hands above the table.
- The continental style of dining is used, with the fork in the left hand and the knife in the right hand.

- Typical meals consist of foods such as soup, fish, salad, potatoes, and tea. *Pierogi* (dumplings with cream cheese and potatoes), *uszka* (a kind of ravioli), and braised pork and *bigos* (cabbage) are popular foods.

Gender Issues

- International businesswomen must contend with almost exclusively male-dominated organizations at almost every decision-making level.

Also Remember This . . .

- Poland joined NATO in 1999 and the European Union in 2004, and is taking steps toward becoming a free-market economy.
- Poland has a strong industrial sector and is a major producer of minerals and steel.
- About 25 percent of the labor force works in agriculture, which has remained in private hands.
- Foreign investment is welcomed to help build the economy and to gain hard currency.
- The World Bank, International Monetary Fund, and other international organizations influence Poland's development.
- Poland has a skilled, low-paid workforce.
- A stock exchange has been established in Warsaw.

ROMANIA

Fast Facts

Monetary Unit: leu

Major Industries: mining, timber, construction materials

Primary Trading Partners: Italy, Germany, France, Turkey, United Kingdom, Russia

Key Exports: textiles and footwear, metals and metal products, machinery and equipment

Key Imports: machinery and equipment, fuels and minerals, chemicals

Major Cities: Bucharest (cap.) (2.1 mil.), Constanta (349,000), Iasi (338,00), Timisoara (325,000)

Ethnic Groups: Romanian (90%), Hungarian (3%), Roma, German, Ukrainian, French (7%)

Primary Religions: Romanian Orthodox (87%), Protestant (7%), Roman Catholic (6%)
Languages: Romanian (official), Hungarian, German

Reducing Communication Noise

Greetings

- Shake hands with men and women upon meeting and leaving, though wait for the woman to extend her hand first. In the larger cities it is typical for a man to greet a woman by kissing her hand.
- Women often use the word *Buna* (Good) when greeting, and men say *Salut* (Salutation). Other common greetings are *Buna ziua* (Good day), *Buna dimineata* (Good morning) and *Buna seara* (Good evening).
- Use titles such as Mr., Mrs., or Doctor before the surname.

Conversation

- Soccer is the most popular Romanian sport. They also do well in international competitions in gymnastics, weight lifting, tennis, and rowing. Swimming, skiing, and aerobics are also popular.
- Romanians are proud of their many museums and have excellent orchestras, opera houses, and theaters in the major cities.
- Romanian folk art includes carpets, pottery, woodcarvings, and religious paintings on glass.
- Make eye contact during conversation. Romanians see this as a sign of honesty.

Sensitivities

- Avoid discussing politics, religion, or social conditions. Romanians face challenges in terms of political freedoms, low wages, and corruption.

Key Negotiating Pointers

- Make prior appointments. Be punctual.
- Dress conservatively. Romanian businessmen usually wear a conservative suit and businesswomen may wear tailored suits or skirts and dresses.
- If you are negotiating the purchase of a business, don't expect many clues as to what the business is worth (asset valuation, cash flow analysis, or marketing plans).
- Use an interpreter during the negotiation unless you speak Romanian. Few Romanian businesspeople speak English. Some of the older generation speak French as a second language.
- Emphasize your firm's ability to transfer business skills and technology know-how.

- Stress your firm's links to the global economy.
- Be patient. Negotiations are likely to be time consuming. Organizations in Romania are still bureaucratic and cumbersome. Decision making is likely to be slow.

Day-to-Day Pointers

Business Entertainment Guidelines
- Most business entertainment is done in restaurants.
- Lunch is the main meal of the day, usually eaten between noon and 2:00 p.m. Dinner is normally eaten after 7:00 p.m.
- A 10 to 15 percent tip is appropriate in restaurants.

Table Manners and Food
- Romanians use the continental style of eating, with the fork in the left hand and the knife in the right hand.
- Keep hands (but not elbows) above the table.
- Romanians usually start each meal by wishing each other *Pofta buna* (Enjoy the meal).
- Wine and beer is a part of most meals, and toasting is usually a part of both lunches and dinners. The phrase *Noroc* (Cheers) is used in social situations.
- Romanian food has many ethnic specialties such as *mititei* (spicy, minced beef, pork, or lamb in sausage form), *mamaliga* (cornmeal mush served like mashed potatoes), and *sarmale* (minced meat with rice, rolled in pickled cabbage or grapevine leaves).
- The larger cities have fast-food restaurants like McDonald's.

Gender Issues

- International businesswomen must contend with almost exclusively male-dominated organizations at almost every decision-making level.

Also Remember This . . .

- Romania became a satellite country of the USSR in 1948. The communist regime was overthrown in 1989, and free elections were held in 1990. Romania joined NATO in 2004.
- Romania has attracted some foreign investment because of tax incentives, skilled workers, and its extensive industrial complex.
- Top priorities include cutting inflation, increasing foreign investment, encouraging privatization, modernizing the country, and developing closer ties with members of the European Union.

RUSSIA

Fast Facts

Monetary Unit: ruble

Major Industries: extraction and processing raw materials, machine building from rolling mills to aircraft

Primary Trading Partners: Netherlands, Germany, Ukraine, Italy, China, United States, Switzerland, Turkey

Key Exports: petroleum and petroleum products, natural gas, metals, wood and wood products, coal

Key Imports: machinery and equipment, medicines, meat, grain, sugar, semifinished metal products

Major Cities: Moscow (cap.) (8.7 mil.), St. Petersburg (4.8 mil.), Novosibirsk (1.4 mil.), Nizhnyi Novgorod (1.4 mil.)

Ethnic Groups: Russians (82%), Tartars (4%), Ukrainians (3%), Chuvash (1%), other (10%)

Primary Religions: Russian Orthodox (15 to 20%), Islam (10 to 15%); estimates are of practicing worshippers

Languages: Russian is the official language; ethnic languages are also spoken.

Reducing Communication Noise

Greetings

- Shake hands with a firm grip upon meeting and when leaving. Introductions tend to be direct and informal.

- Typical greetings are *Zdravstgvuyte* (Hello), *Dobr dien* (Good day), *Dobroye utro* (Good morning), or *Dobry vecher* (Good evening).

- The Russians are very status conscious, so address people by a title such as Director, Minister, Mr. (*Gospodin*), Mrs. (*Gospozha*), or Miss with the last name. First names are reserved for close friends and relatives.

- When referring to a group of people use *Dami i Gospoda* (Ladies and gentlemen).

- Use business cards printed in both Cyrillic (the Russian script) and English.

Conversation

- Russians are proud of their art, architecture, literature, ballet, theater, and other cultural achievements. Museums are also a safe topic of conversation.

Features of Russian culture include the Bolshoi Theatre and Pushkin Art Gallery in Moscow, and the Kirov Ballet and the Hermitage in St. Petersburg.

- Hockey, soccer, basketball, volleyball, billiards, and cross-country skiing are popular sports. Chess is also a popular leisure activity.
- There tends to be a lot of touching in Russia compared to many other countries.

Sensitivities
- Avoid discussing politics and social conditions (such as the alcoholism problem), or the negative aspects of Russian history, such as Stalinism.
- Listen, rather than give lots of opinions, regarding the hardships currently taking place.

Key Negotiating Pointers

- Russians have a reputation for being warm and intelligent people, but not hard workers who show a lot of initiative.
- Make prior appointments and be punctual.
- Business dealings go through the appropriate ministry, and business dealings are likely to move quite slowly through the bureaucratic machinery. Having connections can accelerate the process.
- Be prepared to devote a lot of senior executive time. Russians are very status conscious and want to deal with your key decision makers. Use the most impressive title allowed you by your organization.
- Business presentations should be factual and full of technical details. Be prepared to defend the technical aspects and performance standards, particularly of high-tech products. Russians want to know exactly what they are buying. Consider bringing along a specialist.
- Compared to negotiators in many cultures, no long-term personal relationship is necessarily desired or expected by your Russian counterpart.
- Give yourself a lot of room to negotiate. Russian initial demands are often extreme.
- If you are the seller, try to determine if there is genuine interest and ability to pay for your product or service. Beware of giving detailed information if you sense that your counterpart seeks only the information, and not the deal.
- If your counterpart needs your product, particularly if it is high-tech, price may be less of a sticking point than in other countries. Russia lags far behind the West in high technology.
- Be patient. Russian negotiators typically have limited authority, so they frequently check with headquarters. You can also expect the Russians to be slow in making concessions.
- Expect considerable time to pass before you get a response to a proposal. Delaying tactics are common.

- Another common Russian tactic is to stress the tough competition you face as a seller. Quotations from competitors are sometimes revealed. If your counterpart uses these tactics, be sure to point out those areas where your product is of a higher quality and all-around better value.

- You may also find that Russian negotiators obtain concessions from the weakest competitor first, then demand that you make the "required concessions."

- Get help with the financial aspects of your deal. One of your biggest problems in doing business in Russia is how you will get paid. Nobody wants the ruble.

- Expect to make at least one trip to Russia before a negotiation is finalized. Several years may be required to establish a business or joint venture.

- Check and recheck to ensure all items have been considered before making a final agreement. Last-minute demands are common after you think all the details have been resolved.

- You can expect compliance with the spirit, if not the letter, of the agreement.

Day-to-Day Pointers

Business Entertainment Guidelines

- A typical night of entertainment might involve a visit to the circus, or a concert or dinner in a restaurant. It is rare to be invited to a Russian's home.

- Lunch is the biggest meal, while supper is usually light and eaten late in the evening.

- After 8:00 p.m., an orchestra often plays music in restaurants while patrons dance.

- Be aware of multiple toasts, and be prepared to return them. Unless you can handle large amounts of alcohol well, fill your glass with mineral water (usually provided at the table).

- Gift-giving is an old Russian tradition. Meeting people you don't know very well without *gostinets* (presents from a visitor) is considered to be bad manners. Almost any modest gift will be appreciated—especially those items not readily available in Russia, such as quality ballpoint pens, picture books of your home country, cosmetics, liquors, perfume, and chocolate.

Table Manners and Food

- Sit at the table for a while after the meal to compliment your host.

- Keep your hands above the table.

- Typical Russian food includes bread, potatoes, and cabbage and, to some extent, meat. Traditional dishes include *borsch* (vegetable soup) and various kinds of *goulash* (stew). Russians also love *pelmeni* (small Siberian meat pies boiled in broth).

- Pork, chicken, sausage, and cheeses are popular but expensive.

Gender Issues

- International businesswomen must contend with almost exclusively male-dominated organizations at almost every decision-making level.

- In spite of equalitarian principles, Russian women have limited access to key professional positions.

Also Remember This . . .

- Although Russia's natural resources give it great potential for economic growth, expect slow going as Russians address the fundamentals of a free-market economy.

- Russians are experiencing radical political, social, and economic changes. Almost any business deal should be viewed against this backdrop. Their challenges include a poor infrastructure and distribution system, political uncertainties, low tax-collection rates, organized crime, and corruption.

- Trips to Russia should be planned months in advance to arrange visas, contacts, and travel arrangements.

TURKEY

Fast Facts

Monetary Unit: Turkish lira

Major Industries: textiles, food processing, mining (coal, chromite, copper, boron minerals)

Primary Trading Partners: Germany, United Kingdom, Italy, United States, France, Spain, Russia, China

Key Exports: textiles and apparel, foodstuffs, iron and steel products

Key Imports: machinery, fuels, minerals, foodstuffs

Major Cities: Ankara (cap.) (3.6 mil. metro area), Istanbul (9.8 mil. metro area), Izmir (2.4 mil.), Bursa (1.3 mil.)

Ethnic Groups: Turkish (80%), Kurd (20%)

Primary Religions: Muslim (mostly Sunni) (99%)

Languages: Turkish is the official language, based on a Latin alphabet; Kurdish, Arabic, Armenian, English, French, and German are also understood.

Reducing Communication Noise

Greetings

- *Nasilsiniz* (How are you?) or *Merhaba* (Hello) are the usual greetings. A typical response to *Naslsiniz* is *Iyiyim, tesekkur ederim* (Fine, thank you).
- When entering an office one might say *Gunaydin* (Good morning).
- A handshake is appropriate.
- Use professional titles followed by the last name.
- Greetings among friends will be followed by polite inquiries about one's health, family, and work.
- Among close friends, Turks clasp hands and kiss on both cheeks when greeting.
- When meeting with a small group, greet each person in the group.
- Bring plenty of business cards.

Conversation

- Turkish men like to discuss their families, particularly their sons.
- Soccer is Turkey's most popular sport. Volleyball, basketball, wrestling, cycling, and swimming are also popular.
- The area now known as modern Turkey has enormous historical significance. For instance, the oldest known site of human urban habitation is located at Chatalhuyuk (6500 B.C.), in central Turkey. Ephesus and Antioch were established by the Romans in the first century B.C. The Roman Emperor Constantine founded the city of Constantinople (now called Istanbul) in 330 A.D., which later became the capital of the Byzantine Empire.
- *Ramadan* is observed by Muslims, a month where fasting takes place from dawn to dusk.
- Expect animated hand gestures during conversation.
- Western-style clothing is worn for business, though traditional clothing is still worn in rural areas for ceremonial occasions.
- Expect a lot of cigarette smoking. There are few no-smoking areas. If you smoke, be sure to offer cigarettes to those with you.

Sensitivities

- Avoid discussing issues associated with the Kurdish minority, where there are strong biases, the Turkish-Greek dispute over Cyprus, or Turkish-Armenian relations.

Key Negotiating Pointers

- The pace of Turkish negotiations is quite slow.
- Make appointments two or three weeks in advance. A letter of introduction would be helpful.

- Be punctual for meetings. Allow yourself plenty of time. Traffic jams in Istanbul and Ankara are legendary.

- Expect to engage in considerable small talk before getting down to business. There will probably be questions about your background, education, and family.

- Build trust and a strong relationship with your Turkish counterpart. There is not a lot of trust in people outside one's family or closest friends.

- Be gracious and show respect. You will be offered several cups of tea or coffee. Try to at least sip these beverages to show politeness.

- Emphasize group concerns more than individuality or personal assertiveness.

- Be aware that Turks prize a good sense of humor and consider it a sign of intelligence. Be more willing to share in the joy of their humor rather than trying to tell jokes.

- Try to avoid doing business during June, July, or August, when most Turkish businesspeople are on vacation.

Day-to-Day Pointers

Business Entertainment Guidelines

- Meals are considered a social event, and business is seldom discussed.

- Business entertainment is usually confined to restaurants, where service is usually quite efficient. Lunch is usually at midday. Dinner is the main meal and is usually about 7:00 p.m.

- The Turks are great hosts, and may insist on making all arrangements and paying for the meals.

Table Manners and Food

- Turkish cuisine is world-famous, and can be quite lavish. For example, *meze* is a tray or table of hors d'oeuvres that includes stuffed grape leaves, salads, eggplant, and other items. Shish kebabs (chunks of lamb on a skewer) is a favorite. Turkish desserts are very sweet, such as *baklava* (syrup-dipped pastry) and *muhallebi* (milk pudding). *Raki* is a popular alcoholic drink often served with meals.

- Turks usually order each course one at a time, unless in an international hotel, where the meal is ordered at one time.

- Expect your Turkish host to smoke between courses. If you smoke, be sure to offer a cigarette to the others present.

- The famous thick Turkish coffee, or *kahve*, is served in very small cups at nearly every meal.

- The continental style of eating is followed, with the fork in the left hand and the knife in the right hand.

- A tip of 5 percent is customary if a service charge (usually 10 percent) is included in the bill, or a tip of 15 percent if none is included in the bill.

Gender Issues

- Although Turkey is a male-dominated society, businesswomen visiting Turkey will probably do better than in most other countries in this part of the world.
- Turkish women do have a few basic rights. Turkish women gained the right to vote in 1927, and to divorce in 1934.
- About one-third of the Turkish workforce is female.

Also Remember This . . .

- Although most of Turkey is in Asia, it has important European ties, and is often considered a bridge between the East and the West.
- Turkey joined NATO (North Atlantic Treaty Organization) in 1952.
- The Turks share a strong Muslim orientation with Middle Eastern countries. Although 99 percent of Turkey is Muslim, it has been a secular state since 1923.

UKRAINE

Fast Facts

Monetary Unit: hryvnia
Major Industries: coal, electric power, metals, machinery, chemicals
Primary Trading Partners: Russia, Germany, Turkey, Italy, United States, Turkmenistan
Key Exports: coal, electric power, ferrous and nonferrous metals, chemicals
Key Imports: energy, machinery and parts, transportation equipment, chemicals
Major Cities: Kiev (cap.) (2.6 mil.), Kharkov (1.6 mil.), Dnepropetrovsk (1.2 mil.), Odessa (1.0 mil)
Ethnic Groups: Ukrainian (78%), Russian (17%), other (5%)
Primary Religions: Ukrainian Orthodox, Ukrainian Greek Catholic, Roman Catholic
Languages: Ukrainian is the official language (67%); most people are bilingual, also speaking Russian, Polish, Hungarian, or Romanian.

Reducing Communication Noise

Greetings

- The typical greeting is *Pryvit* (Hi) or *Dobryi den'* (Good day), which are used informally and formally when shaking hands. Don't be surprised if the greeting

is excluded, however. Men often wait for a woman to extend her hand offering to shake.

- Ukrainians use titles and *Pan* (Mr.), *Pani* (Mrs.), *Panni* (Miss), or *Panove* ("Sirs" or "Gentlemen"). When referring to a group of men or women, use *Pani ta Panove* (Ladies and gentlemen).

- First names are reserved for close friends and relatives. In business conversations, refer to your counterpart by his or her first name and add the person's father's name after the first name. For example, for a man whose first name is Aleksandr and his father's name is Victor, you should refer to him as Aleksandr Victorovich. If the person is a woman whose first name is Julia and her father's name is Victor, refer to her as Julia Victorovna.

- It is sometimes hard to remember and pronounce double names. Ukrainians and Russians use a lot of nicknames, so in time you may be asked to call them by a nickname or first name. At this time you can ask them to call you by your first name.

- Have business cards printed in Cyrillic. Ukrainian is a Slavic language written in the Cyrillic alphabet of thirty-three letters.

- Bring plenty of business cards.

Conversation

- Ukrainians like to talk about nature and the outdoors, and love technology and gadgets.

- Popular activities are camping, mountain climbing, hiking, swimming, volleyball, fishing, and skiing. Soccer, ice hockey, and basketball are major sports.

- Ukrainians treasure their folk songs and legends.

- Urban people sometimes have *dachas* (country houses) where they relax. People without *dachas* often have a small plot of land near the city where they grow a garden.

- Christmas is the most popular holiday, celebrated on December 25 by Catholics and January 7 by Orthodox Christians.

- Many Ukrainians read their Ukrainian literature. The Ukrainian literacy rate is 99 percent.

- Establish eye contact during a conversation, though don't do it constantly.

- Don't take it personally if your Ukrainian counterpart doesn't smile much. Smiles are usually reserved for close friends.

- Use limited hand gestures. Approval is expressed by giving the "thumbs up" gesture.

Sensitivities

- Avoid discussing politics and social conditions or their independence from the former Soviet Union.

- While Ukrainians might criticize Ukrainian life, they don't want to hear it from you.
- Crossing one's arms during a conversation is considered disrespectful. Don't sit with one ankle resting on the other knee.
- Keep your space during discussions—usually about two feet.

Key Negotiating Pointers

- Build rapport with your Ukrainian counterpart.
- Business dealings go through the appropriate ministry, and business dealings are likely to move quite slowly through the bureaucratic machinery.
- Make prior appointments and be punctual. Don't be surprised if appointments are sometimes canceled.
- Be patient. Getting a yes will probably involve several discussions. Your Ukrainian counterpart wants to know about you, the details of what you want and how it is going to work, and what other bureaucrats have agreed to it.
- Expect to be told no (*ni*) a lot. Though Ukrainians are gracious, they are also often very direct. Be polite but firm in your response. Saying no is related to the lack of risk-taking traditionally found in their communistic history. The word *yes* is *dobre* in Ukrainian and *da* in Russian.
- Make presentations factual, including technical details.
- Think in terms of a joint venture arrangement where possible. This tends to be the preferred international business arrangement.
- Be prepared for a win-lose rather than win-win approach to negotiations. Compromising on even insignificant details sometimes doesn't come easily.
- Get an agent who can help you work through the government bureaucracy. Ukrainian regulations are complicated and often in a state of flux.
- Don't assume you have completed the negotiation until you have a signed contract.

Day-to-Day Pointers

Business Entertainment Guidelines

- Most business entertainment is done in restaurants. Expect long waits for food.
- The main meal, *obid*, is eaten at midday. This meal consists of two main courses—the first being soup and the second being a meat or fish dish.
- Business entertainment should focus more on building a personal relationship than business aspects of the deal.
- The evening meal, *vechera*, is usually eaten about 6:00 or 7:00 p.m.
- Gift-giving is important in the Ukraine. It is very common to give gifts to business partners, especially during holidays. Gifts are considered a social gesture

and will not be considered a bribe. Many things are in short supply, so anything from highlighters, thermos-type products, to dress shirts will be appreciated. Giving high-quality local products and flowers would be an acceptable gesture, and shows respect for the Ukrainian culture and people. Knowing gift guidelines and the rich holiday traditions will enhance your business prospects.

Table Manners and Food

- Keep your hands (not elbows) on the table rather than in your lap.
- The basic Ukraine staples are vegetables, breads, dairy products, potato (*kartoplya'*), and starchy foods. Corn-on-the-cob is typical.
- The most popular Ukrainian dishes are made of cereal grains and flour pastes, such as *varenyky* (dumplings), *holubtsi* (cabbage leaves stuffed with ground meat and rice), and *kasha* (cooked or baked cereal).
- Your Ukrainian counterpart will probably toast to good health, linger over the meal, and engage in lively conversation.
- You will probably have a bottle of water (*voda*) and bottle of vodka (*gorilka*) on your table. Expect your counterparts to drink all the vodka. In fact, be braced for a lot of drinking in general—of vodka, champagne, or cognac.
- The fork is held in the left hand, and the knife in the right.
- It is considered impolite to leave food on your plate.

Gender Issues

- Though both parents work outside the home in a typical Ukrainian family, work organizations are almost exclusively male-dominated at most levels.
- There is a high regard for women, who are considered by many to be the moral leaders of the nation.
- Businesswomen may experience some chivalry from men. Ukrainian men may open doors for women, though not necessarily *organizational doors*.

Also Remember This . . .

- Ukraine became officially independent from the former Soviet Union in 1991.
- This is a period of great transition for Ukraine, learning the meaning and value of private enterprise after being accustomed to Soviet work patterns.
- Ukraine has enormous potential as a food producer. One-third of the world's black soils are in Ukraine.
- Ukraine has great potential in both the agricultural and industrial sectors. Growth and foreign investment will hinge on modernization of farms, along with addressing corruption, political opposition, and continued state subsidies to unprofitable businesses.

Negotiating in Latin America

The Business Environment of Latin America

Latin America generally refers to Mexico, Central and South America, and the Spanish-speaking Caribbean. Although Mexico is geographically part of North America, culturally it is usually considered part of Latin America. Business practices differ in the many different cultures collectively referred to as *Latin*.

With over 400 million people, a large market exists in Latin America. In addition, vast natural resources make Latin America a potentially strong economic force in the world. Political and economic policies have heretofore hampered progress.

There are generally huge differences in the distribution of wealth. Although the small middle class is growing in countries such as Brazil and Mexico, economic and political power remains concentrated in the hands of a few people.

Cultural Factors That Affect Negotiating in Latin America

Use of Time

The typical Latin American sees time as abstract—more a series of events than in terms of hours or minutes. There is no sense of urgency in the traditional way of life, rooted in the seasons of agriculture. It is natural in Latin America to consider a 10:00 a.m. appointment as meaning roughly 10:30 a.m. or 11:00 a.m.; in fact, that is considered *prompt*.

Latin Americans are more present-oriented than future-oriented. They accept many things as "just happening," rather than applying logical or technical analysis and planning.

Individualism vs. Collectivism

A key to understanding Latin negotiators is to understand the Spanish-Portuguese culture. Both Spain and Portugal dominated colonial Latin America, and status could be achieved only by adapting to their standards. While North Americans came to the New World to flee the oppression of the Old, the Spanish and Portuguese brought their traditional system with them, and they considered themselves still part of the mother country rather than colonizers. Their social and economic style was based on the manorial lifestyle of Europe, a system where status is connected to birth and bloodlines, and where loyalty is primarily to individuals rather than to laws or the constitution of the land. Overall, you will find Latin Americans very ethnocentric—intensely proud of their own country more than the region as a whole.

The Latin view of individualism is quite different from that in North America. North Americans believe in the dignity of the individual as defined by what he or she does or accomplishes in life—for example, what occupation a person chooses. The Latin American emphasizes the inherent uniqueness of each person. The individual is valued not for what he or she does, but for whom he or she is.

It is also important to understand the concept of *machismo* in the role of the Latin American negotiator. North Americans usually connect this concept with sexual overtones. In Latin America, it is more the "essence of being masculine." Whether the male is tall, short, skinny, fat, ugly, or handsome, a *macho* is confident. He has charisma and is a good talker, both eloquent and witty. He is a man for whom no task is impossible. You will encounter him often during your negotiations.

Role Orderliness and Conformity

There is generally low need for role orderliness and conformity in Latin America. In negotiations, a *macho* shows his dislike of plans, schedules, and legal details and a preference for ad hoc and freewheeling decisions.

Latin Americans have a strong sense of dignity. Words and actions are easily interpreted as insults to the individual's inner worth and are highly explosive in their effects. To promote harmony among different social strata, a complicated system of etiquette and diplomacy has evolved for interpersonal relations. This may lead to "group think" in some negotiating situations, where the negotiating

team follows the leader's choices. This relates to the traditional patterns, where a lower-status person does not correct the high-status person openly or put forward conflicting ideas.

Personal relationships are the key to negotiations, as they are to most functions in Latin America. People take priority over institutions, laws, and regulations. When negotiating with Latin Americans, this need for a personal relationship is critical before anything else can be accomplished. The only way to get anything done in Latin America is through a "friend" or a "friend of a friend."

Don't be surprised if your negotiating counterpart asks you for a favor—it is part of the Latin American tradition of starting a personal relationship. The very fact that the favor was asked shows that he or she feels a personal relationship is started, and you are expected to produce. If you refuse bluntly to help ("No, I can't do that; there's a company policy . . ."), then the friendship tie is broken. If you really cannot accommodate the request, give a "Latin no." You might say, "I'll see what I can do." This means that you will try, and that you care. If the person asks about it again, or indirectly brings up the subject, continue the indirect no: "I'm still trying." This will usually not be an offense to the person.

Patterns of Communication

Verbal Communication

Latin negotiators are likely to have a lot of voice inflection, gestures, and emotion. While individuals from North America tend to consider softer tones, fewer gestures, and less emotion as the sign of a poised individual, in Latin America expressiveness and emotion in talking is tied to the Latin concepts of individualism and *machismo*.

Expect to get interrupted frequently. This is not seen as being impolite so much as eagerness to share points of view with you.

Nonverbal Communication

You can expect the physical space to be quite close among Latin Americans compared to the United States and Canada. People in the United States and Canada stand at arm's length when conducting business face-to-face, but Latin Americans stand much closer. Latins often complain than North Americans are impersonal and don't want to get close to them—personally or figuratively. Embracing is common among men who are established business acquaintances; similarly, women may briefly kiss the other's cheek.

You will probably shake hands unless you get to know your counterpart quite well. Handshaking is softer than in North America; firm handshakes may be perceived as hostile. North American negotiators sometimes mistakenly think that the soft Latin handshake is an indication that the Latin negotiating counterpart is unassertive and will not negotiate a very effective agreement on his or her own behalf. Only later does the North American negotiator learn that the Latin American negotiator was in fact very effective.

There is no general rule on eye contact. On the one hand, some Latin Americans are taught that it is respectful to look down when with someone in a position of authority. This can sometimes look shifty to a North American who does not know the cultural influence at work. On the other hand, sustaining eye contact is considered important in Argentina.

Latin America is a good place to be expressive in your hand, arm, and facial gestures. Smiles are valued in Latin America.

HOW NEGOTIATIONS WORK IN LATIN AMERICA

Negotiating Factors

1. *Pace of Negotiations*	Slow
2. *Negotiating Strategies*	
Opening Offers vis-à-vis Settlement	Moderate initial demands
Presentation of Issues	One at a time
Presentations	Informal
Dealing with Differences	Argumentative, whether right or wrong; passionate
Concessions	Slow
3. *Emphasis on Personal Relationships*	High
4. *Emotional Aspects*	
Sensitivity	Valued
Degree of Emotions	Passionate
5. *Decision Making*	
Overall Method	Impulsive, spontaneous
Emphasize	Concepts
Emphasis on Group/Team	Low: Decisions from top person
Emphasis on Face Saving	Extreme
Influence of Special Interests on Decision Makers	Expected, condoned

6. *Contractual and Administrative Factors*

Need for an Agent Average
Degree of Contract Specificity Moderate
Degree of Paperwork/Bureaucracy Moderate
Need for an Agenda Low

ARGENTINA

Fast Facts

Monetary Unit: peso

Major Industries: food processing (especially meat packing), motor vehicles, consumer durables, textiles

Primary Trading Partners: Brazil, Chile, United States, China, Spain, Germany

Key Exports: edible oils, fuels and energy, cereals, feed, motor vehicles

Key Imports: machinery and equipment, motor vehicles and parts, chemicals, plastics

Major Cities: Buenos Aires (cap.) (13.3 mil. metro area), Córdoba (1.5 mil.), Rosario (1.3 mil.), Mendoza (988,000)

Ethnic Groups: Caucasian (97%) (descendants of Spanish-Italian immigrants), mestizo (Spanish-Indian mix), Indian, and other non-Caucasian groups (3%)

Primary Religions: nominally Roman Catholic (92%) (less than 20% practicing); Protestant (2%), Jewish (2%), other (4%)

Languages: Spanish is the official language; many people speak English, German, French, and Italian.

Reducing Communication Noise

Greetings

- Greet each person present, not the group as a whole. A handshake and a slight nod to show respect is also appropriate.

- In some areas, such as Buenos Aires, an embrace with a peck on both cheeks is common among friends.

- Address people as *señor*, *señora*, or *doctor* when being introduced.

- When approaching someone such as a customs official for information, greet the official before asking questions.

- A common greeting is *Buenos días*, or *Buen día* in Buenos Aires (Good day). Say good-bye by using common phrases such as *Adios* or *Hasta luego*.

Conversation

- Argentines appreciate compliments about their children and the meal, and like to talk about the beauty of local parks and gardens.
- Many Argentines are opera fans. Buenos Aires is on the world's opera circuit, and the Colón is one of the finest opera houses in the world. In addition, the Tango dance originated in Argentina, and many Argentines appreciate American jazz.
- Soccer is the national sport, and Argentines love to talk about it. Horse-racing, rugby, tennis, and polo are also popular.
- Though your counterpart may speak English, give serious consideration to learning Spanish. The Argentines are very proud, and an effort to learn Spanish—at a minimum, a few phrases—will be appreciated.
- Maintain eye contact as you would in most Western countries.

Sensitivities

- Avoid discussing politics and religion, even though you can expect urban Argentines to be cosmopolitan, progressive, and often vocal about politics and social conditions.
- Argentines are proud and often view Brazilians, those from the United States, and others as uncultured.

Key Negotiating Pointers

- Argentines have a reputation as tough negotiators. Be patient and expect concessions to come very slowly and grudgingly.
- Make prior appointments and be punctual, though your counterpart may arrive up to thirty minutes late without being inappropriate.
- Nurture the relationship with your counterpart. Argentines are very social, and friendship is a key part of the negotiating process.
- Find a contact who can introduce you to the top person in the organizational unit where you want to do business. Dealing with mid-level managers will be very time consuming and usually fruitless. Decisions are made from the top down.
- Avoid behavior that might be construed as personal criticism of your counterpart.
- Get a written agreement. Try to close key loopholes. Expect contracts to be fairly lengthy and detailed.

Day-to-Day Pointers

Business Entertainment Guidelines

- Meals are a social event. Limit business discussions.
- Evening meals are likely to start very late (8:00 p.m. or 9:00 p.m.). There are many late-night restaurants, theaters, and clubs in Buenos Aires.

- If you are invited to a private home for dinner, bring a small gift such as flowers or candy. Avoid personal items such as a tie or other articles of clothing.
- Tipping is not required but is becoming more common in many restaurants.

Table Manners and Food

- Keep your hands (but not elbows) above the table.
- It is considered poor manners to clear one's throat or blow one's nose at the table.
- Vegetarians have a hard time here. Beef is an Argentine staple; Argentines lead the world in per capita beef consumption.
- Baked stuffed beef and *empanadas* (meat pies) are favorite foods. French cuisine is widely available.

Gender Issues

- Argentine men show great respect for women in their conversation. However, this doesn't necessarily translate into doing serious business with international businesswomen.
- Argentine men may be easy to warm up to on a personal level, but difficult on a business level. International businesswomen often find Argentine men chauvinistic—for example, they do not discuss business over dinner with Argentine women present.

Also Remember This . . .

- Argentina can be a tough place to do business. There is a long history of fascism, political instability, foreign debt, and inflation. Recent political developments would indicate a strong movement toward a free-market economy, however.
- Argentines are proud, educated, and sophisticated, and they identify very strongly with European traditions. Many Argentines believe Buenos Aires is the cultural counterpart of Paris.
- Argentina is going through several economic reforms, focusing on privatization, reducing foreign debt and historically high inflation, and other areas.
- Agriculture is the mainstay of the Argentine economy, although industry is developing. The country is a major exporter of beef, hides, and wool.

BRAZIL

Fast Facts

Monetary Unit: real
Major Industries: textiles and other consumer goods, shoes, chemicals

Primary Trading Partners: United States, Argentina, the Netherlands, China, Germany, Mexico, Nigeria, Japan
Key Exports: iron ore, soybean bran, orange juice, footwear
Key Imports: capital goods, chemical products, oil, electricity
Major Cities: Brasilia (cap.) (1.8 mil.), São Paulo (18.3 mil., metro area), Rio de Janeiro (6.0 mil.), Belo Horizonte (2.3 mil.)
Ethnic Groups: Caucasian (55%) (mainly of Portuguese descent), mixed heritage (38%), black (6%), other (1%)
Primary Religions: Roman Catholic (90%, nominally)
Languages: Portuguese is the official language; Spanish, English, and French are widely spoken.

Reducing Communication Noise

Greetings

- Shake hands upon meeting. When leaving a small group, shake hands with all who are present.
- When greeting, good friends often embrace. Women often kiss each other on alternating cheeks.
- Brazilians tend to use first names, but do not do so until you are asked. Brazil differs from Spanish-speaking Latin America in the use of formal names. You can usually address people by a title and last name instead of middle name (e.g., Paulo Pedro Alveres is Senhor Alvares). Often you can address people by a title and their first name (e.g., Doña Maria).
- A common greeting is *Come vai?* (How are you?)
- Bring plenty of business cards.

Conversation

- Brazilians enjoy talking about their country's rapid development, its industry, and the natural resources of the country, including the beautiful beaches.
- Soccer is the national sport. Brazil has won several World Cups. Pele, the legendary soccer player, is from Brazil. Basketball is also popular, and volleyball is widely played on the beaches.
- Be expressive in your speech. Brazilians enjoy conversation and are likely to be very expressive and passionate in their viewpoints. Brazilians are comfortable with showing emotion and enjoy good jokes and love to laugh. Though Brazilians tend to be warm, friendly, and outgoing, don't ask personal questions (such as age or salary). Don't be surprised, however, if you are asked personal questions.
- Learning a few Portuguese phrases can earn you points.
- Try to get comfortable with the closer physical distance in Brazil than in the

United States. Your counterpart may be only about one foot from you if you are talking while standing up.

Sensitivities

- Avoid talking about politics or religion.
- Avoid voicing your opinions on the deforestation of Brazilian forests.
- If you are from the United States, don't refer to yourself as an American, since Brazilians also see themselves as Americans.
- Avoid speaking in Spanish to Brazilians; this may be offensive even though they understand the language.
- Don't refer to Brazilians as Latin or South Americans. Brazilians consider themselves independent from the rest of South America.
- Avoid using the American "okay" sign, with the thumb and index finger forming a circle. This is an obscene gesture in Brazil.

Key Negotiating Pointers

- Brazilians like to bargain. Like U.S. negotiators, they tend to make concessions slowly and grudgingly.
- Be punctual for your negotiating session, though your counterpart will probably arrive a few minutes after the appointed time. An exception is in São Paulo, where punctuality is practiced.
- Negotiators are likely to move at a faster pace in São Paulo than in other parts of Brazil.
- Engage in general conversation before you get down to business.
- Develop a solid relationship with your Brazilian counterpart.
- Put some flair into your presentations. Try to be expressive.
- Avoid public statements that could possibly embarrass your counterpart.
- Be aware that some use of phony facts may occur at the early stages of the negotiation.
- Brazilians expect deception among negotiators who do not know one other.
- Don't mistake for anger the passion with which Brazilians may argue their points.
- Get a written agreement. Be clear about delivery times and payment details.
- Speak English or use an interpreter unless you speak Portuguese.
- A knowledgeable local is essential to help you maneuver through the government bureaucracies.

Day-to-Day Pointers

Business Entertainment Guidelines

- Meals are considered to be a social event. Business is occasionally discussed during meals in São Paulo or Rio.
- If you are invited to a private home for dinner, bring a small gift such as candy, wine, or a small figurine.
- In restaurants, the check is requested with the phrase *A conta, por favor*. Tips are usually included in the bill. If not, 10 to 15 percent is appropriate.

Table Manners and Food

- Avoid touching food with your fingers while eating. Wipe your mouth before taking a drink.
- Conversation after a meal often takes place over a cup of strong black coffee (*cafezinho*).
- In Rio, the favorite dish is *feijoada*, consisting of black beans with beef, pork, sausage, tongue, and—yes—sometimes a pig's ears, nose, and tail. *Feijoado* is the Brazilian national dish.
- A favorite national drink is *caipirnha*, a tasty drink made with *pinga* (sugar cane liquor), sugar, and lemon.

Gender Issues

- Overall, international businesswomen find a favorable business climate in Brazil.
- There is less *machismo* in Brazil than in Mexico. Brazilian women often fill professional jobs in education, medicine, and journalism, and are sometimes small-business owners. Brazilian women are slowly starting to attain managerial positions.
- Brazilian men tend to stare at and make comments about women passing by on the street.

Also Remember This . . .

- Brazil is a good long-term market with almost 190 million people. It has the largest economy in Latin America, and has the eighth largest economy in the world. U.S. goods are highly valued and sought-after, and there is generally a positive attitude about doing business with the United States.
- Brazil is going through several economic reforms, focusing on privatization, reducing corruption and the historically high inflation, and other areas.
- The Brazilian economy has been helped by substantial foreign investment in the past few years.

- Although Brazil has large oil reserves, it must import about one-fourth of its oil because it lacks oil refining capacity.
- *Carnaval*, a five-day festival preceding Ash Wednesday, is a world-famous event in Rio de Janeiro, and is celebrated throughout Brazil.

CHILE

Fast Facts

Monetary Unit: peso
Major Industries: copper, other minerals, foodstuffs, fish processing
Primary Trading Partners: United States, Japan, China, South Korea, the Netherlands, Brazil, Italy, Mexico, Argentina
Key Exports: copper, fruit, fish products, paper and pulp, chemicals, wine
Key Imports: petroleum, chemicals, electrical and telecommunications equipment, industrial machinery vehicles
Major Cities: Santiago (cap.) (5.3 mil. metro area), Vina del Mar (319, 000), Concepción (318,000)
Ethnic Groups mestizo (Spanish-Indian mix) (95%), Indian (3%)
Primary Religions: Roman Catholic (89%), Protestant (11%)
Languages: Spanish is the official language; English, Portuguese, German, and Italian is spoken in various areas.

Reducing Communication Noise

Greetings

- Common greetings are *Buenos días* (Good morning), *Buenas tardes* (Good afternoon), *Buenas noches* (Good evening), *Cómo está?* (How are you?), and *Gusto de verte!* (Nice to see you).
- A handshake is appropriate when meeting someone for the first time. Chileans greet close friends and relatives with an *abrazo* (a full embrace, while patting each other on the back). *Abrazos* are given between men and women only if they are close friends or relatives.
- Appropriate titles are *señor* (for a man), *señora* (for a married woman), *señorita* (for an unmarried woman), or professional titles (*doctor, director, professor*). Be sure to use the person's professional title when introducing them in public. *Don* (for men) and *Doña* (for women) are used with a person's first name to show special respect and familiarity.
- Men stand when a woman enters the room; they will also open doors for a woman.

Conversation

- English is widely understood among businesspeople, but there are relatively few bilingual people in the population as a whole.
- Maintain eye contract and an upright posture during conversation.
- Chileans are known for their witty sense of humor.
- *Fútbol* (soccer) is the most popular sport. Other popular activities include swimming, tennis, cycling, going to parks, fishing, and rodeos.
- Chileans take pride in their literacy, nation, and heritage. Famous Chilean writers include Nobel Prize poets Gabriela Mistral and Pablo Neruda (also a famous political activist).
- Dress is quite sophisticated in Santiago and other urban areas, following European fashions.

Sensitivities

- Since most Chileans are mestizo, social class is a greater sensitivity than race. The working class resentfully call the elite *momios* (mummies).

Key Negotiating Pointers

- Be punctual for meetings, though your counterpart may arrive a few minutes later. Business is conducted on a more timely basis in Santiago than in other parts of Chile, yet "fashionably late" can mean fifteen minutes late for business meetings.
- Build a solid relationship. Get to know your Chilean counterpart on a casual, personal basis before business aspects are approached. Light conversation precedes any business discussions. Your Chilean host will appreciate it if you try to use a few words of Spanish.
- Ask about the health and welfare of your counterpart's family.
- Give your presentations some flair, with an emphasis on enthusiasm more than an excessive amount of facts.
- Don't say anything in public that could embarrass your Chilean counterpart.
- Get a written agreement, with delivery and payment details spelled out.

Day-to-Day Pointers

Business Entertainment Guidelines

- "Fashionably late" can mean more than an hour late for dinner parties.
- Most business entertainment will be done in restaurants, but it is not unusual for a Chilean to invite you to his or her home.
- The main meal is eaten at midday, between 12:30 and 2:30 p.m. A lighter meal is eaten between 8:00 and 10:00 p.m.

- Teatime is customary during the afternoon between 4:30 p.m. and 6:00 p.m.
- A 5 to 10 percent tip is customary in restaurants.

Table Manners and Food
- Many dishes include fish, seafood, chicken, beef, beans, eggs, or corn.
- Some favorite dishes include *empanadas de horno* (meat turnovers with beef, hard-boiled eggs, onions, olives, and raisins) and *cazuela de ave* (chicken soup).
- It is considered impolite to ask for second helpings.
- The continental style of eating is used, with the fork in the left hand and the knife in the right.

Gender Issues

- Visiting international businesswomen can be more effective in Chile than in most Latin American countries.
- Women make up about 30 percent of the Chilean workforce, and many women hold key political and business positions.

Also Remember This . . .

- Chile is one of the most prosperous Latin American countries and has a strong middle class. Chile's 94 percent literacy rate is one of the highest in Latin America.
- There is a modern business climate in Chile, with its experts and investments integrated into world markets.
- Chile is sometimes called the "Switzerland of South America" for its natural beauty. Because it stretches over 4,000 miles (6,400 kilometers), there are many different climate changes, from subtropical in the north, to subarctic in the south.
- Chileans have strong roots in the provinces and communities where they grew up. This often makes it difficult for employees and their families to move to other regions of the country.

COLOMBIA

Fast Facts

Monetary Unit: peso
Major Industries: textiles, food processing, oil

Primary Trading Partners: United States, Venezuela, Ecuador, China, Mexico, Brazil

Key Exports: petroleum, coffee, coal, bananas, flowers

Key Imports: industrial equipment, transportation equipment, consumer goods, chemicals

Major Cities: Bogotá (cap.) (7.6 mil. metro area), Cali (1.7 mil.), Medellín (1.6 mil.), Cartagena (745,000)

Ethnic Groups: mestizo (Spanish-Indian mix) (58%), Caucasian (20%), mulatto (black-Caucasian mix) (14%), black (4%), other (4%)

Primary Religions: Roman Catholic (90%) is the state religion, although freedom of religion is guaranteed.

Languages: official language is Spanish; English is widely spoken in business.

Reducing Communication Noise

Greetings

- Shake hands with men upon meeting, but not too vigorously. Women offer a verbal greeting and may kiss each other on the cheek if they are acquainted.

- *Abrazos* (hugs) are common among close friends or relatives only.

- Address people by title (such as *señor, señora,* or *doctor*) when being introduced. First names are not used among strangers.

- Individuals bear two family names: The last name is the mother's family name, and the middle name is the father's family name and the official surname. Therefore, a person named Pedro Muñoz Gomez is called Señor Muñoz.

- Common terms are *Buenos días* (Good day), *Cómo está?* (How are you?), and *Adios* (Good-bye). *Chao!* and *Nos vemos!* are informal parting phrases. Smiles are particularly valued in Colombia.

- Bring plenty of business cards.

Conversation

- Colombians are proud of their history of democracy and independence. Other good conversation topics include Colombian art, coffee, and the beautiful countryside.

- Soccer (*fútbol*) is the most popular sport. Bicycle racing, swimming, track and field, and bullfights are also popular. Auto racing and bullfights draw large crowds. Wealthy Colombians belong to golf or tennis clubs.

Sensitivities

- Avoid discussions of current politics or drugs.

- Don't be critical of bullfighting.

- U.S. foreign policy is often seen as overbearing.

Key Negotiating Pointers

- Colombian negotiators are gracious and formal. Colombians are generally receptive to Western businesspeople.
- Be punctual even though your counterpart may not be. Colombian negotiators stress individuality more than punctuality.
- Be prepared for sometimes long discussions over black Colombian coffee before serious business is transacted.
- The pace of negotiations is slow.
- Focus on the top person in the negotiating team, probably the head of the family firm.
- Avoid embarrassing your counterpart in front of others. Try to find ways to make him or her look good.
- Put flair into your presentations.
- Get a written agreement that summarizes the key aspects of agreed-to points. Expect contracts to be fairly lengthy and detailed.

Day-to-Day Pointers

Business Entertainment Guidelines

- Courtesy and etiquette are emphasized. Business is sometimes discussed over meals, but let your Colombian counterpart bring up the subject.
- Lunch is the main meal of the day, usually eaten between noon and 2:00 p.m. Many businesses and schools close during this time, and family members eat lunch together.
- Supper is usually between 7:00 p.m. and 8:00 p.m.
- In restaurants, tipping is not mandatory, but a 10 percent tip for good service is appreciated.

Table Manners and Food

- Social conversation over meals is prized.
- Overeating is considered impolite. Though the host may offer more helpings, politely refuse them.
- Colombians generally eat starchy foods, such as potatoes, rice, and noodles, and enjoy stews and thick soups. A popular dish is chicken with rice.

Gender Issues

- There is an overall receptivity to international businesswomen doing business in Colombia.
- There are very few Colombian women in professional or management positions. Only about one-third of the workforce is women.

- Some traditional values prevail, where the father is the provider for the family. The mother is usually responsible for home duties.

Also Remember This . . .

- Colombia is a developing country whose economy has been heavily dependent on agriculture. A very small number of Colombians hold most of the country's wealth and political power.

- Although Colombia has a reputation for sound financial management, progress is limited by a decaying infrastructure, violence, and illegal drug trade.

- Colombia is a leading coffee producer, but Colombians drink less coffee than North Americans. Oil, however, has overtaken coffee as the main legal export.

- Many wealthy Colombians send their children to U.S. colleges and universities.

COSTA RICA

Fast Facts

Monetary Unit: colón

Major Industries: microprocessors, food processing, textiles, clothing, construction materials

Primary Trading Partners: United States, the Netherlands, Guatemala, Japan, Mexico, Brazil

Key Exports: manufactured products, coffee, bananas, textiles, sugar

Key Imports: raw materials, consumer goods, capital equipment, petroleum

Major Cities: San José (cap.) (1.5 mil. metro area), Alajuela (172,000), Cartago (118,000)

Ethnic Groups: Caucasian, including mestizo (Spanish-Indian mix), (95%), black (3%), Indian (1%), Chinese (1%)

Primary Religions: Roman Catholic (77%), Evangelical Protestant, other Protestant, Jehovah's Witness (14%)

Languages: Spanish is the official language; English is widely spoken in the bigger cities and by businesspeople.

Reducing Communication Noise

Greetings

- Common greetings are *Buenos días* (Good morning), *Buenas tardes* (Good afternoon), and *Buenas noches* (Good evening).

- Men shake hands, including everyone in the group. Women more often greet

each other with a light kiss on the cheek. Once a business or personal relationship is established, a kiss on the cheek is common between men and women.

- The Costa Rican people are called *ticos* by other Central Americans, and by themselves as well. This is because the rural people end words or phrases with the suffix *tico* instead of the more common Spanish diminuitive *tito*.

- Professional titles are used either with or without a surname, depending on the situation. Appropriate titles are *señor* (Mr., for a man), *señora* (Mrs., for a married woman), or *señorita* (for an unmarried woman). The titles *Don* or *Doña*, followed by the first name, are used for respect and authority. Be sure to use the person's professional title when introducing them in public.

- Typical titles are *doctor* (Ph.D or physician), *profesor* (teacher), *ingeniero* (engineer), and *abogado* (lawyer).

- First names are used among friends, coworkers, and subordinates.

- Keep in mind that people stand very close to each other when talking.

- Western dress is worn throughout the country.

- Bring plenty of business cards, printed in both Spanish and English.

Conversation
- Costa Ricans love to talk about their beautiful country, such as rainforests, volcanoes, and nature preserves. Ecotourism is very popular.

- *Fútbol* (soccor) is Costa Rica's most popular sport. Basketball, baseball, volleyball, surfing, and autoracing are also popular. Golf and polo are enjoyed by the wealthy.

- Men are called *ticos* and women, *ticas*, but in mixed company the reference is *ticos*.

- Television programs and movies from the United States are popular.

- There are many festivals, carnivals, and bullfights.

- Maintain sustained eye contract. It is generally assumed that a person with poor eye contact cannot be trusted. Costa Ricans use their hands a lot when they talk.

Sensitivities
- *Ticos* avoid confrontation where possible.

Key Negotiating Pointers

- Make prior appointments and reconfirm before arrival.

- Be gracious and courteous. Socializing is a key part of the business relationship. Quiet, understated behavior is valued.

- Be punctual even though your counterpart may arrive later. Don't be shocked if deadlines are not strictly observed.

- Be well prepared and organized, since business meetings themselves are quite formal. Keep your jacket on during business meetings.
- Get to know your Costa Rican counterpart on a casual, personal basis before business aspects are approached.
- Show respect just as you would to your most valuable client. Dignity and honor are very important. Demeaning your counterpart, especially in public, could ruin the deal.
- Be patient if you have a hard time getting a commitment. Top decision makers tend to consult all those involved. Be prepared to make several trips to finalize the agreement.
- Don't mistake graciousness and lack of disagreement, or even a verbal agreement, for a definite yes. The person probably just doesn't want to hurt your feelings or say no face to face.
- Find a mentor who knows who's who. Contacts are very important.
- Have your proposals printed in both Spanish and English. Your Costa Rican counterpart will probably speak excellent English, but his or her support staff may not.

Day-to-Day Pointers

Business Entertainment Guidelines

- Socializing is an important part of business relations. Meals are considered a social event and business is seldom discussed. Meals are to be enjoyed by active conversation.
- Business entertainment is usually confined to restaurants, at either lunch or dinner.
- After an evening out, call, send a thank-you note, or send a gift such as flowers, wine, or a plant, if invited to a person's home.
- Expect a lot of gift giving at various special occasions.

Table Manners and Food

- *Casado* (rice, beans, eggs, meat, and plantain) is a typical lunchtime meal. Rice and beans in various combinations make up almost every meal.
- Coffee is enjoyed by *ticos* of all ages.
- A 10 percent tip is usually included in the bill. A further tip is not required or expected.

Gender Issues

- International businesswomen can expect better treatment than in the rest of Latin America, but keep in mind that *machismo* is strong.

- Most women have not traditionally worked outside the home, but a growing number are entering the workforce. About one third of the workforce is now women.
- Although the husband is definitely the center of the family unit, women maintain their own identity in legal and business matters.

Also Remember This . . .

- Costa Rica has one of the most stable democratic traditions in Latin America, and has a policy of nonintervention in the affairs of foreign governments.
- There is a strong work ethic in most segments of Costa Rican society. Its gross national product per capita has doubled in the last generation.
- Costa Rica has one of the best medical systems and urban public education systems in Latin America.
- Ecotourism is popular as tourists are drawn to Costa Rica's protected areas.

CUBA

Fast Facts

Monetary Unit: peso
Major Industries: sugar, petroleum, tobacco, construction, nickel, steel
Primary Trading Partners: Mexico, Canada, the Netherlands, Russia, Spain, France
Key Exports: sugar, nickel, tobacco, fish, medical products, citrus, coffee
Key Imports: petroleum, food, machinery, chemicals
Major Cities: Havana (cap.) (2.6 mil. metro area), Santiago de Cuba (555,000), Camaguey (355,000), Holguín (319,000)
Ethnic Groups: mulatto (51%), Caucasian (37%), black (11%), Chinese (1%)
Primary Religions: predominately Roman Catholic, although highly secularized
Languages: Spanish is the official language; English is spoken by many people.

Reducing Communication Noise

Greetings
- Greetings in business are brief. Common greetings are *Qué tal?* (How are you?), *Buenos días* (Good morning), *Buenas tardes* (Good afternoon), and *Buenos noches* (Good evening).
- A handshake and polite smile is appropriate. Women often greet each other with an *abrazo* (hug) and a kiss on the cheek, along with a verbal greeting.

- Titles are often used with or without a surname, such as *señor* (Mr.), *señora* (Mrs.), *señorita* (Miss), or *Compañero/Compañera* (Comrade). Be sure to use the person's professional title when introducing him or her in public.

- First names may be used after you've gotten to know your Cuban counterpart, but wait for that person to first offer to do so. As in most other parts of Latin America, the person's last name is the mother's family name and the second-to-last name is the father's name and used as the person's surname.

- Keep in mind that people stand very close to each other when talking, often touching or tapping each other when making a point.

Conversation
- Expect Cubans to be very brief in the use of hand gestures when they talk. Don't be put off by interruptions, though don't interrupt your Cuban counterpart.

- Maintain eye contract.

- Some Spanish words and expressions are unique to Cuba, such as *pelotear* (to pass the buck) and *rebambaramba* (a free-for-all).

- Sports are highly emphasized in Cuba. Baseball is Cuba's most popular sport. Boxing, basketball, swimming, volleyball, and cycling are also very popular. Dominoes is a national pastime, played especially by males. Most Cubans love their festivals, dancing, and music. The *rumba*, *mambo*, and *cha-cha-cha* originated in Cuba.

Sensitivities
- Expect Cubans to be impassioned in their opinions about many things, such as the economy, international politics, or baseball. Be gracious as a listener.

- Avoid discussing issues such as Cuba's relations with the United States, or politics in general.

Key Negotiating Pointers

- The pace of Cuban business is relaxed. Cubans prefer an easygoing, informal approach to business relationships.

- Be punctual, even though your counterpart may arrive later.

- Get to know your Cuban counterpart on a casual, personal basis before business aspects are approached.

- Remember that Cuba is a socialist state. Getting things done can be cumbersome as you try to deal with the government bureaucracy.

- Be patient and keep a sense of humor. The negotiations are likely to be slow and interrupted.

- Be sure not to publicly embarrass your Cuban counterpart.

- Put some flair and expressiveness in your presentations.
- Find an agent who can introduce you to key contacts.

Day-to-Day Pointers

Business Entertainment Guidelines

- Meals are considered a social event and business is seldom discussed.
- Business entertainment is usually confined to restaurants. Restaurants are state-owned, except for expensive home restaurants. Expect long waits.
- If invited to a Cuban home, you will probably be offered black coffee, wine, or a soft drink. It is okay to graciously decline such offers if you wish.

Table Manners and Food

- The staple Cuban meal is *arroz y frijoles* (rice and beans). Rice is served at most meals, with potatoes, *boniatos* (sweet potatoes), *yuca* (cassava), *plátanos* (plantains), and tomatoes. Roast pork is eaten on special occasions. Seafood is typical in coastal areas. Tropical fruits are eaten in season.
- Coffee is usually served sweet and strong after meals.
- Keep your hands above the table.

Gender Issues

- International businesswomen will be treated with respect, but typical of Latin America, there is still a strong *machismo* aspect of doing business there.
- Cuban women are a key factor in the Cuban workforce—almost 40 percent of the labor force. They hold a majority of Cuba's specialist positions, and occupy leading government and administrative posts.

Also Remember This . . .

- Cuba lies about 90 miles (145 kilometers) south of the United States. The United States has a 99-year lease on Guantánamo Bay, signed in 1934.
- The breakup of the Soviet Union in the early 1990s seriously hurt Cuba's economy. The government has responded with a number of reforms to help conditions, such as opening free-trade markets for produce and crafts, and has been promoting self-employment.
- Education and health care is a priority in Cuba. Its literacy rate is the highest in Latin America. Life expectancy and infant mortality rates are the best in Latin America.

ECUADOR

Fast Facts

Monetary Unit: U.S. dollar
Major Industries: petroleum, food processing, textiles, wood products
Primary Trading Partners: United States, Panama, Peru, Italy, Colombia, China, Venezuela, Brazil, Chile, Japan
Key Exports: petroleum, bananas, flowers, shrimp
Key Imports: vehicles, medicinal products, telecommunications equipment, electricity
Major Cities: Quito (cap.) (1.8 mil. metro area), Guayaquil (2.6 mil. metro area), Cuenca (286,000), Machala (185,000)
Ethnic Groups: mestizo (Spanish-Indian mix) (65%), Indian (25%), Spanish (7%), black (3%)
Primary Religions: Roman Catholic (95%)
Languages: Spanish is the official language; English is spoken in business by many people; Quenchua and other Indian languages are also spoken.

Reducing Communication Noise

Greetings

- A handshake is appropriate, including between men and women, upon meeting and departing.

- Close friends greet each other with an "air kiss" where they "kiss the air" while brushing or touching cheeks. *Abrazos* (a full embrace, while patting each other on the back) are given between men and women only if they are close friends or relatives.

- As with most Hispanics, there are two surnames: the first one from the father, followed by that of the mother. The father's surname is commonly used when addressing someone.

- Address people by a title such as *señor* (for a man), *señora* (for a married woman), or *señorita* (for an unmarried woman), *doctor*, or *doctora* when being introduced. The title *Don* or *Doña*, followed by the first name, is a common greeting among friends. Be sure to use people's professional title if they have one when introducing them in public.

- Common greetings are *Buenos días* (Good morning), *Buenas tardes* (Good afternoon), *Buenas noches* (Good evening), and *Cómo está*? (How are you?).

- Don't use first names unless invited to do so.
- Bring plenty of business cards, printed in both Spanish and English.

Conversation
- English is widely understood among businesspeople but is not widely spoken outside tourist areas.
- *Fútbol* (soccer) is Ecuador's favorite sport, followed by volleyball and basketball. Track, tennis, and boxing are also popular. Sports are mainly enjoyed by males and much less so by females.
- Several festivals and fairs are held in various regions throughout the year.
- There are various museums and cultural sites in Ecuador. A quite active cultural life in Quito is available to the wealthy.
- Western-style clothing is worn for business in urban areas.
- Expect animated hand gestures during conversation.

Sensitivities
- Avoid discussing the role of indigenous groups within Ecuador. Many members of indigenous groups feel they have limited participation in society.
- Be aware that social space is quite close in Ecuador—usually about one foot from the other person. Don't back away.

Key Negotiating Pointers

- The pace of Ecuadorian business is relaxed, though it is more formal and reserved in Quito than in other regions.
- Expect negotiators from Guayaquil to be entrepreneurial, sophisticated, and connected to the outside world (it's a port). Quiteños tend to be more formal, less effusive.
- Make appointments one or two weeks in advance. Be punctual for meetings, even though your counterpart may arrive later.
- Build a strong personal relationship with your Ecuadorian counterparts.
- Try to keep the same negotiating team, since Ecuadorians feel they are negotiating more with people than a company.
- Make sure you have the proper contacts. An Ecuadorian business consultant or lawyer can be helpful. Friendship and kinship influence many business relationships.
- Give your presentations some flair. Don't use an excessive amount of facts and figures. Feelings are more important than objective facts in making decisions.
- Be patient. Expect delays and several versions of the contract before closure.
- Be aware that there are large divisions between rich and poor in Ecuador, and

there is the assumption that the powerful people are entitled to special privileges that come with their office.
- Have documents translated into Spanish.

Day-to-Day Pointers

Business Entertainment Guidelines
- Expect business entertainment to be more formal in Quito than in Guayaquil.
- The midday meal is the most important of the three meals, and is the usual business meal. A heavy lunch with alcohol is typical. Guayaquil is hot, so beer is more common. Quito is cooler, so hard liquor is more typical.
- Business entertainment is usually done in a restaurant, though you may be invited to an Ecuadoran's home after you have established a good relationship. You should consider this an honor.
- Bring flowers, chocolates, or pastries if invited to a home for a meal. Avoid marigolds or lilies, associated with funerals.
- The person who invites a guest to a restaurant is expected to pay for the meal.

Table Manners and Food
- The type of food favored depends on the region of the country. *Serranos* (those from Quito and the mountainous regions) prefer corn and potatoes, while *Costeños* (those from coastal regions) favor rice, beans, and bananas.
- Fresh fruits, fish, and chicken are staple items. Soup is usually served at the midday and evening meals. *Arroz con pollo* (rice and fried chicken), *locro* (a soup made with potatoes, cheese, meat, and avocados) are favorite dishes.
- It is considered rude to leave food on one's plate.
- Try to reciprocate if your host makes a toast.
- Ecuadoran men will be unaccustomed to seeing women drinking hard liquor, though wine is acceptable.

Gender Issues
- International businesswomen can expect tough going in Ecuador, where *machismo* is a model for men.
- Traditional roles are followed in most families, where the man is the unquestioned head of the household. Women, however, are beginning to work outside the home in urban families.

Also Remember This . . .
- There are a lot of regional differences and ethnic diversity in Ecuador. Indigenous peoples maintain a strong cultural identity. Quito is the political, cultural,

and economic center of Ecuador. There is a huge rivalry, mostly friendly, between the *Serranos* (Quito) and *Costeños* (the coast). It has influenced politics and economics of the country since the conquistadores.

- Though more than half the population lives at subsistence levels, the economy and standard of living have improved for many Ecuadorans. Challenges of huge foreign deficits and high unemployment have lessened by dollarization of the monetary system and increased foreign investment.

- Ecuador is the world's largest banana exporter.

- The *Archipiélago de Colón* (or Galápagos Islands), about 600 miles (960 kilometers) off the coast, is a naturalist's treasure, and is where Charles Darwin did most of his evolution studies.

GUATEMALA

Fast Facts

Monetary Unit: quetzal

Major Industries: sugar, textiles and clothing, furniture, chemicals, petroleum

Primary Trading Partners: United States, El Salvador, Honduras, Mexico, Costa Rica

Key Exports: coffee, sugar, petroleum, apparel, bananas

Key Imports: fuels, machinery and transport equipment, construction equipment, grain

Major Cities: Guatemala City (cap.) (2.7 mil. metro area), Quezaltenango (101,000), Escuintla (68,000)

Ethnic Groups: mestizo or *ladino* (Spanish-Indian mix) (55%), Amerindian (43%), black (2%)

Primary Religions: Roman Catholic, Protestant, and traditional Mayan beliefs

Languages: Spanish (60%) and Amerindian (40%) (23 dialects)

Reducing Communication Noise

Greetings

- A common greeting when meeting for the first time is *Mucho gusto!* (Pleased to meet you), accompanied by a handshake. Handshakes in Guatemala are usually quite hardy.

- For those whom you've met, common greetings are *Buenos días!* (Good day), *Buenas tardes!* (Good afternoon), and *Buenas noches!* (Good evening). You might then ask, *Cómo está?* (How are you?), or the more casual, *Qué tal?* (How's it going?) if you've established a friendship.

- Close friends greet each other with an "air kiss," where they kiss the air while brushing or touching cheeks. *Abrazos* (a full embrace, while patting each other on the back) are given between men and women only if they are close friends or relatives.
- As with most Hispanics, there are two surnames: the first one from the father, followed by that of the mother. The father's surname is commonly used when addressing someone.
- Address people by a title such as *señor* (for a man), *señora* (for a married woman), or *señorita* (for an unmarried woman), *doctor*, or *doctora* to show respect. The title *Don* or *Doña*, followed by the first name, is a common greeting among friends. Be sure to use people's professional titles if they have one when introducing them in public.
- Don't use first names unless invited to do so.
- Bring plenty of business cards, printed in both Spanish and English.

Conversation

- *Fútbol* (soccer), basketball, and volleyball are Guatemala's favorite sports.
- Several Guatemalan writers are world famous, such as Nobel Prize–winner Miguel Asturias, who often wrote about indigenous peoples and traditions.
- Try talking about Guatemalan music. The *marimba*, similar to a xylophone, is the most popular indigenous instrument and permeates most Guatemalan music. The marimba is often accompanied by flutes and guitars. Many young Guatemalans enjoy Mexican and North American music.
- Guatemalan textiles are known for their bright colors.
- Many ancient arts abound, such as ceramics, wooden masks, black and green jade carvings and jewelry, and silver-work and gold-work.
- Personal space during a conversation is quite close compared to North America and much of Western Europe.

Sensitivities

- Avoid discussing politics, such as Guatemala's long civil war, Guatemalan poverty, or its drug trade.
- *Ladinos* are people who descended from both the Spanish and Maya but relate more to their Spanish heritage. Be aware that many wealthy *ladinos* tend to see the Maya as inferior.

Key Negotiating Pointers

- Make appointments a week or so in advance. Be punctual for meetings even though your counterpart may arrive later, since people are seen as more important than schedules. Arriving after the appointed time is sometimes called *la hora chopina* (the Guatemalan hour).

- The pace of Guatemalan business is relaxed. Guatemalans begin almost any conversation with pleasantries, including business meetings.

- Build a strong personal relationship with your Guatemalan counterparts. Pressure tactics won't work here.

- Guatemalans tend to be warm and polite, and value honesty, personal honor, and work.

- Make sure you have the proper contacts. A Guatemalan business consultant can be helpful.

- Don't use an excessive amount of facts and figures. Feelings are more important than objective facts in making decisions.

- Commitment to the negotiated agreement may waver. Guatemalans often have a sense of fatalism where they believe they have little power to impact events or circumstances due to God's will.

- Be aware that there are large divisions between rich and poor in Guatemala, and there is the assumption that the powerful people are entitled to special privileges that come with their office.

- Have documents translated into Spanish.

Day-to-Day Pointers

Business Entertainment Guidelines

- The midday meal is the most important of the three meals, and is the usual business meal.

- Business entertainment is usually done in a restaurant, though you may be invited to a Guatemalan's home after you have established a good relationship. You should consider this an honor.

- Bring flowers, chocolates, or something for the home if invited to a home for a meal.

Table Manners and Food

- Keep your hands above the table.

- Corn tortillas or *tamalitos* (cornmeal dough wrapped in corn husks and steamed) are eaten with almost every meal.

- Also popular are black beans, rice, greens, and fried *plátanos* (plaintains) with honey, cream, or black beans. Beef, pork, and chicken are usually stewed. Papaya and breadfruit are readily available.

- Fresh fruits, fish, and chicken are staple items. Soup is usually served at the midday and evening meals.

- Expect coffee to be served with a lot of milk and sugar.

- Upon finishing the meal, try to join your Guatemalan hosts as they each thank

all others present at the table with *Muchas gracias,* with the proper response being *Buen provecho* (Good appetite).

- Try to finish everything on your plate.

Gender Issues

- International businesswomen will be treated well in Guatemala, but keep in mind that this is still a very patriarchal society.
- *Ladino* women usually work as secretaries, teachers, or nurses. Mayan women work, though not in an office or formal work environment, usually selling produce or working in community groups.

Also Remember This . . .

- Guatemala is growing its economy mainly in the area of agriculture, where more than half the population is employed. Tourism and manufacturing are also key for future growth.
- Three-fourths of Guatemalans live in poverty, with wealth concentrated among the upper class.
- Attempts by the government to expropriate land belonging to U.S. business interests promoted a U.S.–sponsored invasion of Guatemala in 1954.
- Chronic political instability and violence marked Guatemalan politics during much of the second half of the twentieth century and sometimes political reforms were reversed. In more recent years, the Guatemalan government, a democracy, signed the Dominican Republic–Central American Free Trade Agreement in 2005.
- The government in 2004 took responsibility for much of the country's violence by compensating peasants for land and lives lost during the civil war (1961–1996).
- Seventy-five percent of the cocaine entering the United States passes through Guatemala.

MEXICO

Fast Facts

Monetary Unit: peso

Major Industries: Food and beverages, tobacco, chemicals, iron and steel, petroleum, mining

Primary Trading Partners: United States, Canada, Spain, China, Japan

Key Exports: manufactured goods, oil and oil products, coffee, silver, fruits, vegetables, cotton

Key Imports: metalworking machines, steel mill products, agricultural machinery, electrical equipment

Major Cities: Mexico City (19.0 mil. metro area); Guadalajara (1.7 mil.), Puebla (1.3 mil.), Monterrey (1.1 mil.)

Ethnic Groups: mestizo (Spanish-Indian mix) (60%), Amerindian or predominantly Amerindian (30%), Caucasian (9%)

Primary Religions: Catholic (89%); Protestant (6%)

Languages: Spanish; English is spoken by many in the business community.

Reducing Communication Noise

Greetings

- Shake hands with business acquaintances upon meeting or when you are introduced to someone for the first time. A full embrace is common with closer acquaintances or friends. Women often kiss each other on the cheek.

- Typical greetings are *Buenos días!* (Good morning), *Buenas tardes!* (Good afternoon), *Buenas noches!* (Good evening/night), and *Cómo está?* (How are you?).

- First names are not used unless you know the person well. Address men with the title *señor*, unmarried women by the title *señorita*, and married women by the title *señora,* followed by the surname. *Doña* is a term of respect before a woman's first name, somewhat like *dame* in Great Britain.

- Individuals usually bear two family names: The last name is the mother's family name, and the middle name is the father's family name and the official surname. Thus, Franco Martinez Rodriguez would be called Senor Martinez.

- Bring plenty of business cards in both Spanish and English.

Conversation

- Mexicans are very proud of their country and appreciate it when visitors compliment Mexico's culture, history, and achievements. Try talking about Mexico's geography, art, archaeology, national museums, and beautiful scenery.

- Praise Mexico's economic accomplishments. Mexicans are proud of their progress, independent of U.S. influence.

- Remember in conversation that Mexicans are geographically North Americans, although they are of the Latin culture.

- Your counterpart will appreciate it if you try to speak a few phrases of Spanish.

- Try to get comfortable with the closer physical distance in Mexico. Your counterpart is likely to stand much closer to you than you are perhaps used to.

Sensitivities
- Some Mexicans still resent the U.S. annexation of the southwest.
- Avoid comparisons with the United States, or issues related to immigration of Mexicans into the United States.
- Some of the border industries, or maquiladoras, have been criticized for not meeting U.S. guidelines for safety, wages, or the environment.

Key Negotiating Pointers

- A half-hour or more past the designated meeting time is considered prompt in Mexico, so don't expect meetings to start at the precise time (*hora Americana*, or American time, as it is sometimes jokingly called). In extreme cases, don't be shocked if meetings are delayed, canceled, forgotten, or sometimes even ignored.
- Don't worry about establishing a formal agenda.
- Be prepared to take a while before the content of the negotiation is addressed. Building rapport and friendship is essential. Take time to build a solid relationship.
- Your host might do business with an unexpected visitor even if you arrived first and are in the middle of a meeting.
- Mexicans like to bargain. Don't make your initial offer an insult, but give yourself some room for movement from your original offer.
- You will probably be dealing with the top person in the organizational unit (perhaps a family member). Pay attention to the issue of face; embarrassing your counterpart could be very costly.
- Mexicans are expressive in their verbal communication. Don't take it personally if there are loud exchanges.
- Use lots of detail in your presentations—charts, graphs, and models—to overcome initial suspicions.
- Get your agreements confirmed in writing, but try to stay away from detailed contracts. Contracts are considered a goal to be strived for more than a binding obligation.
- Ask in advance if you can speak English during the negotiation. Your negotiating counterpart may speak very good English, but staunchly refuse to speak it during a negotiation. Consider the use of an interpreter if you don't speak Spanish.

Day-to-Day Pointers

Business Entertainment Guidelines
- You are generally invited to a person's home only if you are known very well.
- Lunch breaks may be as long as three hours, and business is often conducted during this time.

- The main meal of the day is eaten in the early afternoon. A light dinner, or *cena* or *merienda*, is usually eaten between 8:00 p.m. and 9:00 p.m.

Table Manners and Food
- Keep both hands above the table.
- Guests do not usually leave directly after a meal.
- Corns, beans, and chilies are staple foods. They are combined with spices, vegetables, and meats or fish. Tortillas, made from cornmeal or flour, are eaten either alone as bread or as part of a meal. Other popular foods are *frijoles refritos* (refried beans), *tortas* (hollow rolls stuffed with meat, cheese, or beans), quesadillas (tortillas baked or fried with cheese), and tacos (folded torillas filled with meat, cheese, and onions). Enchiladas are tortillas filled with meat and covered with a chili sauce.
- Avoid tap water in many parts of Mexico. It is usual to order mineral water even in better restaurants.

Gender Issues
- International businesswomen must work hard for acceptance in business circles. They must be cordial, but firm.
- *Macho* attitudes predominate.

Also Remember This . . .
- Mexico is a large and growing market of over 105 million people.
- Mexico signed NAFTA in 1993 with the United States and Canada and has experienced some growth since that time. NAFTA lowered trade barriers and resulted in an increased number of border industries where U.S. investment employs Mexican employees.
- In recent years the government has sold state-owned companies, attracted foreign investment, and liberalized trading regulations.
- Pemex, the government-owed petroleum company, is one of the largest oil companies in the world. Tourism is important for foreign exchange and employs many people.

PERU

Fast Facts

Monetary Unit: nuevo sol
Major Industries: mining of metals, petroleum, fishing

Primary Trading Partners: United States, China, United Kingdom, Chile, Japan, Spain, Brazil, Colombia
Key Exports: copper, zinc, gold, petroleum
Key Imports: machinery, transportation equipment, foodstuffs, petroleum
Major Cities: Lima (cap.) (8.1 mil. metro area), Arequipa (837,000), Trujillo (725,000), Chiclayo (599,000)
Ethnic Groups: Amerindian (45%), mestizo (Spanish-Indian mix) (37%), white (15%), other (3%)
Primary Religions: Roman Catholic (81%), unspecified, none, or other
Languages: Spanish and the indigenous Quechua and Aymara languages are all official languages.

Reducing Communication Noise

Greetings

- Common greetings are *Buenos días* (Good morning), *Buenas tardes* (Good afternoon), and *Buenas noches* (Good evening).

- Both men and women shake hands when meeting and leaving. Peruvian men greet close friends with an *abrazo* (a full embrace, while patting each other on the back).

- Titles such as *señor* (for a man), *señora* (for a married woman), or *señorita* (for an unmarried woman), or a professional title such as *doctora*, are used with the last name. Be sure to use the professional title when introducing a person in public.

- Peruvians, as with most Hispanics, have two surnames: the first from the father, and the second from the mother. Only the father's surname is usually used when addressing another person.

Conversation

- Peruvians are taught English as a second language, and most businesspeople can speak it well.

- Maintain sustained eye contact.

- *Fútbol* (soccer) is Peru's most popular sport. Basketball, volleyball, and gymnastics are also popular.

- Traditional music is important to most Peruvians, though young Peruvians like international music.

- Peru is a favorite destination for archaeologists and tourists, with famous ruins such as Cuzco, Chan Chan, and Machu Picchu. The Incas and several of South America's most advanced cultures lived in pre-Colombian Peru.

- Hand gestures are animated during conversation.

- Western business clothing is worn for business.
- Personal space is quite close in Peru, usually about one foot.

Sensitivities
- Don't joke about Peruvian lifestyle. It won't be appreciated.
- Avoid talking about your Peruvian counterpart's ancestry, the government, or politics.

Key Negotiating Pointers

- You will probably be received favorably overall, since Peruvians are very interested in foreign investment.
- The pace of Peruvian business is relaxed.
- Make appointments two to three weeks in advance. Try to make appointments in the morning, and make yourself available for a possible lunch invitation.
- Be punctual even though your counterpart may arrive later. People are considered more important than schedules.
- Find a local mediator (*enchufado*) who can establish key contacts for you. It is important to do business with those in the small upper class that control resources in Peru.
- Be polite when disagreeing. Try to express differences in a positive manner. For example, it would be more helpful to say, "Here is what we might be able to do," rather than, "We can't really do that."
- Take time to build a strong personal relationship.
- Make presentations that are appealing to the eye and that stress the personal benefits for your Peruvian counterpart and related parties. Deemphasize facts and figures.
- Get an agreement that specifies delivery and payment terms. Don't expect that there will necessarily be strict adherence to the contract, however. Peruvians do not see themselves as governed by rules and laws, as many Westerners do.
- Have your business cards and printed materials translated into Spanish.
- Remember that little work gets done between January and March, when many Peruvians are on vacation.

Day-to-Day Pointers

Business Entertainment Guidelines
- Business entertaining is typically done at prestigious restaurants, usually for a late dinner about 9:30 p.m.
- A good deal of casual conversation should accompany any business meal. You

may or may not get into a business discussion. Let your Peruvian host take the lead in this.

- Gift giving is typical after the first formal meeting, usually during a social situation. Something representing your home region or a company logo gift will be appreciated.
- Dress in well-tailored suits. Official parties usually require tuxedos and cocktail dresses or evening gowns.

Table Manners and Food

- Proper table manners are important. For instance, a polite guest eats all the food that is offered. Try to be tactful in your excuses for not eating something.
- The main staples are rice, beans, fish, and tropical fruits. Soups are also common. *Ceviche* (raw fish seasoned with lemon and vinegar) is a popular dish on the coast. Fresh vegetables are eaten in season.
- The continental style of eating is followed, with the fork in the left hand and the knife in the right hand.

Gender Issues

- International businesswomen should expect to face clearly male-dominated organizations.
- Men are the undisputed head of the household. Women account for only about 25 percent of the workforce, mainly in urban areas.

Also Remember This . . .

- Peruvians are quite nationalistic, though there are deep social and political divisions among Peruvians.
- Peru has a relatively wide economic base, with a variety of industries it can use for growth. Government reforms have cut the hyperinflation from 7,600 percent in 1990 to a more manageable level.
- Peru remains one of the world's largest cocoa producers, and dependence on the drug trade has been a big challenge for the country.
- Peru has one of the longest workweeks in the world, with businesses open six days a week.

VENEZUELA

Fast Facts

Monetary Unit: bolívar
Major Industries: petroleum, iron ore mining, construction materials

Primary Trading Partners: United States, the Netherlands Antilles, Dominican Republic, Colombia, Brazil, Mexico

Key Exports: petroleum, bauxite, aluminum, steel, chemicals, agricultural products

Key Imports: raw materials, construction materials, machinery and transport equipment

Major Cities: Caracas (cap.) (3.5 mil. metro area), Maracaibo (1.9 mil. metro area), Valencia (1.5 mil.)

Ethnic Groups: mestizo (Spanish-Indian mix) (67%), Caucasian (21%), black (10%), Indian (2%)

Primary Religions: Roman Catholic (96%, nominally), Protestant (2%)

Languages: Spanish is the official language and spoken by almost everyone; students must take English in high school.

Reducing Communication Noise

Greetings

- Shake hands and smile politely upon meeting. Men greet close friends with an *abrazo* (a full embrace), while patting each other on the back. Women greet each other with an *abrazo* and a kiss on the cheek. *Abrazos* are given between men and women only if they are close friends or relatives.

- Venezuelans are very title-conscious. Address people as *señor*, *señora*, or *señorita*, followed by the surname. Be sure to use a person's professional title when introducing him or her in public.

- Common greetings are *Buenos días* (Good morning), *Buenas tardes* (Good afternoon), and *Buenas noches* (Good evening). Greetings often include polite inquiries about the other person's health.

- Bring plenty of business cards.

Conversation

- Baseball is Venezuela's most popular sport. Horse racing, bullfighting, soccer, fishing, and hunting are also enjoyed.

- Be respectful in conversation of religious or historical figures.

- English is widely understood among businesspeople.

- Maintain eye contact during conversation.

- Try to get comfortable with the close physical distance.

Sensitivities

- Avoid discussing politics and Venezuela's foreign policy.

- Don't sit in a slouched position or put your feet up on any object.

Key Negotiating Pointers

- The pace of Venezuelan business is relaxed. Venezuelans prefer an easygoing, informal approach to business relationships.
- Be punctual even though your counterpart may not be.
- Get to know your Venezuelan counterpart on a casual, personal basis before business aspects are approached. Be aware, however, that many Venezuelan businesspeople are very busy and many cut the small talk shorter than you think. Let your host take the lead in this.
- Make your presentations factual. Venezuelans are shrewd businesspeople and do not want to be left with any doubts about the deal.
- Be patient and keep a sense of humor. The negotiations are likely to be slow and interrupted.
- Be consistent in your answers to questions. You may be asked the same questions repeatedly.
- Avoid embarrassing your Venezuelan counterpart publicly.
- You will be serve *un cafecito* (a thick, black coffee in a small cup) when visiting a home, business, or the office of a government official. Accept it graciously or you will offend your host.
- Appearances are important in Venezuela. Dress fashionably to give an aura of success.

Day-to-Day Pointers

Business Entertainment Guidelines

- Business entertainment is usually confined to restaurants.
- Meals are considered a social event and business is seldom discussed.
- Dinner is usually late (about 8:00 p.m. or 9:00 p.m.).
- After an evening out, call or send a thank-you note or a good-quality pen or flowers (orchids are the national flower).

Table Manners and Food

- Don't sit at the head of the table. Those seats are for the mother and father of the family.
- Most of the food consists of casseroles, meat pies, stews, and pasta dishes. *Arepa* is a thick fried pancake made from white corn flour and filled with butter, meat, and cheese.
- Hot chocolate is almost as popular as coffee.

Gender Issues

- The concept of *machismo* is alive and well in Venezuela, but international businesswomen can still operate effectively there.

Also Remember This . . .

- Venezuela is the most urban country in Latin America.
- Family continues to be a dominant factor in business, with nepotism a way of life.
- Petroleum is the cornerstone of the economy, and Venezuela is a member of OPEC (Organization of Petroleum Exporting Countries).
- Petroleum revenues have helped fund a modern infrastructure.

Negotiating in North America

The Business Environment of North America

The economy of North America (the United States and Canada) is the largest in the world. There is a climate of free enterprise where most laws are designed to promote competition rather than restrict it. Big corporations dominate the business environment, particularly in the manufacturing and oil sectors. Small and medium-size businesses are prevalent in the service, retail, and construction industries.

U.S. and Canadian businesspeople try to keep up to date on the latest management techniques and ideas. Anyone planning to do business with North Americans should be aware of such management trends as Six Sigma, customer relationship management, strategic thinking, and participative management (giving nonsupervisory employees more power to participate in decision making). In the United States, management gurus such as Jim Collins, Peter Drucker, W. Edwards Deming, Daniel Goleman, Joe Juran, John Maxwell, Tom Peters, and Michael E. Porter strongly influence management thinking.

Fixed ideas about the behavior of North American negotiators are particularly dangerous because of the enormous heterogeneity in the backgrounds of the negotiators themselves. How one might behave in Manhattan may be quite different from one's behavior in Jackson, Mississippi, or Calgary, Alberta, or Montreal, Quebec. The gender, racial, and ethnic mixes of the U.S. and Canadian workforces are going through unprecedented demographic changes. For exam-

ple, in the United States, women are now almost half the workforce, there are vast increases in the Hispanic and Asian populations, and large numbers of immigrants are entering the country. Caucasian males, who once dominated the U.S. workforce, are now a minority and are expected to be increasingly so in the future.

Although the United States and Canada have strong civil rights laws, employees can be routinely dismissed individually or in large groups for economic or performance reasons. For example, a scene feared by a U.S. employee is being called into the boss's office on a Friday afternoon, being terminated, and then being asked to clear out his or her desk immediately before being escorted out of the building. North American organizations would generally find their employee protection laws less stringent than in Europe.

U.S. businesses are organized by state rather than at the federal level, but once a business is established in one state, it can operate in any of the other states. It is generally advisable to organize in the state where you do the most business. However, liberal incorporation laws, tax breaks, and other considerations make states such as New York and (especially) Delaware favorite incorporation sites. In Delaware there is no need for any one of the incorporators to be a U.S. citizen.

Usually, foreign investors face few problems in North America (unless there are security-related reasons, such as in the defense, communications, and airline industries). In fact, a French company has the same status as a Delaware company incorporated in the state of Ohio.

An American's Report Card

How do American negotiators stack up in their global negotiating skills? Let's look at their report card, as shown in Exhibit 8-1. It itemizes the criteria that will make you a masterful negotiator. This assessment is based on discussions with hundreds of Americans who negotiate internationally as well as with their international counterparts in other countries.

The Seven SINs

There are many challenges in keeping a firm footing on the international negotiating terrain. There are, however, seven main areas where U.S. negotiators tend to stumble. They are what I call the seven SINs (Slips in International Negotiating). These SINs are areas where American negotiators tend to score a C or lower in terms of key international negotiating skills:

Exhibit 8-1. The American negotiator's report card.

Global Business Negotiating Performance

Skill	Grade	Comments
Planning the negotiation	B	Most American negotiators would almost rather take a beating than do any kind of business plan, but their logical orientation helps them along.
Win-win approach	C +	Competitiveness is hard to overcome.
Cultural IQ	C –	Often well-traveled but not well-versed as to how their counterparts really think and behave.
Adapting the negotiating process to the host country environment	C –	Old habits are hard to change, especially when they work so well in the massive U.S. market.
Patience	D +	Are you kidding? "Time is money."
Listening skill	C +	Listening is especially hard for busy Americans
Using language that is simple and accessible	C	The English language is complicated enough, and we complicate it even more with jargon, slang, and acronyms.
High aspirations	B +	Often a strong point.
Personal integrity	A	American negotiators have a reputation for sticking to their word.
Building solid relationships	B –	No global warming on our part. "Sounds really good, but I've got 'real' business to do," is a typical approach.
Overall Grade	C +	

SIN 1: Falling into the win-lose trap

SIN 2: Ignoring cultural gaps

SIN 3: Failing to recognize the host country's negotiating obstacles

SIN 4: Being in too much of a hurry

SIN 5: Not listening for communication barriers

SIN 6: Wearing cultural blinders with respect to relationships and emotions

SIN 7: Using language that is hard to understand

Cultural Factors That Affect Negotiating in North America

Use of Time

The pace of business is vigorous in North America, particularly in the United States. Whether a negotiation takes place over the telephone, in an office, or over a business meal, emphasis is put on getting through the content of the negotiation as efficiently as possible. Don't be surprised, however, if final decisions are occasionally bogged down in detailed analysis by financial, strategic planning, legal, or other managers. This slow, exhaustive review is sometimes irreverently referred to as a *paralysis of analysis*. Financial analysis of one- to five-year returns on investment are typical.

There is often more of an emphasis on short-term profits than on long-term growth, although this is more the case in the United States than Canada. Many shareholders demand quick results.

Individualism vs. Collectivism

Individualism is prized in North America. With no aristocracy in either Canada or the United States, one earns social status largely through individual competitiveness that leads to business success. Although family commitments and outside interests are extremely common and deeply held, a preoccupation with business success is usual, particularly in the United States. The fierce competition of New York City executives typifies this preoccupation. However, executives in the midwestern, southern, and western parts of the United States, and most of Canada, do not stress individualism to the same degree.

Team negotiations with, say, seven or more individuals are very unlikely unless the negotiation is very complex and critical to the company's future. Even with several team members present, there are normally only one or two key decision makers on whom you should focus most of your attention. These one or two key players usually "call the shots"—that is, they have the authority to make decisions that can consummate a business deal, or consummate the deal subject to the review of various financial, legal, and other technical experts in the company. Be aware that while many U.S. and Canadian companies are trying to find ways to involve workers in key decisions through participative management techniques, any such involvement normally impacts operational decisions rather than business negotiations.

Role Orderliness and Conformity

There is a low need for role orderliness and conformity in North American organizations compared with those in other regions of the world. More emphasis is put on the content than on the form of the negotiation. *How* business is done tends to get less emphasis than getting it done efficiently. U.S. negotiators sometimes say, for example, "Let's not stand on ceremony—let's just get on with it."

North Americans are generally quite informal in their business dealings, although in French-speaking Canada there is a bit more formality than elsewhere in North America. The use of first names in business characterizes North American informality.

An exception to this informality is the significant role that attorneys often play in finalizing negotiations, particularly in the United States. This sometimes leads to the feeling that U.S. negotiators have a "home field advantage" because of the unpredictable nature of what might be decided in a U.S. court of law. U.S. contracts tend to be lengthy and are reviewed in detail by attorneys. This is largely because U.S. organizations tend to be very concerned about potentially costly lawsuits.

Patterns of Communication

Verbal Communication

North American verbal communication is direct and open. This means that a U.S. or Canadian negotiator is likely to tell you directly, "I'm sorry, but we can't accept your offer." If your North American counterpart is unwilling to make further concessions, she may tell you, "This is our bottom line—our final offer."

The English language as used by North Americans has many slang expressions that make understanding difficult. Each region of the United States and Canada has its own forms of expression. Be sure to ask for clarification if you do not understand what is being said.

Silence is avoided in conversation, and interruptions are common. Don't be surprised or take it personally if a North American negotiator, particularly one from the United States, finishes your sentence for you if you hesitate when you are speaking.

Nonverbal Communication

North Americans like more space in their organizational lives than individuals in most other regions of the world. A distance of three feet is typical between people in business situations. Very little touching takes place. Handshakes, for example, are usually firm and brief. You rarely see two North American business-

people hugging each other upon greeting or leaving (an exception is in French-speaking Canada).

Some North American executives are known to be "back slappers"—those who give others a light slap on the back to show camaraderie or encouragement. Even this gesture is brief and often not appreciated by others.

"You're Really a Porker!"

A few years ago I was teaching a seminar in Toronto and needed to get a shot for a trip overseas. I went to an instant care clinic near the seminar site. A Chinese doctor, who seemed to be about half my size, was studying my chart and suddenly looked up and said in somewhat broken English, "You're really a big guy. You're really a porker!"

Quite surprised, I said, "I'm a what?" He repeated, "You're really a porker!"

Now I'm 6'1" and usually around 185 pounds, and I'll admit that I would like to keep my weight perhaps 10 pounds lighter. But I don't think of myself as unusually overweight.

Intercultural expert that I am, I attributed his assessment of my weight to perhaps trying to work into his vocabulary a new phrase he'd heard. So, I said as pleasantly as I could, "Thank you."

And oh, I immediately started eating more fish and salads and pumped up my workout routine a bit.

HOW NEGOTIATIONS WORK IN NORTH AMERICA

Negotiating Factors

1. *Pace of Negotiations* Fast

2. *Negotiating Strategies*
 Opening Offers vis-à-vis Settlement High initial demands
 Presentation of Issues One at a time
 Presentations Formal
 Dealing with Differences Direct
 Concessions Slow

3. *Emphasis on Personal Relationships* Fairly low

4. *Emotional Aspects*
 Sensitivity Moderate
 Degree of Emotions Moderate

5. *Decision Making*

Overall Method	Group consensus
Emphasize	Logic
Emphasis on Group/Team	Moderate: Decisions from middle managers
Emphasis on Face-Saving	Moderate
Influence of Special Interests on Decision Makers	Low

6. *Contractual and Administrative Factors*

Need for an Agent	Low
Degree of Contract Specificity	High
Degree of Paperwork/Bureaucracy	Moderate
Need for an Agenda	High

 # CANADA

Fast Facts

Monetary Unit: Canadian dollar

Major Industries: processed and unprocessed minerals, food products, wood and paper products

Primary Trading Partners: United States, Japan, United Kingdom, China, Mexico

Key Exports: motor vehicles and parts, wood pulp, timber, petroleum

Key Imports: machinery and equipment, petroleum, chemicals, motor vehicles

Major Cities: Ottawa (cap.) (1.1 mil. metro area), Toronto (5.2 mil.), Montreal (3.6 mil.), Vancouver (2.1 mil.)

Ethnic Groups: British Isles origin (28%), French origin (23%), other European (15%), indigenous Indian and Inuit (2%), other (mostly Asian, African, Arab) (6%), mixed background (26%)

Primary Religions: Roman Catholic (46%), Protestant (38%), other (16%)

Languages: English and French are official languages; English predominates in Ontario, Manitoba, and the other Western provinces, and French predominates in Quebec.

Reducing Communication Noise

Greetings

- Shake hands firmly upon greeting and leaving.
- *Hello* is a common greeting for English-speaking people. In the French parts

of Quebec, the handshake should be a little bit less firm, and *Bonjour* is appropriate; exchanging light kisses on each cheek is typical.

- First names are not typically used in business situations, except by close friends.
- Use business cards printed in both French and English for French-speaking clients.

Conversation

- Canadians like to talk about the history, culture, and geography of their individual province and of Canada as a whole.
- Canadians are sports-minded. Ice hockey is the most popular sport. Curling, boating, swimming, baseball, football, skiing, fishing, hunting, lacrosse, soccer, and rugby also have large followings.
- Try to become familiar with the Canadian political system, geography, and current events. Also recognize that Canada is the biggest trading partner of the United States.
- Most Canadians speak English, and many speak French. French-speaking associates will appreciate your efforts to speak French.
- Good eye contact is usually considered to be direct eye contact for perhaps five to seven seconds, with breaks of two or three seconds. This sustained eye contact is perceived as a sign of interest, sincerity, and truthfulness.

Sensitivities

- Don't behave in any way that might be perceived as condescending. If you are from the United States, be aware that Canadians are sometimes conscious about being "talked down to" by Americans.
- Avoid making comparisons with the United States. Canadians are proud of their accomplishments and independence.

Key Negotiating Pointers

- Canadians tend to be restrained in their negotiating style, keeping their emotions in check. Don't come on too strong. Hard sells do not work well in Canada.
- Make prior appointments and be punctual.
- Be friendly, but get to the point in your discussions.
- Etiquette is important. Perhaps due to their British and French heritage, Canadians tend to be patient and genteel.
- Expect the pace of negotiations to be quite fast in the larger cities, such as Toronto or Montreal, and a bit slower in the Western provinces, where the atmosphere is more friendly and relaxed.
- Focus attention on your counterparts in top management.

- Expect your counterpart to ask you to split the difference, a common tactic by Canadian sellers when asking the buyer to pay more.
- Leave yourself ample room to make concessions. Canadians tend to have high initial demands as both buyers and sellers.
- Canadians tend to make concessions in a deescalating pattern—generous at first, then tapering off.
- Respect deadlines. The Canadians are time-conscious.
- Expect detailed and lengthy contracts.
- Be sure to translate documents into French for French-speaking associates.

Day-to-Day Pointers

Business Entertainment Guidelines
- Business entertainment normally takes place in restaurants or clubs.
- Dinner is usually the business meal, served between 5:00 and 7:00 p.m., and often continuing for two or three hours.
- Dress well for dining in restaurants: usually a coat and tie for men, and dresses or nice pants for women.
- *Cheers* is the traditional toast in most situations. In French-speaking areas, use *Sante* (To your health).
- If you are invited to a private home, bring an inexpensive gift or flowers or send flowers to your host.

Table Manners and Food
- In French-speaking areas, keep your hands (but not elbows) above the table.
- Place your utensils together on the plate when finished eating.
- The Canadian cuisine reflects its multicultural heritage. In the Western provinces, there is fish, beef, Pacific salmon, ethnic dishes, and a variety of foods. In Quebec, there is a definite French influence, with pea soup, meat pies, French pastries and breads, cheese, and lamb. In Newfoundland and Nova Scotia, the most important foods are fish, lobster, and crabs.

Gender Issues
- International businesswomen will be in a comfortable business climate in Canada.
- Except in some of the more rural parts of Quebec where there are strong family traditions, international businesswomen in managerial and professional positions are welcomed.
- Canadian women make up almost half of the workforce, and occupy key professional and managerial positions.

Also Remember This . . .

- Canada has one of the strongest economies in the world, and is the United States' largest trading partner.
- Canada is the second largest country in the world, after Russia.
- Canada is a leading supplier of gold, silver, copper, uranium, oil, natural gas, agriculture, and wood pulp.
- More than a third of Canada's population lives in Ontario.
- Canada signed the North American Free Trade Agreement (NAFTA) in 1993.

 # UNITED STATES

Fast Facts

Monetary Unit: U.S. dollar

Major Industries: petroleum, steel, motor vehicles, aerospace, telecommunications, chemicals, electronics

Primary Trading Partners: Canada, Mexico, Japan, China, Germany

Key Exports: capital goods, automobiles, consumer goods, industrial supplies and raw materials

Key Imports: crude oil and refined petroleum, machinery, automobiles, consumer goods, industrial raw materials

Major Cities: Washington, D.C. (cap.) (571,000), New York (18.5 mil. metro area), Los Angeles (12.2 mil. metro area), Chicago (8.7 mil. metro area), Houston (2.0 mil.)

Ethnic Groups: Caucasian (69%), Hispanic (13%) (Hispanics can be of any race), black (12%), Asian (4%), Pacific Islander, American Indian, Alaskan, or claiming more than one race (2%)

Primary Religions: Protestant (52%), Roman Catholic (24%), Mormon (2%), Jewish (1%), Muslim (1%), other (10%), none (10%)

Languages: predominantly English; sizable Spanish-speaking minority

Reducing Communication Noise

Greetings

- Shake hands firmly and briefly with both men and women upon meeting and leaving, and smile. American greetings are informal. A peck on the cheek or a hug may be used between women or between men and women who have been acquaintances for a long time.
- First names are used in most business situations. Possible exceptions would be

to use *Mr., Mrs.,* or *Miss* for a very senior person in age and rank, or in formal situations.

- Common greetings are *Pleased to meet you* and *How do you do?* More casual greetings include *Hello, Howdy* (in the West), and *Aloha* (in Hawaii).
- Business cards are routinely exchanged in a business setting, though not in social settings.

Conversation

- Americans enjoy talking about business, travel, current trends, and world events. Going to the movies and restaurants are popular leisure activities.
- Baseball, football (American), basketball, golf, tennis, and bowling, are popular spectator and participant sports. Hunting and fishing are popular in rural parts of the country. Soccer has become popular in recent years among children but has yet to catch on as a major national public sport.
- Expect for people to ask you in social gatherings, "What do you do?" (i.e., "What kind of work do you do?") and "Where do you work?" ("For what organization do you work?").
- Americans like their physical space, and usually stand about three feet from each other during conversation.
- Good eye contact is usually considered to be direct eye contact for perhaps five to seven seconds with breaks of two or three seconds. This sustained eye contact is perceived as a sign of interest, sincerity, and truthfulness.

Sensitivities

- Americans like discussing politics. Do more listening than talking.
- Don't criticize the United States. Even though Americans may be self-critical about their environment, they are usually patriotic and don't appreciate negative opinions from others.

Key Negotiating Pointers

- Make prior appointments and be punctual. Although Americans are very time-conscious, business meetings sometimes start ten to fifteen minutes after the appointed time.
- Be cordial but get to the point of the discussions after a limited amount of small talk. Americans sometimes suggest that "we dispense with the formalities and get down to business." Expect negotiations to move quickly.
- Be polite, but be direct and candid in your comments. U.S. negotiators will expect you to "tell it like it is," which means to be open in your communication. Indirect answers may be mistaken for lack of confidence, insincerity, or even dishonesty.
- Don't expect large U.S. negotiating teams. Unless the negotiation is very com-

plex, a typical American negotiation team probably consists of one to five persons.

- Make proposals and presentations detailed, factual, and formal. Be sure to have copies for those present.
- Leave yourself some room to negotiate. U.S. negotiators often have very ambitious initial demands.
- A common tactic is for U.S. sellers to tell buyers to "take it or leave it."
- Expect U.S. negotiators to concede grudgingly, saving concessions until the end of the negotiation.
- Use patience to your advantage. U.S. negotiators sometimes make concessions in order to conclude the negotiation and get on to other business.
- Respect deadlines. Americans are extremely time-conscious.
- Expect contracts to be very detailed and lengthy.

Day-to-Day Pointers

Business Entertainment Guidelines

- Business entertaining is usually done in restaurants.
- Dinner is the main meal of the day, but business breakfasts, lunches, and dinners are common. Dinners start about 7:00 to 9:00 p.m. and continue for one-and-a-half to two hours.
- You may discuss business during a meal.
- In restaurants, tips are not usually included in the bill. A 15 to 20 percent tip is typical.

Table Manners and Food

- Napkins are usually placed in the lap. The left hand often rests in the lap during the meal.
- Americans usually eat with the fork in the right hand. The fork is switched to the left hand and the knife is held in the right for cutting.
- It is generally considered poor manners to rest one's elbows on the table, but many Americans are casual about this.
- There is a rich variety of foods, reflecting diverse cultural backgrounds. Beef, pork, and chicken are popular meats, though many Americans are eating a higher portion of vegetables and fruits for health reasons.
- The large number of fast-food restaurants reflects the busy U.S. lifestyle, as well as food preferences.

Gender Issues

- Compared to other countries, U.S. women occupy more key professional and managerial positions.

- Businesspeople can expect to do business with women as well as men in every region of the country, in many different product lines and services. However, an Old Boy Network still remains in some business sectors.
- Women make up about half the workforce.
- Both parents often work outside the home. Only about 6 percent of the U.S. population lives in a "traditional American family": father at work, with mother and children at home.

Also Remember This . . .

- The United States has the world's largest and most diverse economy, though not the highest per capita income. It is the financial capital of the world.
- American society is prosperous as a whole, though there is a widening gap between income levels.
- The United States is an extremely diverse country, with a wide variety of ethnic, racial, and other backgrounds in the workplace.

Negotiating in the Middle East and North Africa

The Business Environment of the Middle East and North Africa

The region encompassing the Middle East and North Africa is a very diverse area, covering countries such as Saudi Arabia, Israel, Egypt, the United Arab Emirates, Syria, Iran, Iraq, Jordan, Lebanon, Oman, Algeria, and Morocco. The Arabs are relatively small in number, mainly centered in Saudi Arabia, Jordan, Iraq, and the Gulf States (e.g., the United Arab Emirates and Oman).

Negotiating, or bargaining, is part of the everyday life of Middle Easterners, particularly the Arab population. By bargaining, Arabs are able to make their own decisions, to mix socially with people at work, and to earn a living for their families. Just as the average North American would not think of bargaining even if he or she ended up with more profit, the average Arab would not think of doing without it even if he would end up with more profit.

Religion plays a large part in both the history and present-day business environment of the Middle East. Throughout much of the area, there is no separation between church and state as is the case in the United States. Political and religious differences predominate in the area, affecting any attempts to do business among countries in the region. For example, one cannot travel or do business between Israel and any Arab country except Egypt, where there have been diplomatic relations between the two countries since the 1978 Camp David ac-

cords. Anything close to a Middle Eastern Economic Community doesn't seem likely in the near future.

Be aware that *Hebrew* is the Semitic racial term for people from the twelve tribes, whose founder is Abraham. A *Jew* is one who believes in the tenets of Judaism. An *Iranian* is a native of Iran, speaks the Farsi or Persian language, and is not an Arab. Though the Farsi language is written in Arabic characters, Farsi is not Semitic-based. Judaism is the predominant religion for the Jews, and Islam is the predominant religion for the Arabs and Iranians. A *Muslim*, one who practices Islam, is not necessarily an Arab or an Iranian. (The most populous Muslim nation is Indonesia.)

The Islamic culture is based on the teachings of Mohammad. Muslims pray five times a day, bowing to the ground, facing Mecca. Each summer, during Ramadan, twenty-nine days are devoted to fasting during daylight hours. Normal working routines are sharply curtailed during this time.

Cultural Factors That Affect Negotiating in the Middle East and North Africa

Use of Time

Time in the Middle East and North Africa, as in most parts of the world, is not as precise as it is in North America. That is, Middle Easterners will often arrive half an hour late for a meeting, but this is on time for this person. Nor are appointments held in the esteem that they are in North America. The fact that your negotiating partner does not show up at all should not necessarily be taken personally.

Middle Easterners and North Africans don't believe that schedules should rule their lives. Hurrying a Middle Easterner or North African through a negotiation is an insult. Similarly, it is believed to be unlucky or unwise to plan too far ahead. There is some feeling of awe about the future, that if you plan in detail you take on too much upon yourself and invite disaster.

Individualism vs. Collectivism

There is a strong *we* orientation in Middle Eastern and North African cultures, particularly when dealing with government or quasi-government Arab organizations, such as oil companies. The exception is the Arab family merchant/businessman who prides himself on his ability to make his own far-reaching decisions. Success is defined more in terms of group memberships or group accomplishments than in individual accomplishments.

Do not try to save time in your negotiations by ruling out the discussion of any ideas that are not useful to the group as a whole. There is a great deference to those in positions of status and power. Such a tactic would be considered rude by their spokesperson and cause confusion and uncertainty among the underlings.

Role Orderliness and Conformity

There is a relatively high need for role orderliness and conformity in most Middle Eastern and North African countries. Solid personal relationships are vital to the success of negotiations. Before the content of the negotiation is addressed, the parties spend a good amount of time chatting about things that have nothing to do with specific business issues.

Middle Eastern and North African negotiations, particularly those in Arab countries, often seem chaotic to most Western negotiators: people coming in and out of the room when you are meeting, many telephone interruptions, or your counterpart stopping to talk about other matters when you are addressing a key point. You should expect such interruptions to take place.

For the Arab, it is masculine to read poetry, use intuition, and be sensitive. It's feminine to be cool and practical. Therefore, when you are negotiating, it sometimes helps to be a little emotional, or your sincerity may be doubted.

Patterns of Communication

Verbal Communication

Verbal communication in Israel is generally quite direct and open. Verbal communication in Arab countries, by contrast, is quite indirect, vague, and expressive by North American standards. In such high-context cultures, the speaker does not feel obligated to be specific as long as the receiver of the message can infer the message. For example, Arabs will seldom give you a direct no, even if they disagree with your idea, plan, or suggestion. If you ask whether something is a good choice and the person hesitates, then agrees, the hesitation is a strong clue that he or she might actually disagree were it not for the courtesies involved. So a white lie in the name of good manners and someone's feelings is considered better, just as it is to a lesser extent in North America.

U.S. negotiators are very quick to say, "I don't know, but I'll find out." This is not a good idea in most Arab countries of the Middle East. A person of status is not expected to hesitate over an answer. If you don't know, try to stall. Then quickly and privately find the answer or risk losing respect and power.

Don't be alarmed if Arabic-to-English translations sound very exaggerated.

The Arab language is conducive to exaggeration. For example, there are common endings of words that are meant to be emphasized, along with numerous rhetorical devices to achieve even more exaggeration. Fantastic metaphors are common, and many adjectives are often used to modify the same word.

Arabs generally have a strong feeling that information is critical, and they are therefore masters at incremental disclosures—slow at letting you know what is really on their minds. The *truth* is considered something that can be cruel, dangerous, and rude, as well as a matter of negotiation.

Nonverbal Communication

Gestures are quite expressive in Middle Eastern and North African countries, and negotiators generally maintain direct eye contact with their counterparts and have closer physical distance than in most Western countries. These combined behaviors are sometimes viewed as "coming on too strong" by some Western negotiators. Arab men tend to touch each other (but not Arab women, except in private). Embracing upon meeting and holding hands in public is typical in Arab countries. This touching is not sexual, but a display of friendship.

If an Arab makes a short jerk upward with his head, he means no. Often it's accompanied by a *tsk* sound. If he tilts his head sideways, it means yes (yes, I heard you, not necessarily yes, I agree).

HOW NEGOTIATIONS WORK IN THE MIDDLE EAST AND NORTH AFRICA

Negotiating Factors

1. *Pace of Negotiations*	Moderate
2. *Negotiating Strategies*	
Opening Offers vis-à-vis Settlement	High initial demands
Presentation of Issues	One at a time
Presentations	Informal
Dealing with Differences	Usually passionate
Concessions	Slow
3. *Emphasis on Personal Relationships*	High
4. *Emotional Aspects*	
Sensitivity	Valued
Degree of Emotions	Passionate
5. *Decision Making*	
Overall Method	Group consensus

Emphasize	Concepts
Emphasis on Group/Team	Low: Decisions from top person
Emphasis on Face Saving	Extreme
Influence of Special Interests on Decision Makers	Expected, condoned

6. *Contractual and Administrative Factors*

Need for an Agent	High
Degree of Contract Specificity	Low
Degree of Paperwork/Bureaucracy	Moderate
Need for an Agenda	Low

ALGERIA

Fast Facts

Monetary Unit: Algerian dinar
Major Industries: petroleum, light industries, natural gas, mining
Primary Trading Partners: United States, Italy, France, Spain, Canada, Brazil, Belgium, Germany, China, Turkey
Key Exports: petroleum, natural gas, and petroleum products
Key Imports: capital goods, foodstuffs, beverages, consumer goods
Major Cities: Algiers (cap.) (3.9 mil. metro area), Oran (752,000), Constantine (530,000), Annaba (247,000)
Ethnic Groups: Arab-Berber (99%), European (1%)
Primary Religions: Sunni Muslim (state religion) (99%), Christian and Jewish (1%). Although Islam is the state religion, Algeria is not an Islamic Republic.
Languages: Arabic is the official language; Tamazight, spoken by the Imazighen, is also a national language; French is widely spoken.

Reducing Communication Noise

Greetings

- Shake hands when meeting and leaving. An embrace by members of the same sex is also typical, sometimes following the French tradition of kissing each other on the cheeks when embracing. Men shake hands with women unless one or both the parties have a religious prohibition.

- Typical Algerian welcomes are *Ahlan wa sahlan* (May your way be easy) or *Marhaban bikoum* (Hello to you).
- Address others by their title and family name in a business setting.
- Expect hand gestures along with or instead of conversation. For example, to show thanks, your counterpart might place a flat right hand to the heart to show appreciation or thanks.
- Though your male counterpart may wear Western-style clothing, traditional attire could include long, flowing robes or a long shirt, vest, and loose-fitting pants. Head coverings are typical. About half of the urban women wear Western-style attire.

Conversation

- Algerians value family, intelligence, courage, and social status.
- Soccer is the most popular sport, though only men attend matches at stadiums.
- Basketball, volleyball, and handball are other popular sports. Although women participate in sports such as track, it is far less so than for men.
- Algerian jewelry and textiles are traditional arts that continue to be popular. Swords and daggers are typical of the intricate metalwork. Wool Algerian rugs are known for their bold colors and geometric form.
- Algerians are also proud of their hand-tooled leather items, such as boots and saddles.

Sensitivities

- Avoid discussing political or religious issues, such as the ongoing dispute between Algeria and Morocco over the western Sahara. There are also widely differing views within Algeria because of tension related to large gaps between the rich and the poor, corruption, materialism, and crime.
- Most Algerian men have a mustache, a traditional symbol of manhood. Any remark that might be construed as an insult about the mustache could be very damaging to the relationship.
- Don't let the bottom of your foot point towards others.

Key Negotiating Pointers

- Expect your Algerian counterparts to be courteous and formal and to be more candid than those from most other Middle Eastern and North African countries.
- Algerians are used to bartering in their everyday lives, normally in outdoor *souks* (markets) where businesses sell their goods.
- Be punctual even though your counterpart may not be.
- Expect the pace of the negotiation to be slow.

- Building a good relationship is vital. Expect considerable small talk before you get to the business content of your discussions. Trust must be established before business can proceed.

- Reliance on God influences negotiations. Various commitments will be kept *Insha'allah* (if God wills).

- Be prepared to get a written contract and to renegotiate it later since it will probably be seen as a list of general guidelines rather than a specific, firm commitment.

- Get an agent who can make the right connections for you. After you have gotten to know your counterpart, however, you will probably want to deal directly with that person.

Day-to-Day Pointers

Business Entertainment Guidelines

- Dinner is the main meal, usually eaten after 5:00 p.m.
- Expect to socialize for an hour or so after the meal.
- Tipping is discretionary in restaurants.

Table Manners and Food

- Before eating, Algerians wash their hands and say *Elhamduli Allah* (Praise be to God).

- Some foods such as meats and desserts are eaten with the right hand, though utensils will probably be used in most business settings.

- A very popular Algerian dish is *couscous*, a pastalike semolina made from wheat, which is often cooked with lamb or chicken and vegetables. Another popular dish is *tajine*, a meat-and-vegetable stew named for the pot in which it is cooked.

- Meals are usually followed by tea.

Gender Issues

- Algeria is a male-dominated society and local women are virtually nonexistent in business organizations. Algerian women are therefore traditionally restricted to domestic roles, while men are responsible for income.

Also Remember This . . .

- France first established control of the region in 1847. A bloody Algerian War ensued from 1954 to 1962. Independence was achieved in 1962.

- Islamic fundamentalists opposing the military brought Algeria to a virtual civil war in the 1990s.

- The violence that had characterized Algeria for a decade has started to subside

in recent years. The county's first presidential elections in twelve years were held in 2004.

- As in other Islamic countries, Islam is practiced daily through dietary rules, dress, five daily prayers, and repeated references to *Allah*.
- The normal business hours are Saturday through Wednesday. The holy day for Muslims is Friday.

EGYPT

Fast Facts

Monetary Unit: Egyptian pound
Major Industries: tourism, textiles, food processing, chemicals, cement, petroleum, pharmaceuticals
Primary Trading Partners: Italy, United States, Syria, Germany, Spain, France, China, United Kingdom, Saudi Arabia
Key Exports: crude oil and petroleum products, cotton yarn, raw cotton, textiles, metal products, chemicals
Key Imports: machinery and equipment, foods, fertilizers, wood products, durable consumer goods
Major Cities: Cairo (cap.) (11.1 mil. metro area), Alexandria (3.8 mil.), Giza (2.6 mil., part of Cairo metro area)
Ethnic Groups: Egyptian (98%), Berber, Bedouin, and other (2%)
Primary Religions: Muslim (mostly Sunni) (94%), Coptic Christian and other (6%)
Languages: Arabic is the official language; English and French widely understood by educated classes

Reducing Communication Noise

Greetings
- Shake hands with everyone present upon arriving and leaving. Men should wait for women to extend their hands first. Greetings tend to be expressive and elaborate, with the host welcoming the visitor many times.
- Titles are important. Address people by a title (such as *Mr., Mrs.,* or *Miss*) with the first name, or with the last name if the individual is of a high level or a governmental official.
- Use business cards that are printed in both Arabic and English.

Conversation

- Egyptians enjoy talking about their culture's past and present achievements. Egyptian cinema and television programming are known throughout the Middle East and North Africa.
- Soccer is the national sport. Tennis, swimming, and horseback riding are available in sports clubs.
- Egyptians tend to be expressive and emotional in their conversation. A favorite term is *ma'alesh*, generally meaning "don't worry" or "never mind" about concerns that are not serious or that you can doing nothing about.
- Physical space among those of the same sex is closer in Egypt than in most parts of the world. It is much further apart for members of the opposite sex.
- Egyptians may offer unsolicited advice. This is considered polite and caring.

Sensitivities

- Avoid discussing religion.
- Many Egyptians like discussing politics. Do more listening than talking.

Key Negotiating Pointers

- Egyptians are used to bartering in their everyday lives, normally in outdoor *souks* (markets) where businesses sell their goods.
- Egyptians are quite Westernized and are used to doing business with North Americans and Europeans.
- Be punctual even though your counterpart may not be. Don't be shocked if meetings are delayed, postponed, or occasionally ignored.
- Allow plenty of time to get where you are going in Cairo. Traffic is among the heaviest in the world.
- Building a good relationship is vital. Take time to socialize before you get to the content of your discussions. Trust must be established before business can proceed.
- The pace of the negotiation will be slower than in North America, Western Europe, or Israel, but faster than in the rest of the Middle East and North Africa.
- Do not be put off by frequent telephone calls, visitors, or many cups of tea during your negotiating meeting.
- Reliance on God influences negotiations. Various commitments will be kept *Insha'allah* (if God wills).
- Be prepared to get a written contract and to renegotiate it later. A contract is more valued by Egyptians than by most others in the Middle East and North Africa, but it remains a list of general guidelines rather than a specific, firm commitment.

- Get an agent who can make the right connections for you. After you have gotten to know your counterpart, however, you will probably want to deal directly with that person.

Day-to-Day Pointers

Business Entertainment Guidelines

- Lunch is the main meal of the day and usually extends from about 2:00 p.m. to 4:00 p.m. Dinner may not be served until 10:30 p.m. or later.
- If your client is male, invite him and a few of his associates and their wives to a European-style restaurant.
- Business may be discussed over meals, but let your host bring up the subject.

Table Manners and Food

- It is usually considered inappropriate to eat everything on your plate. Leftover food is seen as a compliment to the host for providing so well or, in a restaurant, a sign of your wealth (you can afford to leave food on the plate).
- Since this is a Muslim country, don't use your left hand to shake hands, touch others, point, or give or receive objects.
- When Western eating utensils are used, the continental style is observed, with the fork in the left hand and knife in the right.
- Do not eat, drink, or smoke in front of a Muslim in the daytime during Ramadan.
- Rice, bread, fish, lamb, chicken, turkey, and stuffed vegetables are common foods. Beef is expensive but is available in the large hotels. Bread is eaten with every meal.
- Nonalcoholic beverages are generally served, although alcohol consumption is becoming more widely accepted.

Gender Issues

- For an Arab country, this is a relatively good place for an international businesswoman to do business.
- Egyptians are liberal by Arab standards, with less segregation of the sexes.
- Although women earn only about one-fourth of Egypt's income, women are part of social and business life in Egypt more than most other parts of the Middle East and North Africa.

Also Remember This . . .

- Along with playing a role in industrial pursuits, the Suez Canal is an important source of income for Egypt. Over one-third of the population is employed in agricultural jobs.

- Although large portions of the population remain impoverished, Egypt has improved confidence in foreign investment and lowered inflation through economic reforms.
- Egypt held its first-ever multiparty elections in 2005.
- Cairo has a modern subway, the first in the Middle East.

ISRAEL

Fast Facts

Monetary Unit: shekel
Major Industries: food processing, high tech projects, diamond cutting and polishing, textiles and clothing
Primary Trading Partners: United States, Belgium, Hong Kong, Switzerland, United Kingdom
Key Exports: machinery and equipment, software, cut diamonds, agricultural products, chemicals
Key Imports: raw materials, military equipment, investment goods, rough diamonds, oil, grain
Major Cities: Jerusalem (cap.) (696,000), Tel Aviv (366,000), Haifa (280,000)
Ethnic Groups: Jewish (80%), non-Jewish (mostly Arab) (20%)
Primary Religions: Judaism (80%), Muslim (mostly Sunni) (16%), Christian (2%), Druze and other (2%)
Languages: Hebrew is official language, although Arabic is the official language of Arabic minority; most Israelis speak English.

Reducing Communication Noise

Greetings
- Shake hands upon meeting and leaving. Good friends may pat each other on the back or shoulders.
- First names are generally used. Israel is very informal, and titles are even less important than in the United States; for example, first names or nicknames are even used in the military.
- *Shalom* (meaning peace) is used for *Hello* and *Good-bye*.

Conversation
- Israelis enjoy lively, candid discussions. There is much to talk about. Israel is a study in contrasts: old versus new, tradition versus change.

- Most Israelis enjoy talking about their families. Visiting with family, friends, and neighbors is the most popular leisure-time activity.
- Soccer and basketball are the favorite sports.

Sensitivities
- Israelis love to talk about politics. Be careful here, however. If you engage in a political discussion, be aware of the diversity of opinion that exists in Israel, and do more listening than talking. Don't criticize the government, even if your counterpart seems antigovernment.
- Don't drive or smoke on the Sabbath in religious areas.

Key Negotiating Pointers

- Make prior appointments and be punctual even though Israelis are sometimes casual about time.
- Be friendly, but firm.
- Expect the negotiating pace to be brisk and the style to be aggressive. Be tough and bargain hard. Soft sells may not get heard.
- Be patient. Conserve concessions.
- Don't be put off by expressive, strongly stated positions by your counterpart.
- Get local legal and accounting help. Religious laws strongly influence business transactions.

Day-to-Day Pointers

Business Entertainment Guidelines
- Lunch is more common than dinner for business entertaining.
- If you are invited to a private home, bring a book, candy, or flowers.

Table Manners and Food
- The host or oldest person will begin eating first.
- Dietary restrictions for pork and shellfish are common.
- The diverse backgrounds of immigrant Jews have resulted in a diverse cuisine. Popular dishes include *kabobs* (meat and vegetables on a skewer), Russian *borscht* (beet soup), and chicken soup. Vegetable salad is a staple eaten almost every day. *Falafel* (pita bread filled with fried chick peas) is a national food.

Gender Issues

- Though *macho* attitudes prevail, international businesswomen can successfully do business in Israel.

- The father has traditionally exercised great authority in the home, but women have gained more influence both inside and outside the home in recent years. Women serve in combat positions in the military, for example.
- The female clothing restrictions of more conservative Middle Eastern countries do not apply in Israel—women can wear whatever they want.

Also Remember This . . .

- Israel's economy is modern and well developed. Israel has a fast-growing technological base that offers opportunities for investment, licensing, and franchising agreements and joint ventures.
- Although Israel is surrounded by Arab neighbors, business and social customs for the most part are different.
- Most Israeli workers belong to a labor union. Israeli unions are strong influences in the workplace.
- *Jewish* describes a religion and a culture that unites people called *Jews*, rather than an ethnic group.
- The peace process and global market trends substantially impact growth, inflation, and unemployment.
- Business dress is informal and casual.

 # KUWAIT

Fast Facts

Monetary Unit: Kuwaiti dinar
Major Industries: petroleum, petrochemicals, cement, shipbuilding and repair, desalination
Primary Trading Partners: Japan, South Korea, United States, Singapore, Taiwan, Germany, United Kingdom, Saudi Arabia
Key Exports: oil and refined products, fertilizers
Key Imports: food, construction materials, vehicles and parts, clothing
Major Cities: Kuwait City (cap.) (1.7 mil. metro area), as-Salimiya (147,000)
Ethnic Groups: Kuwaiti (45%), other Arab (35%), South Asian (9%), Iranian (4%), other (7%)
Primary Religions: Muslim (85%: 70% Sunni, 30% Shiite); Christian, Hindu, Parsi, and other (15%)
Languages: Arabic (official); English is widely spoken.

Reducing Communication Noise

Greetings

- Shake hands with everyone present both at the beginning and ending of a meeting. Shake hands with a light, brief grip.

- Greetings are elaborate. Customary terms are *Salahm alaykum* (Hello) upon meeting, then *Kaif halak*? (How are you?) as you are shaking hands. Other common greetings are *Sabaah al-khayr* (Good morning) and *Massa' al-kayr* (Good evening). *Shukran* means "Thank you."

- Men often embrace each other and kiss both cheeks, though this will not be expected of you as a visitor during negotiations.

- For address, the first name should be preceded by Mr., Sheik, Excellency (for ministers), or Your Highness (for members of the royal family) with the first name. For example, Sheik Rashid Abdul Mohammed is addressed as Sheik Rashid; Prince Mohammed Abdullah is Your Highness Prince Mohammed.

- Use business cards that are printed in Arabic and English.

Conversation

- Though most Kuwaiti businessmen understand basic English, speak plainly and slowly. Avoid jargon.

- Kuwaitis usually like to talk about their country's history, the excellence of the coffee or tea, and the gold *souk* (shopping area), carpets, and other shopping concerns. Kuwaitis will be happy to tell you about the Old City Gates or National Museum in Kuwait City.

- Expect Kuwaitis to sit and stand very close to you, and they may rest a hand on your shoulder, tap your forearm with a finger, or exhibit touching in everyday conversation. Hand holding among men walking down the street is a common sight.

- Don't be surprised by the loud voices, animated facial expressions, and wide arm gestures exhibited by two Arabs talking. What might seem like an argument is probably a discussion about business or everyday affairs.

- Eye contact should be maintained, and hand and arm gestures should be open. Expect personal space to be very close, even in a formal negotiation.

Sensitivities

- Avoid talking about religion, Middle Eastern politics, or the role of women.

- Don't tell off-color jokes or use profanity in any way.

- Don't ask about the women or female children in a Kuwaiti man's family. It is okay, however, to inquire about the family in general or about his children.

- Avoid telling your negotiating counterpart that you admire a particular object. He will probably feel obligated to give it to you.
- The bottom of one's foot should never face another person.

Key Negotiating Pointers

- Kuwaiti businessmen have a reputation for being shrewd and knowledgeable about negotiations.
- Get an agent when first doing business in Kuwait. Connections are critical, and your agent can introduce you to the right people and save you a lot of time. Though you have an agent, your counterpart may later want to deal directly with you.
- Remember that you may be dealing not only with Kuwaitis but with those from other Arab countries and non-Arab countries. Kuwaitis account for only 40 percent of the Kuwait population.
- Make prior appointments. Be punctual, though this probably will not be reciprocated. Don't take it personally if your meeting is delayed, rescheduled, or ignored.
- There may be more than one meeting going on in your meeting place at the same time. It is typical for there to be several interruptions during your meeting, with a steady stream of people coming in.
- Be prepared for social banter for several hours—or sometimes even several meetings—before you get down to business. Let your host decide when it's time to talk business.
- Get your proposal translated into Arabic. Even if your counterpart speaks excellent English, some of his associates may not.
- Be patient. Don't press for an immediate yes or no during negotiations. This will be viewed as too aggressive. Allow time for deliberation.
- Bargaining usually starts with inflated proposals and proceeds with a series of ritualistic concessions. A hard-sell approach will not work very well.
- You must build a level of confidence and trust. Price should be discussed as if it is a matter between friends. Maintain mutual respect at all times. Kuwaiti negotiators see themselves as doing business with the person rather than with the company or contract.
- It may require frequent visits to build the relationship. It is probably futile to conduct business via telephone or the mail. In-person visits are therefore preferable.
- Expect to be reminded of the competition.
- Be sure to get a written contract, and be prepared to renegotiate it later. Recognize that you will probably run into resistance on getting a detailed written contract. The contract will be written in Arabic as well as English.

- Expect deadlines to often be ignored.
- The meeting normally concludes with an offer of coffee or tea, and is usually the time when future meetings are arranged.
- Reliance on God influences negotiations, whether it be adherence to a meeting schedule or compliance with a contract. These meetings will be kept *Insha'allah* (if God wills).

Day-to-Day Pointers

Business Entertainment Guidelines

- Business entertainment usually takes place over lunch in fine restaurants, often located in luxury hotels.
- Lunch usually takes place between 1:00 and 5:00 p.m.
- Try the local food. Your host will be delighted to explain the different dishes.
- Reciprocate if you receive a gift, but check with your home office legal staff if it is other than a modest token of your appreciation.

Table Manners and Food

- Since this is a Muslim country, do not use your left hand to touch others, point, or give or receive objects.
- Do not eat, drink, or smoke in front of a Muslim in the daytime during the Ramadan feast.
- All drinks are nonalcoholic, and include soft drinks, mineral water, and fruit juices.
- Try to drink the coffee and tea, which are served at almost any meal or business meeting.
- Kuwaiti food is composed mainly of rice with mildly spiced lamb or chicken. Lamb is the most prestigious meat. Muslims do not eat pork.

Gender Issues

- Kuwait is a male-dominated society, and local women are virtually nonexistent in business organizations.
- Visiting women should cover their arms and legs (wear a long skirt and a loose-fitting, long-sleeved blouse) and dress not to attract attention to their bodies. As a visiting woman, you need not wear a veil. Avoid direct eye contact with men, and don't respond to approaches on the street.
- Local women are seldom present for business dealings. If a local woman is there, however, men should not expect to shake hands or even be introduced.

Also Remember This . . .

- Although Kuwait is today the prototypical oil state, what is now Kuwait City was settled only about 300 years ago. Since that time, there have been many territorial disputes.
- An oil concession was granted to a U.S.–British joint venture in 1934 known as the Kuwait Oil Company, and it soon became clear that Kuwait had massive oil reserves. Kuwait has about 10 percent of the world's crude oil reserves, and among the Gulf States, these reserves are second only to those of Saudi Arabia.
- Today, Kuwait's health care, education, and general standard of living are very high.
- Although Islam is the official state religion, the Kuwaiti constitution guarantees freedom of religion.

MOROCCO

Fast Facts

Monetary Unit: dirham

Major Industries: phosphate rock mining and processing, food processing, leather goods, textiles, tourism

Primary Trading Partners: France, Spain, United Kingdom, Italy, United States, Germany, Russia, Saudi Arabia, China

Key Exports: clothing, fish, chemicals, transistors, minerals, fertilizers (including phosphates)

Key Imports: crude petroleum, textile fabric, telecommunications equipment, wheat, gas, electricity

Major Cities: Rabat (cap.) (1.6 mil.), Casablanca (3.4 mil), Fez (942,000), Marrakech (753,000)

Ethnic Groups: Arab and Berber (99%)

Primary Religions: Muslim (state religion) (99%); Christian (1%)

Languages: Arabic is the main official language, along with French; French is widely spoken in business, government, and higher education; Berber is the language of a large population of indigenous people; Spanish is spoken in the North, particularly the Tangiers area; English is growing in popularity.

Reducing Communication Noise

Greetings
- Shake hands upon meeting and leaving. Moroccans might also touch the heart after the handshake to show personal warmth.

- If a woman is wearing a veil, wait for her to offer her hand; if she doesn't, a slight nod of the head will suffice.
- Hello is commonly expressed as *Assalam Oualaikoum* (Peace be upon you). This greeting is normally reserved for Muslims meeting one another. Other greetings include *Sbah al Kheir* (Good morning) and *Msa al Kheir* (Good evening), or *Bonjour* (Good day) or *Bonsoir* (Good evening).
- Titles are used both in formal situations and to address acquaintances.
- Use business cards that are printed in both Arabic and English.

Conversation

- Moroccans value family, honor, and generosity.
- Soccer is the most popular sport, along with basketball.
- Morocco is famous for its artisan materials, including pottery and ceramic tile, along with silver jewelry, carpets, and hand-tooled leather.
- The *djelleba* is a hooded, ankle-length article of clothing that is the national garment. The *djelleba* is often worn over Western clothing by both men and women in place of a jacket.

Sensitivities

- Avoid discussing political or religious issues, such as the ongoing dispute between Morocco and Algeria over the western Sahara.
- Avoid saying anything negative about the king. Moroccans are cautious when speaking to foreigners and would not speak of the king, except in positive terms. Moroccans can still go to prison or receive a death sentence for negative comments about the king.

Key Negotiating Pointers

- Self-control is important. Losing one's temper would not be acceptable.
- Western-style clothing is common throughout Morocco when conducting business. Be neat, well-groomed, and appropriately dressed to gain respect. Men should plan to wear a suit. Women can also wear a suit, but should consider pants or a long skirt suit, rather than a suit with a skirt above the knee.
- Moroccans, like many people from the Middle East and North Africa, are used to bartering in their everyday lives, normally in outdoor *souks* (markets) where businesses sell their goods.
- Be punctual even though your counterpart may not be.
- Expect the pace of the negotiation to be slow.
- Building a good relationship is vital. Take time to socialize before you get to the content of your discussions. Trust must be established before business can proceed.

- Do not be put off by frequent telephone calls, visitors, or many cups of tea during your negotiating meeting.

- Reliance on God influences negotiations. Various commitments will be kept *Insha'allah* (if God wills).

- Be prepared to get a written contract and to renegotiate it later, since it will probably be seen as a list of general guidelines rather than a specific, firm commitment.

- Get an agent who can make the right connections for you. After you have gotten to know your counterpart, however, you will probably want to deal directly with that person.

Day-to-Day Pointers

Business Entertainment Guidelines

- Lunch is the main meal of the day and usually extends from about 2:00 p.m. to 4:00 p.m. Dinner may not be served until 8 p.m. or later.

- Meals in Morocco are an important time for conversation, so try to join in when you can.

- Business may be discussed over meals, but let your host bring up the subject.

Table Manners and Food

- Moroccans eat with their fingers from a communal dish, using only their right hand. Eating from a common dish is not particularly common in a business setting, however, unless the guest is from the Middle East or Africa.

- Don't point at people or let the bottom of your foot point toward a person.

- Since this is a Muslim country, don't use your left hand to touch others, point, or give or receive objects.

- It is generally considered impolite to cross one's legs.

- Mutton, beef, chicken, and lamb are the main meats in the Moroccan diet, although turkey is increasingly common. Popular dishes included *kefla*, ground beef or mutton, seasoned and cooked over charcoal, and *tajinge*, a term that refers to a "main dish" and can be made of almost any combination of meat and vegetables or fruit. *Couscous* is also popular, made from a grain/pasta called couscous, and served with a medley of steamed vegetables and often chicken, beef, or lamb.

- Milk and dates are often served, particularly the first time a guest comes to a Moroccan home. This is more of a personal tradition rather than a professional one. Mint tea is the national drink. Sodas, such as Coke and Fanta, are also very popular.

Gender Issues

- Although Moroccan women have been traditionally restricted to domestic roles, most Moroccans live in urban areas, where women are better educated and work outside the home. With younger Moroccans, those in their twenties and thirties, women and men play an increasingly equal role.

- A Moroccan law was approved in 2004 that rendered the status of females and males equal before the law.

Also Remember This . . .

- Morocco lies in the northwest corner of Africa and is across the Strait of Gibraltar, only twelve miles from Spain. With this strategic location, Morocco's history is full of foreign invasions from the Phoenicians to the Romans, Greeks, Arabs, and others.

- Moroccan culture is deeply rooted in Islam, though there is some movement from a conservative to a more moderate expression of the faith.

- Morocco was the first country to sign a peace and friendship treaty with the United States. It was signed in 1787 and is still in force.

- Agriculture is the mainstay of the economy, employing about 40 percent of the labor force. Cannabis (hashish) is an important illegal export.

SAUDI ARABIA

Fast Facts

Monetary Unit: riyal

Major Industries: crude oil production, petroleum refining, basic petrochemicals

Primary Trading Partners: United States, Japan, South Korea, China, Taiwan, Singapore, Germany, United Kingdom

Key Exports: petroleum and petroleum products

Key Imports: machinery and equipment, foodstuffs, chemicals, motor vehicles, textiles

Major Cities: Riyadh (cap.) (3.7 mil.), Jeddah (2.7 mil.), Mecca (1.6 mil.), Taif (410,000)

Ethnic Groups: Arab (90%), Afro-Asian (10%)

Primary Religions: Muslim (100%)

Languages: Arabic; English is widely spoken in business.

Reducing Communication Noise

Greetings

- Shake hands with everyone present with a light, brief grip upon meeting and leaving. There is a great deal of handshaking in Saudi Arabia. Greetings are elaborate.

- Saudi women are seldom present for business dealings. If a Saudi woman is there, however, men should not expect to shake hands or even be introduced.

- Saudi men often embrace each other and kiss both cheeks. This is not expected of those who are not accustomed to this from other cultures.

- Address people by a title—such as *Mr., Sheik, Excellency* (for ministers), or *Your Highness* (for members of the royal family)—with the first name. For example, Sheik Mohammed Abdul Waheb is addressed as Sheik Mohammed; Prince Abdullah Ibn Feisal is Your Highness Prince Abdullah.

- Customary greeting are *Salahm alaykum* (Hello) upon meeting, then *Kaif halak?* (How are you?) as you are shaking hands. Other common phrases are *Sabaah al-khayr* (Good morning), *Massa' al-kayr* (Good evening), and *Shukran* (Thank you).

- Use business cards printed in Arabic and English.

Conversation

- Saudis usually like to talk about their country's history, their city, or their taste in art. Try talking about the rapid growth of technology and the excellence of the coffee or tea.

- Although most Saudi businessmen understand basic English, speak plainly and slowly. Avoid jargon.

- Don't be surprised by the loud voices, animated facial expressions, and wide arm gestures exhibited by two Arabs talking. What might seem like an argument is probably a discussion about business or everyday affairs.

- You should maintain eye contact and use open hand and arm gestures.

- Don't praise an object too much. Your Saudi host will probably insist on giving it to you.

- Try to get comfortable with the closer physical space in Saudi Arabia than in Western countries. Expect Saudis to sit and stand very close to you, rest a hand on your shoulder, tap your forearm with a finger, or exhibit touching in everyday conversation. Hand holding among men walking down the street is a common sight. Backslapping by Westerners is not appreciated.

- A man who has made several trips to Saudi Arabia shouldn't be shocked if his counterpart takes his hand while walking. This is only a sign of friendship and has no sexual overtones.

Sensitivities

- Avoid talking about religion, Middle Eastern politics, or the role of women. Remember that religion and politics are intertwined in most of the Middle East.
- Don't tell off-color jokes or use profanity in any way.
- Don't ask about the women or female children in a Saudi man's family. It is okay, however, to inquire about the family or his children.
- The bottom of one's foot should never face another person.

Key Negotiating Pointers

- Saudi negotiators have a reputation for being shrewd and knowledgeable about money making.
- Make prior appointments and be punctual even though your counterpart probably will not be. Don't be surprised if your meeting is delayed, rescheduled, or ignored.
- Be prepared for social banter for several hours—or sometimes even several meetings—before you get down to business. Let your host take the lead in this.
- Build a level of confidence and trust. Price should be discussed as if it is a matter between friends. Maintain mutual respect at all times. Saudi negotiators see themselves as doing business with the person rather than with the company or the contract.
- It may require frequent visits to build the relationship. It is probably futile to conduct business via telephone or written correspondence.
- Be patient. Don't press for an immediate yes or no during negotiations. This will be viewed as too aggressive. Allow time for deliberation.
- Bargaining usually starts with inflated proposals and proceeds with a series of ritualistic concessions. Hard sells do not work very well.
- There may be more than one meeting going on in your meeting place at the same time. It is typical for there to be several interruptions during your meeting, with a steady stream of people coming in.
- Expect deadlines to often be ignored.
- The meeting normally concludes with an offer of coffee or tea, and this is usually the time when future meetings are arranged.
- Reliance on God influences negotiations, whether it be adherence to a meeting schedule or compliance with a contract. Meetings will be kept *Insha'allah* (if God wills).
- Be prepared to get a written contract and to renegotiate it later. You will probably run into resistance getting a detailed written contract. Try, however, to get the details in writing as soon as possible after agreement on the broad concepts. The contract is written in Arabic as well as English. A contract written in English is legal in Saudi Arabia.

- Get your proposal translated into Arabic. Even if your counterpart speaks excellent English, some of his associates may not.
- Get an agent when first doing business in Saudi Arabia. Connections are critical, and your agent can introduce you to the right people and save you a lot of time. After you have gotten to know your counterpart, however, he will probably want to deal directly with you.

Day-to-Day Pointers

Business Entertainment Guidelines

- Business entertainment usually takes place over lunch at a hotel or a restaurant. There are no nightclubs, and not a large selection of restaurants.
- Lunch usually takes place between 1:00 and 5:00 p.m.
- Try the local foods. Your host will be glad to explain the different dishes.
- Gift giving is not considered appropriate by government officials but is common among business associates in the private sector. Reciprocate if you receive a gift, but check with your home office legal staff if it is other than a modest token of your appreciation.

Table Manners and Food

- Since this is a Muslim country, do not use your left hand to shake hands, touch others, point, or give or receive objects.
- Try to drink the coffee and tea.
- Do not eat, drink, or smoke in front of a Muslim in the daytime during the holy month of Ramadan.
- Saudi food is mainly of rice with mildly spiced lamb or chicken. Lamb is the most prestigious meat. Muslims do not eat pork.
- No alcohol is served in Saudi Arabia, though nonalcoholic beer is occasionally available.

Gender Issues

- Saudi Arabia is a male-dominated society and is one of the most difficult places in the world for women to do business. It may even be difficult to get a visa to enter the country at all. It is, however, possible for international businesswomen to conduct business effectively in Saudi Arabia. This should be done only after consulting someone who knows the individual Saudi negotiators. Women should also develop any resources available, such as expatriate spouses and local support networks.
- Women earn less than 10 percent of the nation's income. Local women are virtually nonexistent in professional or managerial jobs.
- Both Arab and any other women must cover their arms and legs (wear a long

skirt and a loose-fitting, long-sleeved blouse) and dress not to attract attention to their bodies. As a non-Arabic woman, you need not wear a veil under any circumstances, though you are encouraged to wear the *abaya* (a black silk, capelike cover) in public. Women are not allowed to drive.

- Arab wives are seldom seen during any business transaction, even in a Saudi home. However, Arab wives sometimes accompany their husbands on business trips abroad and should generally be treated as other guests.

Also Remember This . . .

- Although Saudi Arabia has a growing economy, based almost exclusively on oil and oil products, it hasn't kept pace with fast population growth and this has led to frequent deficits.

- The government is slowly considering increased foreign investment and tourism in order to combat relatively high unemployment and wide economic swings resulting from fluctuations in world oil prices.

- Expatriate workers form the bulk of the labor force.

- Saudi Arabia has the world's largest oil reserves, and Saudi Aramco Oil Company is the world's largest oil company. Most oil company activity is based in the Dharan-al Khobar area in the eastern province.

- Dress in lightweight and light-colored clothing. This is a hot place. Afternoon temperatures regularly exceed 100 degrees.

 # THE UNITED ARAB EMIRATES

Fast Facts

Monetary Unit: U.A.E. dirham
Major Industries: petroleum and petrochemicals, fishing, aluminum, cement, fertilizers, commercial ship repair
Primary Trading Partners: Japan, South Korea, India, Thailand, China, Germany, United Kingdom, France, United States
Key Exports: crude oil, natural gas, re-exports, dried fish, dates
Key Imports: manufactured goods, machinery and transport equipment, chemicals, food
Major Cities: Abu Dhabi (cap.) (540,000), Dubai (1.5 mil. metro area), Sharjah (401,000)
Ethnic Groups: Emirian (19%), other Arab and Iranian (23%), Southeast Asian (50%), other expatriates (8%)

Primary Religions: Muslim (96%) (80% Sunni, 16% Shiite); Christian, Hindu, and other (4%)

Languages: Arabic (official); Persian, Hindi; English is spoken by many members of the business community.

Reducing Communication Noise

Greetings

- Shake hands with everyone present with a light, brief grip upon meeting and leaving. There is a great deal of handshaking in the U.A.E. Greetings are elaborate.

- Local women are seldom present for business dealings. If a local woman is there, however, men should not expect to shake hands or even be introduced.

- Local men often embrace each other and kiss both cheeks. This will not be expected of those from other cultures who are not accustomed to this.

- Address people by a title—such as *Mr., Sheik, Excellency* (for ministers), or *Your Highness* (for members of the royal family)—with the first name. For example, Sheik Rashid Abdul Mohammed is addressed as Sheik Rashid; Prince Mohammed Abdullah is Your Highness Prince Mohammed.

- Customary greetings are *Salahm alaykum* (Hello) upon meeting, then *Kaif halak* ? (How are you?) as you are shaking hands. Other common greetings are *Sabaah al-khayr* (Good morning) and *Massa' al-kayr* (Good evening). *Shukran* means "Thank you."

- Use business cards that are printed in Arabic and English.

Conversation

- Although most Emirian businessmen understand basic English, speak plainly and slowly. Avoid jargon.

- Emirians usually like to talk about their country's history, Dubai's extraordinary development as a tourist and financial center, the rapid growth of technology, the excellence of the coffee or tea, and Persian carpets. Sizable crowds turn out to watch the local nobility race their prized camels.

- Expect Emirians to sit and stand very close to you, and they may rest a hand on your shoulder, tap your forearm with a finger, or exhibit touching in everyday conversation. Hand holding among men walking down the street is a common sight.

- Don't be surprised by the loud voices, animated facial expressions, and wide arm gestures exhibited by two Arabs talking. What might seem like an argument is probably a discussion about business or everyday affairs.

Sensitivities

- Avoid talking about religion, Middle Eastern politics, or the role of women. Remember that religion and politics are intertwined in most of the Middle East.

- The body of water that the U.A.E. borders to the east is referred to in the U.A.E. as the Arabian Gulf, not the Persian Gulf.

- Don't tell off-color jokes or use profanity in any way.

- Don't ask about the women or female children in a Emirian man's family. It is okay, however, to inquire about the family in general or about his children.

- Avoid telling your negotiating counterpart that you admire a particular object. He will probably feel obligated to give it to you.

- A man who has made several trips to the U.A.E. shouldn't be shocked if his counterpart takes his hand while walking. This is only a sign of friendship, and has no sexual overtones.

- The bottom of one's foot should never face another person.

Key Negotiating Pointers

- U.A.E. negotiators have a reputation for being shrewd and knowledgeable about money-making.

- Get an agent when first doing business in the U.A.E. Connections are critical, and your agent can introduce you to the right people and save you a lot of time. Though you have an agent, your counterpart may later want to deal directly with you.

- Remember that you may be dealing not only with Emirians but with those from other Arab countries and non-Arab countries. Emirians account for about 20 percent of the U.A.E. population.

- Make prior appointments. Be punctual, though this probably will not be reciprocated. Don't take it personally if your meeting is delayed, rescheduled, or ignored.

- There may be more than one meeting going on in your meeting place at the same time. It is typical for there to be several interruptions during your meeting, with a steady stream of people coming in.

- Be prepared for social banter for several hours—or sometimes even several meetings—before you get down to business. Let your host decide when it's time to talk business.

- Get your proposal translated into Arabic. Even if your counterpart speaks excellent English, some of his associates may not.

- Be patient. Don't press for an immediate yes or no during negotiations. This will be viewed as too aggressive. Allow time for deliberation.

- Bargaining usually starts with inflated proposals and proceeds with a series of ritualistic concessions. A hard-sell approach will not work very well.

- You must build a level of confidence and trust. Price should be discussed as if it is a matter between friends. Maintain mutual respect at all times. Emirian

negotiators see themselves as doing business with the person rather than with the company or contract.

- It may require frequent visits to build the relationship. It is probably futile to conduct business via telephone or the mail. In-person visits are therefore preferable.

- Expect to be reminded of the competition.

- Be sure to get a written contract, and be prepared to renegotiate it later. Recognize that you will probably run into resistance on getting a detailed written contract. The contract will be written in Arabic as well as English.

- Eye contact should be maintained, and hand and arm gestures should be open. Expect personal space to be very close, even in a formal negotiation.

- Expect deadlines to often be ignored.

- The meeting normally concludes with an offer of coffee or tea, and this is usually the time when future meetings are arranged.

- Reliance on God influences negotiations, whether it be adherence to a meeting schedule or compliance with a contract. These meetings will be kept *Insha'allah* (if God wills).

Day-to-Day Pointers

Business Entertainment Guidelines

- Business entertainment usually takes place over lunch at one of the U.A.E.'s fine restaurants, usually located in luxury hotels. There are pubs, clubs, and discos also available, though they are frequented mainly by Western business-people and tourists.

- Lunch usually takes place between 1:00 and 5:00 p.m.

- Try the local food. Many Westerners like it, and your host will be delighted to explain the different dishes.

- Gift giving is not considered appropriate by government officials but is common among business associates in the private sector. Reciprocate if you receive a gift, but check with your home office legal staff if it is other than a modest token of your appreciation.

Table Manners and Food

- Since this is a Muslim country, do not use your left hand to touch others, point, or give or receive objects.

- Do not eat, drink, or smoke in front of a Muslim in the daytime during the Ramadan feast.

- Try to drink the coffee and tea.

- Emirian food is composed mainly of rice with mildly spiced lamb or chicken. Lamb is the most prestigious meat. Muslims do not eat pork.

- Although alcohol is available to Westerners at special stores and in hotels and restaurants, do not drink alcohol when with your Emirian counterpart.

Gender Issues

- Though still restrictive, the U.A.E. is much less conservative toward international businesswomen than Saudi Arabia.
- The U.A.E. is a male-dominated society, and local women are virtually nonexistent in business organizations. However, expatriate women from Western countries work in a few professional and managerial positions.
- Women should cover their arms and legs (wear a long skirt and a loose-fitting, long-sleeved blouse) and dress not to attract attention to their bodies. As a Western woman, you need not wear a veil under any circumstances. Western women are allowed to drive in the U.A.E.
- An Arab wife (wives) will seldom be seen in any business transaction, even in a U.A.E. home. However, Arab wives sometimes accompany their husbands on business trips abroad and should generally be treated as other guests in the United States.

Also Remember This . . .

- The U.A.E. is considerably less conservative than its close ally, Saudi Arabia. Though a Muslim country, many of the restrictions of Saudi Arabia are not enforced in everyday life.
- Dubai has recently established itself as a major tourist destination and financial center.
- The U.A.E. was formed in 1971, and consists of seven emirates (or states): Abu Dhabi, Dubai, Sharjah, Ras al-Khaimah, Ajman, Fujairah, and Umm al-Quwain.
- The ruling families of the U.A.E. have a Bedouin heritage going back a couple of generations—nomadic tribes that roamed the desert.
- The discovery of oil in the U.A.E. in 1960 has brought enormous wealth. The U.A.E. has imported a large amount of labor and management personnel from other Arab countries, India, Pakistan, Iran, Europe, and the United States.
- Expatriate workers form the bulk of the labor force. Less than 20 percent of the population are U.A.E. citizens.
- The U.A.E. imports most of its food.
- The workweek runs from Saturday to Thursday. The holy day for Muslims is Friday.
- Dress in lightweight and light-colored clothing. Like Saudi Arabia, this is a hot place. Afternoon temperatures regularly exceed 100 degrees.
- Arabic script is from right to left.

Negotiating in Asia and the Pacific Rim

The Business Environment of Asia and the Pacific Rim

Whether you are buying or selling, Asia and Pacific Rim countries should be a critical part of almost any company's global strategy. The vast potential of the Pacific Rim is certainly being realized with the emergence of China as a major economic player. Japan's economy is second only to that of the United States. The business climate among Pacific Rim countries can be characterized as creative, aggressive cooperation, where there are alliances between government and industry and between banks and manufacturers. There are also strong, interlocked groups of companies such as the *keiretsu* of Japan and the *chaebol* of South Korea.

Characteristic of the area's economic power are the so-called Four Tigers: South Korea, Taiwan, Singapore, and Hong Kong. While the relatively recent impact of China on the world economic stage is pivotal, the Four Tigers remain key. South Korea, the first Tiger, has one of the world's fastest-growing economies, moving from primarily an agricultural market to a low-cost producer of consumer goods for U.S. and Japanese markets. South Korea now seeks to focus on a medium-tech economy rather than the high-volume, low-tech manufacturing that is currently its mainstay. Korean firms have moved some of their manufacturing to the lesser-developed Pac Rim nations such as Thailand, the Philippines, and Malaysia, where labor is less expensive. If you are looking to invest in South Korea, then consider electronics, general machinery, precision

machinery, and chemicals. Although Korean labor costs are rising, they remain much cheaper than in the United States, and the work ethic rivals or surpasses that of Japan. South Korea's biggest challenge probably comes from other Pac Rim countries seeking to become significant low-cost producing players, such as Thailand, Malaysia, and, most of all, China.

Taiwan, another of the Four Tigers, was, until the emergence of China, economically second only to Japan in Asia, and it has long had strong economic links with the United States. Taiwan's foreign reserves are among world's highest. The country specializes in high technology and, with a relatively well-off middle class, is an excellent market for consumer goods. Although trade is vital to Taiwan's economic health, direct investment has been increasing substantially. U.S. companies often have the inside track on huge government contracts, such as electrical and petrochemical plants and military hardware. Various infrastructure projects, such as those involving telecommunications and transportation, also offer excellent opportunities. Taiwan is focusing on improving its image as a quality producer of goods. The country is not under any immediate threat of sovereignty from China, but be aware of China's official Taiwan policy of "one China, one government."

Singapore, the third Tiger, is challenging the financial and technological supremacy of the other Tigers. Singapore built its reputation by attracting U.S. and Japanese manufacturers with its inexpensive skilled labor, political stability, and government-supported factories. The emphasis is now on high-tech, high-capital R&D, and banking and finance. Singapore is turning to the United States to gain access to high-tech research methods, something the Japanese are not usually willing to do. Singaporeans seek a wide assortment of consumer goods, some of which are made by Singapore-based American companies such as Apple Computer Inc., and Hewlett-Packard. Having had a reputation as a pirate of intellectual property, Singapore has provided tougher copyright protection laws in recent years.

Hong Kong, the last of the Four Tigers, has long been a key example of free enterprise in the Pacific Rim, with a vigorous manufacturing and financial center. Speculation has varied widely as to the ultimate effect on business of Hong Kong's return to China, but most experts agree that Hong Kong will continue to be a key Pacific Rim player. The optimism is largely based on the fact that Hong Kong has traditionally depended on China for its natural resources, and this need helped create the free-enterprise, market-driven system that has generated its success.

China, with its enormous human and other resources, is now a key factor in the region's economics and politics, and exerts a major global impact as well.

Negotiating in China can be tough, however. Although this is somewhat changing, foreign trade has traditionally been a state-run monopoly. You are almost always dealing with the Chinese government and its policies, whether it be for a joint venture or a bank, and the bureaucracy is cumbersome. Few things happen quickly, so it is important to have the cash to sustain both the negotiation and the project through its development stages.

The Pacific Rim countries also include Australia and New Zealand, which are culturally and physically separate from the rest of the region. These countries have long-standing free-market economies and close links with the West.

Cultural Factors That Affect Negotiating in Asia and the Pacific Rim

With the exception of Australia and New Zealand, the Pacific Rim countries have in common ancient histories characterized by sophisticated cultural achievements, dynastic rule, and social stratification. For example, China, the world's oldest living civilization, was ruled by a series of dynasties from about 2000 B.C. until the twentieth century. Hong Kong belonged to China until it was ceded to Great Britain in 1842, and is now once again officially part of mainland China. The Taiwanese are descendants of Chinese immigrants who began settling the islands in the seventh century. Japan was founded some 2,000 years ago, and Japan's line of emperors continues to the present. Korea traces its origins back 4,300 years, with a history of kings and dynastic rule. Singapore was under British rule from 1824 until it became an independent nation in 1965.

Use of Time

You can expect extreme patience from your Pacific Rim counterpart. Every stage of the negotiation process is likely to be slower than in North America. This protracted process is due to three main reasons: (1) emphasis is put more on the long-term relationship than on the task of negotiating the deal; (2) the custom is to have several people on each negotiating team; and (3) the decisions tend to be made by the entire group.[1] Negotiations in Singapore and Hong Kong are likely to move more rapidly than in other parts of the Pacific Rim.

Individualism vs. Collectivism

Pacific Rim cultures are as *we* conscious as Americans are *I* conscious. This characteristic has many implications for the business setting. For example, helping one's counterpart to *save face* and recognizing the importance of group consensus are important aids in negotiating.

Decision making is likely to be slow, with approval of the group made at

almost every level. However, once made, decisions can usually be implemented quickly.

Super Nobodies?

We have some mainframe computers that have to be up all the time. What we thought would be a simple negotiation to get our equipment left on at night wasn't exactly straightforward. You would think that the director of the Computer Center could arrange that, but he had to go all the way to the chairman of the bank because no one was willing to make a commitment on something that was different and because the person might be scrutinized for it later—"what if the equipment caught on fire" or "what if the building burned down" and several other "what ifs." One must deal with a lot of people who cannot make decisions, but ultimately, if you circumvent them, could make your life miserable. In China, you deal from the bottom-up and meet a lot of "super nobodies" when it comes to making decisions.

SOURCE: Manager of contracts administration for a global payment services franchise

Role Orderliness and Conformity

The need for role orderliness and conformity helps explain why it is so important for those in the Pacific Rim cultures to build a relationship with their negotiating counterpart. Getting to know one's negotiating counterpart is a way to bring orderliness and certainty to one's world.

Social stratification over the centuries and the influence of the Confucian ethic make proper social relationships extremely important. These relationships form the basis for such social traditions as rituals of courtesy, formality in behavior, excessive politeness, loyalty to and identification with the group, deference to the elderly, avoidance of direct conflicts, and extreme modesty when speaking of one's status, accomplishments, and family.

Patterns of Communication

Verbal Communication

There are strong elements of Confucianism, Buddhism, and Taoism in Pacific Rim cultures, creating such communication values as humility, silence, modesty, and mistrust of words. Verbal communication in Pacific Rim cultures is generally quite indirect. In high-context cultures such as Japan or China, people expect the person to whom they are talking to know what is on their mind. They

give the other person all the necessary information except the crucial piece. This can be illustrated in the way negotiators say no. Instead of saying it directly, as would be the case with most American negotiators, this message may be conveyed by saying, "We will study the matter" or "We want to get more opinions on your idea." This communication pattern makes it imperative that you listen carefully.

Nonverbal Communication

Body language is generally more reserved than in North America. Expressive gestures are seldom seen, and eye contact is almost always brief. Personal space is a little closer than in the United States, but touching in business settings is generally restrained. Brief handshakes or bows, rather than hugs and other forms of touching, are typical.

Notes

1. Frank L. Acuff, "Negotiating in the Pacific Rim," *The International Executive* (May–June 1990): 20–21.

HOW NEGOTIATIONS WORK IN ASIA AND THE PACIFIC RIM

Negotiating Factors

1. *Pace of Negotiations*	Slow
2. *Negotiating Strategies*	
Opening Offers vis-à-vis Settlement	Moderate to high initial demands
Presentation of Issues	Group of issues may be presented
Presentations	Fairly formal
Dealing with Differences	Polite; quiet when right
Concessions	Slow
3. *Emphasis on Personal Relationships*	High
4. *Emotional Aspects*	
Sensitivity	Valued
Degree of Emotions	Usually not visible
5. *Decision Making*	
Overall Method	Group consensus

Emphasize	Logic
Emphasis on Group/Team	High: Decisions from middle and lower-level groups
Emphasis on Face Saving	Extreme
Influence of Special Interests on Decision Makers	Openly influenced

6. *Contractual and Administrative Factors*

Need for an Agent	Average
Degree of Contract Specificity	Moderate
Degree of Paperwork/Bureaucracy	Moderate
Need for an Agenda	Moderate

AUSTRALIA

Fast Facts

Monetary Unit: Australian dollar

Major Industries: mining, industrial and transportation equipment, food processing

Primary Trading Partners: Japan, China, United States, South Korea, New Zealand, India, United Kingdom, Germany, Singapore

Key Exports: coal, gold, meat, wool

Key Imports: machinery and transport equipment, computers and office machines, telecommunications equipment

Major Cities: Canberra (cap.) (326,000), Sydney (3.7 mil.), Melbourne (3.2 mil.), Brisbane (1.4 mil.)

Ethnic Groups: Caucasian (92%), Asian (7%), aboriginal and other (1%)

Primary Religions: Anglican (26%), Roman Catholic (26%), other Christian faiths (24%), non-Christian (11%); other or unknown (13%)

Language: English

Reducing Communication Noise

Greetings

- Shake hands upon meeting and leaving. Australians are informal and shake hands warmly. This may be accompanied by a casual *Good day* (pronounced guday), particularly by men.

- First names are widely used, but do not use first names until you are invited to do so.

Conversation

- Try talking about physical fitness and recreation. There is a great sporting awareness of Australian football, soccer, rugby, cricket, basketball, tennis, golf, bicycling, and swimming. Many Australians follow the America's Cup yachting event.

- Try to learn how English is used in Australia. There are a number of terms that Americans use, for example, that are offensive in Australia (and vice versa).

- Many expressions are different from English usage in the United States—for example, *no worries* (no problem), *rubber* (eraser), and *bird* (young woman). Men normally refer to their friends as *mate*.

- Australians often use nicknames for common terms such as *uni* (university), *tele* (television), or *barbie* (barbecue).

- Humor is almost always appreciated.

Sensitivities

- Avoid comparisons between Australia and the United States or the United Kingdom.

- Australians value fairness (called a *fair go*). Aggressive or proud behavior will not be welcomed.

Key Negotiating Pointers

- Make prior appointments and be punctual. Australians are easy-going, but they are sticklers about time.

- Be informal, but courteous. Americans tend to feel very comfortable in dealing with Australians, who regard extreme formality as insincere and artificial. Efforts to impress usually are hurtful.

- Try to get connections and introductions at senior executive levels.

- Expect Australian negotiators to be as direct and open in their negotiating style as Americans.

- Don't be afraid to use humor.

- Make presentations detailed and factual, and be prepared to respond evenly to pointed questions.

- Negotiations move crisply. Make brief preliminary comments and then get quickly down to business.

- Keep your administrative requirements to a minimum. Australians don't like being told what to do, and they operate with few rigid lines of authority.

- Stress the practical over the conceptual. Australian negotiators are pragmatic and profit-oriented.

- Make the opening offer fairly close to your *really asking* position, but leave

yourself some room for movement. Australians don't tend to be "blue-sky bargainers" (i.e., haggling for long periods from very high initial offers).

- Expect Australian negotiators to remind you of the competition and to keep the pressure on to make concessions. Patience is another often-used Australian tactic, as they hope to wait it out for you to concede.

- Australians tend to make concessions in a deescalating pattern: generous at first, then tapering off.

- Contracts will be written, specific, and firm.

- Get representation within Australia because of the great distances among locations.

Day-to-Day Pointers

Business Entertainment Guidelines

- Don't discuss business during meals or at social occasions.

- Dinner is the main meal of the day, eaten in the evening. The noon meal is called *lunch*; *supper* is a snack before bed. On Sundays, however, there is often a large noon meal called *dinner*, and a lighter meal (*tea*) in the evening.

- In restaurants, tipping is not traditional, though it is becoming more popular.

Table Manners and Food

- If you are visiting in someone's home, you receive a plate already served, rather than helping yourself to the various dishes.

- When yawning, cover your mouth and excuse yourself. It is considered a sign of boredom.

- All varieties of meat and fish are available. Popular meals are fish and chips and pasties (turnovers filled with meat).

Gender Issues

- International businesswomen can readily do business in Australia, but there is a strong Old Boy Network.

- Women should not plan on having a drink with their Australian male counterparts after dinner. Australian men often prefer to do this with their male mates.

Also Remember This . . .

- Australia is technologically progressive and sophisticated.

- Australian labor unions are a strong workplace influence.

- If you engage in golf, tennis, or another competitive sport, sportsmanship will be applauded. Your Australian counterpart commonly says *Bad luck* when you miss a tennis shot or golf shot.

CHINA

(People's Republic of China)

Fast Facts

Monetary Unit: *yuan* (the currency is called *renminbi*)

Major Industries: mining and ore processing, machine building, armaments, textiles and apparel, petroleum

Primary Trading Partners: United States, Japan, South Korea, Germany, Taiwan

Key Exports: machinery and equipment, plastics, optical and medical equipment, iron and steel

Key Imports: machinery and equipment, oil and mineral fuels, plastics, optical and medical equipment

Major Cities: Beijing (cap.) (10.9 mil. metro area), Shanghai (12.7 mil. metro area), Tianjin (9.3 mil. metro area)

Ethnic Groups: Han Chinese (92%), Zhuang, Uygur, Hui, Yi, and numerous other nationalities (8%)

Primary Religions: officially atheist; Daoist, Buddhist, Christian (3–4%), Muslim (1–2%)

Languages: Standard Chinese, *Putonghua*, or Mandarin, is the national language and is spoken by over 70 percent of the population; other dialects include Wu (in Shanghai), Min, and Yue (Cantonese).

Reducing Communication Noise

Greetings

- Those from outside of Asia are normally given a brief handshake upon meeting in business situations. It's okay to extend your hand first, which will usually be interpreted that you are glad to meet the person, especially with people who are younger or whose status is lower that yours. The most common form of greeting is a nod or slight bow from the shoulders (not from the waist).

- The Chinese are quite formal and use titles and last names. First names are used only among close friends.

- The family name always comes first in Chinese, so that Yao Ming is Mr. Yao.

- A common greeting is *Ni hao ma?* (How do you do?) and is somewhat formal. A more informal greeting is *Zenmoyang?* (How's it going?)

- Be sure to bring plenty of business cards, translated into standard Chinese on one side.

Conversation

- Try talking about the weather, the sights, Chinese culture, shopping, the excellent food, life in your country, your family, and your personal hobbies.
- The Chinese like to share with Westerners the progress that China has made over the past several years.
- The country should be referred to as the People's Republic of China, or simply China.
- Personal distance is generally greater among business associates than in the West. The Chinese are not a touchy society in a business environment, and do not like to be touched or patted on the back or shoulders.

Sensitivities

- Avoid talking and joking about sex, government, religion, and communism. Also avoid talking about Taiwan, though it may be a favorite topic of discussion among the Chinese.
- Avoid excessive use of the word *I*—a reference that is perceived as self-centered. Keep your comments group-oriented.
- Don't use a map showing an independent Taiwan.

Key Negotiating Pointers

- Make prior appointments and be punctual.
- Use your own intermediary, or *zhongjian ren*. This person can help with initial and further meetings. The successful businessperson in China is increasingly the person who can contact key people in a short period of time. The intermediary can also help with potential conflicts or misunderstandings. Chinese negotiators prefer this, even if they speak excellent English, so as not to lose face. This is consistent with the emphasis Chinese put on *guanxi*, or personal connections.
- Give your counterparts advance notice as to what you would like to accomplish in China. This is a courtesy that they will appreciate, and will reduce any concern they may have about being surprised by your intentions.
- Demonstrate respect and build a solid relationship. Politeness, rank, and protocol are essential. A good deal of small talk is important before getting to the content of the negotiations. Trust and mutual connections are important.
- Never do or say anything that might embarrass your counterpart. Be subtle and sensitive in your disagreements. Try not to ask direct questions. Your Chinese counterpart is proud to deal with you as an overseas client even though he probably can't make key decisions alone.
- Focus on long-term benefits, though increasingly many leaders pay attention to short-term benefits because of demands made by their global customers.

- The Chinese see the negotiation as a long courting process. Expect slow decision making that must work its way through a cumbersome bureaucracy.

- Remember that while your negotiating counterpart may not be able to make a decision to go forward on a project, he may be able to veto it or hinder your progress in the bureaucracy.

- The highest-ranking person of your negotiating team should lead the group when entering a business meeting. This highest-ranking person should be the spokesperson.

- Be reserved and dignified in your personal style. Loud, overly expressive behavior is perceived as very offensive.

- Presentations should be detailed, technical, and factual. Speak often of trust and cooperation between you and your counterpart. Keep your presentations brief if a large group is involved.

- Chinese negotiators are characterized by a soft sell and hard buy. Give yourself plenty of room to negotiate. Extreme initial offers are the norm. The Chinese will be offended if there are not sizable concessions.

- Expect long periods where there is no movement in the Chinese negotiating position. Realize that there may be people not present during your discussions who will strongly influence the Chinese negotiating team.

- There is another reason to give yourself a lot of negotiating room. A common Chinese tactic is to pressure you into lowering your price by holding out the promise of their huge market.

- Be patient and persistent. Several trips to China will probably be necessary before you reach a business agreement. Keep your return plans flexible.

- Don't go it alone in China. The Chinese prefer to deal with a group than a single negotiator. Be sure to have technically competent engineers and other experts with you.

- Emphasize that you *specialize* in China, if you feel you can justify it.

- Beware of the Chinese shaming tactic, whereby your Chinese counterparts suggest that you have broken the bond of friendship if you do not agree to the final contract proposals that they have made.

- Be patient in agreeing to a contract. Entering into a formal agreement can take months, with many translations and lengthy reviews. English rather than Chinese versions are usually signed. Though the Chinese do not have a reputation for following the contract, there is now more awareness about the importance of compliance.

Day-to-Day Pointers

Business Entertainment Guidelines

- You are likely to be treated very graciously when visiting China, and this will include an evening dinner party (banquet) at a hotel or restaurant. Try to recip-

rocate as soon as you can, preferably on the same trip. Always allow your Chinese hosts to issue the first invitation.

- Include everybody with whom you have dealt in making the invitation list for your banquet. Who has the ultimate authority on the Chinese team is often ambiguous, so this will avoid the risk of excluding the most important person. Include Chinese spouses and spouses accompanying you.
- Business is not usually discussed during meals.
- *Gambai* (bottoms up) is the usual toast. Raise your glass in a toast, even if you fill your glass with water instead of alcohol. Toast the deal you are making and the friendship of your company with the other side.
- Traditionally, only modest gifts, such as a logo gift, were considered appropriate. More expensive gifts are now more typical, but should be given within the policy guidelines of your organization and legal guidelines of your country, if any.

Table Manners and Food

- Expect to eat at a round table with dishes in the center, and to take food from serving plates to individual bowls. Don't pass serving dishes around. Use chopsticks to reach for food.
- Try to sample every dish.
- Hold the bowl close to your mouth when eating rice.
- Dishes typically consist of rice, potatoes, tofu, cornmeal, and noodles. In restaurants, pork, beef, chicken, or fish are popular. There are many regional specialties, such as duck in Beijing or spicy dishes in the Szechwan province. Chinese dumplings (*jiaozi*) are also popular.
- Never leave rice on your plate.
- If you don't want more tea, leave some in your cup.
- The serving of fruit signals the end of the meal.

Gender Issues

- International businesswomen will find acceptance, though hardly with open arms.
- Women make up over half the Chinese labor force, and equality between the sexes is a key communist tenet. Still, few women reach key government positions.
- When Chinese women hold key positions, however, they are treated with respect, even if this is not the case in their personal lives.

Also Remember This . . .

- The Chinese have one of the highest gross domestic products in the world, but with its large population, one of the lowest per capita incomes. While there is

a very uneven distribution of wealth, there is a growing middle class in urban areas.

- The Chinese economy grew rapidly in the 1990s and is expected to remain strong in the foreseeable future. The government is investing heavily in infrastructure projects such as massive road construction, yet faces major challenges from pollution, corruption, and rising unemployment.

- The government both supports and tries to contain the growing private sector, and urban areas have a growing middle class. Shenzhen, near Hong Kong, is seen by many Chinese as a symbol of a modern international city with everything from its international restaurants to a stock exchange.

- The Chinese government allows the exercise of religious beliefs within certain guidelines. Buddhists, Daoists, Muslims, and Christians practice there.

HONG KONG, CHINA

Fast Facts

Monetary Unit: Hong Kong dollar

Major Industries: textiles, clothing, tourism, electronics, plastics, toys, watches and clocks

Primary Trading Partners: China, United States, Germany, Japan, United Kingdom

Key Exports: clothing, plastic articles, textiles, electric goods

Key Imports: foodstuffs, transport equipment, raw materials, semimanufactured goods

Major City: Hong Kong (7.0 mil.)

Ethnic Groups: 98% Chinese

Primary Religions: Eclectic mixture of local religions (90%), Christian (10%)

Languages: Chinese (especially the Cantonese dialect); business is conducted in English.

Reducing Communication Noise

Greetings

- Shake hands lightly upon greeting and leaving. A nod or slight bow from the shoulders may accompany a handshake.

- Typical greetings are *Neih hau ma* (How are you?) and *Neih sik msik a* (Have you eaten?).

- Address people by title. The family name traditionally comes first, so Lee Chen is Mr. Lee, or Li Wong is Madame Li.

- Expect that many of your Hong Kong Chinese counterparts will have a Western given name. These names are usually added before the family name. These names are used in business or dealing with Westerners. For example, Steven Chang Tsang might be called either Mr. Chang or Steven Chang in business, or Chang Tsang among Chinese business circles or for legal and formal purposes.
- The term for *thank you* is pronounced doe-jay, from the Cantonese dialect.

Conversation

- Acceptable topics of conversation include general inquiries about one's health, business conditions, the excellent cuisine, and Hong Kong shopping.

Sensitivities

- Avoid discussing the political situation in China or in Hong Kong.
- Avoid wearing blue and white, the Chinese colors for mourning.

Key Negotiating Pointers

- Make prior appointments, since Hong Kong appointment calendars are usually quite full. Be punctual. Although a thirty-minute courtesy time is usually allowed, your counterpart will probably be punctual.
- Prepare a detailed agenda for negotiating sessions, and send this in advance of your trip.
- Don't plan a short visit. Hong Kong is a high-pressure business environment, though the pace of the negotiations remains slower than in most Western countries. While decisions are made crisply, it takes time to build trust and personal confidence.
- Expect the tone of the negotiation to be generally formal and reserved, with emphasis on politeness and mutual respect. Don't be shocked, however, if you encounter Hong Kong negotiators who are louder and more assertive than you may have thought. Hong Kong is a busy place, and a certain amount of aggressiveness sometimes exists.
- Be gracious and respectful, but limit small talk. Expect your counterpart to get to the point after initial formalities.
- Avoid asking direct questions that might embarrass your counterpart. An open conflict could cost you the deal.
- A favorite tactic of Hong Kong negotiators is to remind you of the competition when they ask sellers to lower their price. A favorite approach when asking buyers to pay more is to use facts and information as a basis for building a consultative relationship. This documented information is to help the seller make the sale.
- Hong Kong negotiators tend to make concessions in the escalating pattern,

beginning with a low amount and continuously increasing it at subsequent sessions.

- Personal trust will probably be placed above the fine legal points of the deal.
- Terminology in contracts is less problematical than in mainland China, due to experience in dealing with the West.
- Negotiations will be conducted in English, but speak slowly and avoid slang. Politely check for understanding.
- Hong Kong Chinese tend to discuss all aspects of the deal, saving concessions (discounts) until the end.
- Work through an agent or commissioned representative.

Day-to-Day Pointers

Business Entertainment Guidelines

- A lunch or dinner banquet is a key part of the negotiating process. Breakfast meetings are not popular.
- Come hungry. Eight- to twelve-course meals are common.
- The most common toast is *yum sing*. Toasting is an important part of the social etiquette. There will probably be a welcoming toast by your host, and it is customary for you to reciprocate by rising and thanking the host on everyone's behalf at the end of the meal.
- The Chinese retire early and usually leave immediately after a dinner banquet.
- Offer to pay the bill in a restaurant, though your offer will not be accepted. Never offer to split the bill; this would be considered loss of face.
- Gifts are routinely exchanged between business associates as well as friends during the Chinese New Year (usually around February).
- In restaurants, a 10 percent service charge is usually added to the bill, but it is customary to add another 5 percent. Where no service charge is added, 10 percent is acceptable.

Table Manners and Food

- Don't eat or drink before your host does.
- Hong Kong is world famous for its cuisine. Chinese dishes are often prepared with pork, fish, chicken, and vegetables, with rice as the staple food.

Gender Issues

- Hong Kong is one of the best places in the Pacific Rim for international businesswomen to do business.
- Women are on local negotiating teams, influenced by the large amount of busi-

ness done with the United States, Canada, and other Western countries, and the equalitarian principles of mainland China.

Also Remember This . . .

- Great Britain returned Hong Kong to mainland-Chinese rule in 1997 as the Hong Kong Special Administrative Region. It is a self-governing region of the People's Republic of China. Although China is only officially responsible for defense and foreign affairs, it has considerable influence over Hong Kong's domestic affairs as well.

- Hong Kong consists of Hong Kong Island, the New Territories (a small portion of the mainland), the Kowloon Peninsula, Lantau Island, and more than 200 smaller islands.

- Hong Kong is very cosmopolitan—a blend of Asian and European cultures—and has a highly educated and motivated workforce.

- Hong Kong has severely limited land resources, with a very tight supply of office and industrial property. Its busy harbor is a key to its business.

INDIA

Fast Facts

Monetary Unit: rupee
Major Industries: textiles, chemicals, food processing, steel
Primary Trading Partners: United States, United Arab Emirates, China, United Kingdom, Singapore, Switzerland, Belgium
Key Exports: clothing, gems and jewelry, engineering goods, chemicals
Key Imports: petroleum, machinery, gems, fertilizer
Major Cities: Greater New Delhi (cap.) (15.3 mil.), Greater Bombay (Mumbai) (18.4 mil.), Greater Calcutta (Kolkata) (14.3 mil.), Bangalore (4.5 mil.), Chennai (Madras) (4.4 mil.)
Ethnic Groups: Indo-Aryan (72%), Dravidian (natives) (25%), Mongoloid and other (3%)
Primary Religions: Hindu (81%), Muslim (13%), Christian (2%), Sikh (2%)
Languages: Hindi and English and twelve other official languages; English is the language of business and national connection; the central government recognizes only Hindi as the official language, and different states have different official languages.

Reducing Communication Noise

Greetings

- Shake hands lightly upon meeting and leaving. Men do not usually shake hands with Indian women in business situations, though educated women will usually shake hands with both men and women from Western countries. A Western woman should not initiate a handshake with a man.

- The traditional greeting is the *namaste*, formed by pressing your own palms together, fingers up, below the chin. A slight bow may be added to show respect.

- Exchange business cards during the first meeting. Consider having business cards translated into Hindi on one side as a sign of respect. Give and receive the card with your right hand and put it away respectfully—don't jam it into your wallet or purse.

- Address people by a title (such as *Mr.*, *Mrs.*, *Professor*, *Doctor*) or with the last name to show respect.

- Names will tell you a lot about a person's background. For example, the suffix *-jee* (as in *Bannerjee*) is a sign of high caste, while *Singh* will be a Sikh. Arabic names will be used by Muslims.

Conversation

- Indians enjoy talking about their rich artistic and architectural heritage and life in other countries.

- Ask about India's thriving motion picture industry, a popular Indian pastime. India's film industry is the largest in the world, both in movies produced and tickets sold. India makes about five times as many movies as Hollywood each year.

- Soccer, cricket, and hockey are popular sports.

Sensitivities

- Avoid personal questions. Polite inquiries about the general state of one's family are appropriate.

- Avoid discussing India's poverty, beggars, politics, and religion. Political and religious upheaval are commonplace in India. Discussion of India-Pakistan relations is a sore subject.

- Don't dwell on the weather. Indian weather is often hot and humid.

Key Negotiating Pointers

- Indians tend to do business with those whom they know, so building a good relationship is very important. Building the relationship will be based on demonstrating business savvy, and exhibiting honor and trustworthiness.

- Arrange meetings well in advance and confirm meetings by phone. Be punctual.

Don't be shocked by a cancellation. Family matters usually outweigh business matters.

- Deal with the highest-level person possible. Decisions are made at the top.
- Negotiations are probably in the early stages if the owner or director is not present during discussions.
- Be reserved and controlled in your overall style and presentations.
- There are few routine courtesies.
- Expect business decisions to be based on intuition and feeling as well as facts, figures, and a great PowerPoint presentation.
- Be patient. Indian bureaucracy is extremely cumbersome. Several visits will probably be necessary to get into serious business items. Expect many meetings as you weave your way through the multilayered levels of management. You may see this as inefficient, but don't tell this to your counterpart.
- Don't expect a direct *no* if your Indian counterpart disagrees with you. An emphasis on social harmony influences the negotiating process. "I'll try" or "We'll see" often means no.
- Pressure tactics, force, or anger will not work in India.
- Indian managers generally have high security needs, and work in very autocratic organizations. This means that middle-level managers with whom you negotiate will check and recheck decisions with various layers of management.
- Contracts must be written in the local language as well as English.
- Get an Indian agent. Knowing the right families is important, and an agent can be helpful.

Day-to-Day Pointers

Business Entertainment Guidelines

- A celebration dinner usually follows a successful negotiation.
- Business entertainment usually takes place in prestigious hotels; restaurants are not usually popular trade meeting places.
- Husbands should be invited to bring along their wives to social functions. The exception is Muslims, where wives are to be kept from public view.
- Business can be discussed during meals, but let your host initiate the discussion.
- Business meals usually take place in the evening. The traffic and humidity limit luncheon meetings.
- In restaurants, a typical tip for meals is 10 percent of the bill.

Table Manners and Food

- Hindus do not let people outside their caste or religion touch their food.
- Use the *namaste* gesture to signify that you have finished your meal.

- Vegetarian diets are common, mainly for religious reasons. Hindus, who consider cows sacred, do not eat beef (or use leather). Muslims do not eat pork and strict Muslims do not drink alcohol. Orthodox Sikhs do not eat beef or smoke.

- Foods vary widely in India according to culture. For example, *roti* (wheat bread) is the staple in the north, and rice is the staple in the south. Curry—eggs, fish, meat, or vegetables in a spicy sauce—is a basic food.

Gender Issues

- India is a tough place for anyone to negotiate in, but particularly women. India is a male-dominated society where women are often not involved in social functions or conversation, much less business. Too, education for women lags significantly behind that of men in India.

- International businesswomen may be accepted, however, if there is a perception that the woman's position and title warrant it. Use of an agent can be helpful in this regard.

- Indian women usually wear a *sari*, a long, colorful dress. Both single and married women may wear a *bindi*, or dot, on their foreheads.

Also Remember This . . .

- India is a diverse and complex country. Regionalism, language, religion, and caste all impact doing business in India. India has been a democracy since 1947 despite its great cultural diversity.

- India has the world's second largest population (after China) and is projected to have the largest population by 2015.

- India remains primarily an agricultural nation in spite of rapid industrial growth. It has slowly moved toward a market economy since the early 1980s. There are efforts to loosen up the degree of state control, eliminating government-set limits on industrial production and permitting foreign investors to own larger shares of individual Indian companies.

- Indians are generally religious and family oriented. Simple material comforts are emphasized. Physical and spiritual purity are highly valued, and humility and self-denial are respected.

- India is the birthplace of several religions—Hinduism, Buddhism, Jainism, and Sikhism—all of which believe in reincarnation.

- The caste system has been legally abolished but sometimes continues in practice.

- Indian immigrants are spread throughout the world. About two million people of Indian descent live in the United States, for example, and have the highest household income of any immigrant group.

INDONESIA

Fast Facts

Monetary Unit: Indonesian rupiah

Major Industries: petroleum, textiles, mining

Primary Trading Partners: Japan, United States, Singapore, South Korea, China, Malaysia, Thailand, Australia

Key Exports: petroleum and liquefied natural gas (40%), timber (15%), textiles (7%), rubber (5%)

Key Imports: machinery (39%), chemical products (19%), manufactured goods (16%)

Major Cities: Jakarta (cap.) (8.2 mil.), Surabaya (2.5 mil.), Bandung (2.1 mil.), Medan (1.8 mil.)

Ethnic Groups: Javanese (45%), Sudanese (14%), Madurese (8%)

Primary Religions: Muslim (88%), Protestant (6%), Roman Catholic (3%), Hindu (2%)

Language: Indonesian is the official language (a form of Malay); many others speak Javanese and Dutch; English is spoken by many businesspeople.

Reducing Communication Noise

Greetings

- Men and women usually shake hands and nod their head when introduced for the first time. After that, it is unusual to shake hands in greeting; a nod or slight bow is appropriate.
- The social kiss takes place in Jakarta—first on the right, then the left cheek as one shakes hands.
- Exchange business cards after shaking hands or bowing.

Conversation

- Indonesians enjoy talking about their culture and traditions.
- Soccer, volleyball, tennis, and bicycling are popular forms of recreation. Indonesians are among the world's best badminton players.
- There tends to be a lot of touching in Indonesia compared to most other Pacific Rim countries.

Sensitivities

- Avoid talking about politics, the role of the Indonesian Chinese, or foreign aid.
- The bottom of one's foot should never face another person.

Key Negotiating Pointers

- Indonesians are used to bargaining in their everyday lives, as they barter for daily goods.
- Be punctual, even though your counterpart probably won't be.
- Negotiations may occur at several levels—between senior executives and technical people at the operating level.
- Build a solid relationship. Loyalty is given more to family and friends than it is to personal concerns or organizations.
- Be patient. Indonesian negotiations are usually long, slow, and frustrating.
- Be restrained in your demeanor. Avoid conflict and embarrassing your Indonesian counterpart publicly.
- Avoid fast concessions: You will be viewed as naive.
- Payments to obtain services are a routine part of Indonesian business life. Be sure to gain legal counsel from the home office in this regard.
- Be aware that mysticism is still sometimes influential and may be a reference point for your counterpart in making a decision.
- View the contract as a guideline rather than a precise statement of duties and responsibilities. Indonesians tend to deal with probabilities rather than facts.
- Get a local agent to help you weave through the complicated Indonesian government bureaucracy.

Day-to-Day Pointers

Business Entertainment Guidelines

- Graciously receive gifts. Be careful about opening them in public, however, so as not to embarrass the giver in front of others (as being too lavish or too miserly).
- In restaurants, tips are usually included with the bill.

Table Manners and Food

- Don't eat or drink until invited to do so by your host.
- Keep both hands above the table.
- There is a strong Muslim influence, so do not use your left hand to shake hands, touch others, point, or give or receive objects.
- Compliments about the food are appreciated.
- Finishing a drink implies you want more.
- Don't eat or drink in front of Muslims in the daytime during Ramadan.
- Rice is the main food, served with vegetables, fish, and hot sauces. Fruits are

often eaten as dessert. Beef and buffalo are common. Muslims do not eat pork or drink alcohol.

Gender Issues

- Indonesia is a challenging environment for international businesswomen, but less so than in many other Muslim countries.
- There are women in senior positions in Indonesian companies.
- Indonesian women have more rights than Muslim women elsewhere, with rights in property settlements, inheritances, and divorce. The women don't wear veils.

Also Remember This . . .

- Indonesia is very diverse, with many different cultures, religions, languages, and business practices.
- Indonesia consists of 13,500 islands, 6,000 of which are inhabited by people.
- Indonesia is one of the most populated countries in the world. It is the most populous Muslim nation.
- Agriculture employs about 55 percent of the labor force.
- There have been several uprisings surrounding the status of the Indonesian Chinese, who dominate much of the business activity, and the ethnic Indonesians. Indonesians are very aware of who is and is not Chinese. There is a strong government influence to integrate groups such as the Indonesian Chinese into the overall society.

JAPAN

Fast Facts

Monetary Unit: yen
Major Industries: metallurgical and engineering industries, electrical and electronic industries, motor vehicles
Primary Trading Partners: United States, China, South Korea, Taiwan, Hong Kong, Indonesia, Australia
Key Exports: semiconductors, office machinery, chemicals, motor vehicles
Key Imports: fuels, foodstuffs, chemicals, office machinery
Major Cities: Tokyo (cap.) (35.3 mil. metro area); Osaka (11.3 mil. metro area), Nagoya (2.2 mil.), Sapporo (1.9 mil.)
Ethnic Groups: Japanese (99%); the balance mostly Korean

Primary Religions: Shintoism and Buddhism (84%), other (16%)
Languages: Japanese; English is often used in business.

Reducing Communication Noise

Greetings

- Take your cue from the Japanese on whether to bow or shake hands. Though Japanese bow to each other, it is common for them to shake hands with Westerners.
- The depth and length of your bow will show the amount of respect you want to show. In general, when bowing to a peer, bow as low and as long as your Japanese counterpart. The Japanese put a lot of emphasis on nonverbal communication. A proper bow (from the waist) is considered very important.
- Address people as *Mr., Miss, Ms.* or *Mrs.* Use the Japanese suffix *san* added to the last name after you have gotten to know the person—as in Jones-san. Never use first names.

Conversation

- Try talking about your negotiating counterpart's hobbies, Japanese food, the beauty of Japanese architecture, sports (especially baseball and golf), and other countries you have visited. Ask questions about Japanese culture.
- Avoid constantly expressing your own opinion about things or appearing to have excessive pride about your home country or about yourself. The Japanese stress the group more than the individual.
- Write down your question if you are having trouble communicating. The Japanese often understand written English better than spoken English.

Sensitivities

- Avoid discussions about World War II, Japanese politics, or trade issues.
- If your Japanese host gives you a personal gift, don't open it in public. Your host might lose face if his associates view the gift as too lavish or too inexpensive.

Key Negotiating Pointers

- Be punctual. Allow considerably more time than you think you will need to get where you're going in Tokyo, since traffic delays can be lengthy.
- Approach a Japanese company with an introduction from a third party—preferably someone who knows you, your background, your organization, and the Japanese organization with which you want to deal. The introduction could be with a letter or in person.
- The business relationship is very important. You must sell yourself before you can sell the product or service. The Japanese will probably want to know your

age, the university you attended, and about your family. Business comes later. Show the same interest in your counterparts.

- Don't go it alone. Expect a team of negotiators from your Japanese counterparts.

- Your proposals should be factual, technical, and detailed.

- Present written material, translated into Japanese, well in advance of discussing a subject. The Japanese don't like surprises. There should be copies for each member of the negotiating team; this will speed the decision-making process.

- Remember that Japanese tend to focus on long-term viability and on property and physical plant, rather than on short-term profit or cash flow.

- Avoid abrupt, direct statements or questions that might embarrass your counterpart.

- Be patient. The group decision-making system, or *ringi*, is slow and involves all levels of the organization.

- Be patient for another reason. Progress may seem slow, but remember that the Japanese negotiators consider a group of issues, rather than resolving issues one at a time, as do many Westerners.

- Remember, a direct *no* to your proposal is considered rude. Surface harmony is very important. The Japanese may therefore say *hai* (yes), but this doesn't necessarily signify agreement. This may only mean, "Yes, I understand your point," or "Yes, it deserves further study."

- Accept that there will be less direct eye contact and more silence that you may be used to. Japanese may frequently be silent during the negotiation. Be patient and allow them to speak first.

- Beware that in Japan, suppliers don't just sell parts; they may also participate in product development.

- The contract must be approved at each level of the company. Implementation can be immediate after the decision is made, however.

- Be prepared to use an intermediary to help resolve a dispute.

Day-to-Day Pointers

Business Entertainment Guidelines

- Most business entertaining is done is restaurants. Let the Japanese issue the first invitation to a dinner; they do a great deal of this, and occasionally want a break.

- Expect to be taken to a nightclub called a karaoke bar where group singing takes place. The typical drink is called *mizuwari* (Scotch and water). You will usually be served this unless you specifically ask for something else. It is important to participate in the singing, even if you have a bad voice.

- After being taken to a karaoke bar, reciprocate by inviting your Japanese counterpart to a restaurant.
- Few business deals are sealed without dinner in a restaurant or a drink at a bar.
- Go easy on the alcohol, since there are many toasts during the course of an evening. *Kanpai* (meaning Cheers) is a typical toast. Match your hosts toast for toast, but try to drink as little as possible. Filling your glass with water is acceptable. If you do not drink alcohol, ask for tea or juice.
- When you begin a business relationship with a Japanese company, you are usually given a gift. After receiving it, present a group gift, such as an item than represents your organization or region of the country, fine wine, rare Scotch, golf balls, books about your area of the country, a subscription to a magazine, or a food gift such as chocolates, candies, cookies, or nuts. Thank your host profusely for any gift that you receive.

Table Manners and Food
- At meals, you receive a disposable set of chopsticks in a paper wrapper.
- When taking food from a communal serving bowl, turn your chopsticks and use the blunt ends so you won't contaminate the food.
- Raise the rice bowl close to your mouth if necessary when eating rice. Use chopsticks to bring food up to your mouth for other dishes.
- Taste the various dishes, one at a time, alternating with rice.
- When you have finished your meal, leave the chopsticks on the chopsticks rest. Do not leave them standing in a bowl of rice or other food.

Gender Issues
- International businesswomen can be effective negotiators in Japan. Some Japanese men are still not comfortable with women in positions of responsibility, but any awkwardness is usually easily overcome once they learn about your qualifications and experience. For this reason, sharing information about your background in advance is important.
- Japanese women you encounter in the negotiating process are likely to be at junior levels. Although Japan historically has had a male-dominated business culture, this has been changing in recent years as younger Japanese businesswomen become more career-focused and companies change their personnel practices.
- Women are slowly working their way up the corporate ladder, particularly at foreign firms in Japan, and are in a few key government positions.
- Higher Japanese prices have also made two-income families a more acceptable idea.
- Women make up about 40 percent of the Japanese workforce.

Also Remember This . . .

- Japan has one of the world's most powerful economies.
- The United States is Japan's biggest trading partner.
- The economy is manufacturing oriented. Nearly all exports are from the manufacturing sector, such as automobiles, televisions, and electronic equipment.
- Japan is heavily dependent on imported raw materials for its industrial base. Almost half of Japan's food is imported.
- After a long slump, the Japanese economy is now beginning to perk up, bringing renewed confidence to its businesspeople.

MALAYSIA

Fast Facts

Monetary Unit: ringgit

Major Industries: Malaysian Peninsula—rubber and palm oil processing and manufacturing, electronics, light manufacturing; Sabah—logging, petroleum production; Sarawak—agriculture processing, petroleum production and refining, logging

Primary Trading Partners: United States, Singapore, Japan, China, Hong Kong, Thailand, Taiwan

Key Exports: electronic equipment, petroleum and natural gas, wood and wood products, palm oil, rubber

Key Imports: electronics, machinery, petroleum products, plastics, iron and steel products, chemicals

Major Cities: Kuala Lumpur (cap.) (3.7 mil. metro area), Kelang (683,200), Johor Bahru (682,100)

Ethnic Groups: Malay (50%), Chinese (24%), Indigenous (11%), Indian (7%), other (8%)

Primary Religions: Islam is the official religion; ethnic Malays are usually Muslim; Chinese on the peninsula are mainly Buddhist; Indians are chiefly Hindu.

Languages: Bahasa Malay is the official language; Chinese speak one of the Chinese dialects; Indians speak Tamil; English is widely spoken in business.

Reducing Communication Noise

Greetings

- Shake hands upon meeting and parting. Expect handshakes that sometimes last ten or so seconds. Sometimes a slight bow or nod is more appropriate with older Malaysian women.

- Address people by a title (such as *Mr.*, *Miss*, or *Mrs.*) to show respect.
- Common Malay greetings are *Salamat pagi* (Good morning), *Salamat petant* (Good afternoon), and *Apa khabar?* (How are you?). *Halo* (Hello) is a casual greeting. A more formal Muslim greeting is *Asaalam alaykum* (Peace be with you). Common Chinese greetings are *Tze pau le ma* (Have you eaten?) or *Ni hau ma* (Are you feeling all right?). Indians typically greet you with *Namaste* or *Vanakam* (Salutations).
- Business cards are exchanged after greetings.

Conversation
- Malaysians enjoy discussing their country's economic successes, the beautiful scenery, sports, and food. They appreciate polite inquiries about the general state of their family.
- Soccer is Malaysia's most popular sport, along with badminton, field hockey, cricket, rugby, and table tennis. Kite flying is popular on the peninsula.
- There are several popular Malaysian handicrafts such as batik (colorful fabrics that are printed using a process in which the areas not to be dyed are coated with wax), pottery, silk weaving, and woodwork.

Sensitivities
- Avoid discussing religion. There has been a history of antagonism among the various groups.
- Don't try to make comparisons between the West and Malaysia.
- The strong international drug trade in Malaysia is a continuing target of the government.

Key Negotiating Pointers

- Malaysians generally practice a soft sell and hard buy.
- Make prior appointments. Be punctual, though your Malaysian counterpart may not be.
- Be prepared for lengthy small talk unrelated to business issues before business items are discussed.
- Build rapport and trust. The relationship forms the basis for the business aspects of the negotiation.
- Expect discussions to be long and detailed. Be prepared to provide a lot of information. Malays are quite detailed in their approach, and they formulate their position gradually and carefully.
- Expect Malay negotiators to generally be courteous. Etiquette is important.
- Respect the concept of face. Status is important. Don't ask direct, probing questions that could be embarrassing.

- Be diplomatic in the rejection of your counterpart's proposal. A direct rejection of the position is sometimes considered to be a rejection of the person.
- Be prepared for much diplomacy from your Malaysian counterpart. Read between the lines to determine the real positions.
- Expect Malay negotiators to graciously but firmly keep the pressure on for you to make concessions and to remind you of the business potential in Malaysia.
- Malays tend to make concessions in an escalating pattern, when they begin with a low amount and continuously increase it at each session.
- Get a written agreement, but remember that Malaysians view written contracts as less important than personal trust.
- Expect a request for an escape clause if things don't work out. Making and keeping contractual commitments is not usually a high priority for Malay negotiators.

Day-to-Day Pointers

Business Entertainment Guidelines

- Business entertainment, normally at restaurants or hotels, is a key part of the negotiating process in Malaysia. Follow important meetings with lunch or dinner.
- Dinner is eaten about 7 p.m. or 8 p.m.
- If treated by your host, send a thank-you note or flowers the next day.
- Gift giving among business associates is not expected or traditional but is acceptable. Give and receive gifts with both hands.

Table Manners and Food

- Do not use your left hand to eat, shake hands, touch others, point, or give or receive objects.
- Drinks are offered and received with both hands.
- A wide assortment of foods are eaten as a result of Malaysia's cultural diversity. Rice is Malaysia's staple food, and fish is very common. Food is generally spicy. Fruits such as durians (large, oval fruits with a prickly rind), bananas, pineapples, and papayas are plentiful.
- Muslims do not eat pork or drink alcoholic beverages, and Hindus and some Buddhists do not eat beef.

Gender Issues

- International businesswomen may experience a few problems doing business in Malaysia, due mainly to the conservative Muslim influence.
- About 45 percent of the population is Muslim, but the Chinese dominate the

business community and will probably be your negotiating counterparts. They tend to be more equalitarian than Muslims.

Also Remember This . . .

- Malaysia was granted independence from Britain in 1957.

- Malaysia's gross domestic product per capita has tripled and poverty has been sharply reduced in the past few decades.

- Malaysia consists of two different and distinct land regions and is very culturally diverse. Peninsular Malaysia, south of Thailand, is one region, and East Malaysia, on the island of Borneo, is the other. East Malaysia, in turn, consists of two states, Sabah and Sarawak.

- The Chinese generally live in urban areas. Ethnic Malays are mostly Muslim and live in rural areas.

NEW ZEALAND

Fast Facts

Monetary Unit: New Zealand dollar

Major Industries: food processing, wood and paper products, textiles, machinery, transportation equipment

Primary Trading Partners: Australia, United States, Japan, China, United Kingdom, Germany

Key Exports: dairy products, meat, wool, fish, machinery

Key Imports: machinery and equipment, vehicles and aircraft, petroleum, electronics, textiles, plastics

Major Cities: Wellington (cap.) (343,000 metro area), Auckland (369,000 metro area), Christchurch (354,000)

Ethnic Groups: European (70%), Maori (8%), Asian (6%), Pacific Islander (4%), mixed, other, and unspecified (12%)

Primary Religions: Christian (67%), none or unspecified (33%)

Languages: English and Maori are the official languages; Maori is used mainly for Maori ceremonies.

Reducing Communication Noise

Greetings

- Shake hands when meeting or leaving. Men should wait for a woman to offer her hand first.

- First names are usually used after initial introductions.
- Typical greetings are *Good day* (pronounced gidday) or a simple *Hello*.

Conversation
- New Zealand, consisting mainly of the North Island and the South Island, is extremely scenic. The capital, Wellington, is on the more populous North Island.
- The weather is a good conversation opener in New Zealand, since it is often so pleasant. New Zealanders also appreciate sincere compliments on their gardens and homes.
- New Zealanders are proud of their beautiful country with many diverse landscapes. The North Island has the largest man-made forest in the Southern Hemisphere, a few snowcapped volcanoes, and geysers and hot springs in its thermal regions. The Southern Alps are on the South Island and provide extraordinary scenery, with many glaciers, lakes, and rivers.
- Try talking about recreational activities. New Zealanders are very sports-minded. Rugby and soccer are popular winter sports, and cricket and tennis are popular during the summer. Mountaineering, hiking (tramping), fishing, hunting (on a restricted basis), river rafting, and skiing are also popular.
- *Kiwi* is a Maori word meaning New Zealander.

Sensitivities
- Avoid discussing religion or racial issues.
- New Zealanders like to talk about national and international politics. As always, do more listening than talking.
- Avoid comparisons with Australia. New Zealanders are proud of their autonomy.

Key Negotiating Pointers

- Make prior appointments and be punctual or early for meetings. Your counterparts will routinely be five minutes early.
- Be informal in your style, yet courteous.
- Expect negotiations to move crisply.
- Be practical in your approach; de-emphasize concepts. Make presentations detailed and factual.
- Leave yourself some bargaining room, but keep opening offers close to your *really asking* position. New Zealanders are not likely to have highly inflated initial positions.
- New Zealanders tend to make concessions in a deescalating pattern: generous at first, then tapering off.

- Expect New Zealander negotiators to remind you of the competition, and to be extremely patient in getting what they want from you.
- Contracts are specific and firm.

Day-to-Day Pointers

Business Entertainment Guidelines

- It is customary that you, as the visitor, invite your customer to lunch at a hotel or restaurant. Otherwise, you will meet in your counterpart's office.
- Dinner is the main meal of the day, usually eaten in restaurants about 7:00 p.m. to 8:00 p.m. A light supper is sometimes eaten late in the day.
- Tipping is not common and is often refused.

Table Manners and Food

- Keep your hands (but not elbows) above the table.
- Place your utensils parallel to the plate to signify that you are finished eating.
- There is a British influence in the diet, with mutton, beef, and pork the key meats. Fish is also a key part of the diet. Potatoes, vegetables, and pudding (dessert) are common.
- Coffee is often served at the end of the meal.

Gender Issues

- International businesswomen can readily do business in New Zealand.

Also Remember This . . .

- New Zealand has a modern industrial economy that boasts a growing prosperity with a strong middle class.
- Although agriculture is important in international trade, only 5 percent of the population is employed in this sector.
- New Zealand is one of the world's largest exporters of wool.
- The Maori were the first settlers of the islands and are a gracious, friendly people who have very close family ties.

PAKISTAN

Fast Facts

Monetary Unit: rupee

Major Industries: textiles and apparel, food processing, pharmaceuticals, construction materials

Primary Trading Partners: United States, United Arab Emirates, United Kingdom, Germany, Hong Kong, Saudi Arabia

Key Exports: textiles, rice, leather goods, chemicals, manufactures, carpets and rugs

Key Imports: petroleum, petroleum products, machinery, plastics, transportation equipment

Major Cities: Islamabad (cap.) (601,600), Karachi (11.8 mil. metro area), Lahore (5.8 mil.), Faisalabad (2.2 mil.)

Ethnic Groups: Punjabi (65%), Sindhi (12%), Baluchi (9%), Pashtuns (8%), other (6%)

Primary Religions: Sunni Muslim (77%), Shiite Muslim (20%), Christian, Hindu, and other (3%)

Languages: English and Urdu official languages; many languages are spoken; Urdu is encouraged as the unifying language; English is used by government and educated elite.

Reducing Communication Noise

Greetings

- Shake hands lightly with men upon meeting and leaving. It is considered inappropriate for men to shake hands with women or touch them in public.

- Address people by a title (such as *Mr., Mrs., Miss,* or *Doctor*) with the last name.

Conversation

- Pakistanis enjoy talking about their own ethnic group and the general progress that Pakistan has made.

- Field hockey, cricket, squash, soccer, and tennis are popular sports. Pakistanis are world-class competitors in field hockey and squash.

- Ask about *ghazal*, a form of Urdu poem. It is enjoyed by all levels of Pakistani society.

Sensitivities

- Avoid discussing politics, religion, or the standard of living.

- Avoid comparisons with India. There is a history of acrimony between the two countries. The territory of Kashmir, in northern India, is in dispute between India and Pakistan.

- Don't expose the bottom of your foot or shoe to another person.

- Don't be offended if you notice that someone is staring at you. Staring is a common practice in Pakistani culture.

Key Negotiating Pointers

- Be punctual. Pakistanis are somewhat casual about time, but are familiar with Western views about time and expect you to be on time.
- Take time to socialize and build rapport before the business content is discussed.
- Expect to be offered several cups of tea or coffee.
- Don't ask direct, probing questions that could be embarrassing.
- Be patient. Pakistani bureaucracy is extremely cumbersome. Several visits will probably be necessary to get to serious business items. Expect many meetings as you weave your way through multilayered levels of government. You may see this as inefficient, but don't mention this to your Pakistani counterpart.
- Expect decisions to be checked and rechecked.
- Don't be put off if your counterpart takes an extreme position on an issue.
- Expect concessions to be made slowly.
- Contracts must be written in the local language as well as in English.

Day-to-Day Pointers

Business Entertainment Guidelines

- The business meal is an important part of the overall negotiating process, where your host is expressing hospitality and getting to know you better. It is appropriate to reciprocate and invite your client to lunch or dinner.
- Do not discuss business during a meal.
- Expect to socialize for a time before the meal, then to leave soon after the meal is over.
- Pakistani businessmen generally don't bring along wives for business entertainment.
- A typical tip for a meal is 10 percent of the bill.

Table Manners and Food

- Western eating utensils are used, although many of the traditional foods are eaten by hand. There is a heavy Muslim influence, so use your right hand to eat, point, and to receive and pass objects.
- Muslims do not eat pork and avoid alcohol. If you are a Westerner, you can buy alcohol at your hotel, but don't drink it in public.
- *Chapati* or *roti*, an unleavened bread similar to a Mexican tortilla, is the mainstay of the Pakistani diet. Pakistani food is usually hot and spicy, with curry a common spice. Lamb, beef, chicken, and fish are common in hotels and restaurants. Kabobs, strips or chunks of meat barbecued on a skewer, are popular.

Gender Issues

- This is one of the toughest places anywhere for Western women to do business.
- Pakistani women have few legal rights, and only a small minority have achieved success in business. Illiteracy is particularly high among women.

Also Remember This . . .

- Pakistan is primarily an agricultural economy, though the industrial sector is growing. Natural resources, such as natural gas, are largely underdeveloped.
- Karachi, the largest city, is the primary business center.
- Pakistan is composed of many diverse ethnic groups, and politics are generally turbulent. The Islamic religion is a unifying force, and most Pakistanis are devout Muslims, believing the will of God (Allah) is evident in all things.

PHILIPPINES

Fast Facts

Monetary Unit: peso
Major Industries: textiles, pharmaceuticals, chemicals
Primary Trading Partners: Japan, United States, the Netherlands, Hong Kong, China, Singapore, Taiwan, Malaysia
Key Exports: electronics and telecommunications, machinery and transport equipment, garments
Key Imports: raw materials, fuels, vehicles, plastic, chemicals, grains
Major Cities: Manila (cap.) (10.7 mil. metro area), Quezon City (1.7 mil.), Davao City (850,000)
Ethnic Groups: Christian Malay (92%), Muslim Malay (4%), Chinese (1%), other (3%)
Primary Religions: Roman Catholic (83%), Protestant (9%), Muslim (5%), Buddhist and other (3%)
Languages: official languages are English and Filipino (based on Tagalog); English is the main language of business, government, and education.

Reducing Communication Noise

Greetings
- Shake hands with both men and women upon meeting and parting. Greetings are friendly and informal.
- First names are commonly used, but do not use them until you are invited to

do so. The exception is for very senior people in rank or age, where a title (*Mr.,* *Mrs.,* or *Miss*) and last name are used.

Conversation
- Filipinos like general discussion about their families and will enjoy hearing about yours. U.S. action movies or locally produced movies are also popular.
- Basketball is a popular national sport. Horseracing and cockfights have many fans.
- There tends to be a lot of touching in the Philippines compared to most other Pacific Rim countries.

Sensitivities
- Avoid discussing politics, religion, social conditions, and corruption.
- Be careful with the issue of U.S.–Filipino relations. Filipino politics are chaotic, and widely differing views are held on the U.S. presence and influence.

Key Negotiating Pointers
- Be punctual even though your Filipino counterpart may not be. Filipinos are casual about time, and meetings or appointments often start about ten to twenty minutes after the appointed time.
- Be sincere. Though Filipinos are fun loving and casual, insincerity is easily detected.
- Be sensitive and avoid direct criticism. Honor is an important virtue to Filipinos, and the perception of open criticism could bring shame on the individual. Candor is sometimes viewed as a lack of culture.
- Keep proposals practical and conservative. Radical changes or innovation are not usually well accepted. Success is often attributed to fate more than to effort or ability.
- Be prepared for a "take it or leave it" tactic when Filipinos are the sellers asking for a lower price.
- When asking the buyer to pay more, Filipinos tend to play with the numbers, stressing percentage figures rather than absolute figures, costs per unit rather than total costs, or rounded figures rather than exact figures.
- Filipinos tend to make concessions in an escalating pattern, beginning with a low amount and increasing it at each session.
- Be aware of subtle bribery. Seek legal counsel from the home office if you have a question.

Day-to-Day Pointers

Business Entertainment Guidelines
- Business entertainment is normally done in restaurants or clubs.
- Don't discuss business over meals.

- Your host will probably invite you out for dinner. Try to reciprocate.
- In restaurants, tips are usually 15 percent.
- Gift giving is important in the Philippines, so be prepared if your host offers you a token of appreciation in this way. A logo gift from your organization or a book or other item from your home locale is usually a safe way to reciprocate.

Table Manners and Food

- Eating heartily is a compliment to your host.
- Leave a small portion on your plate to indicate that you have finished eating.
- Filipino cuisine is diverse, reflecting the influence of many cultures. Rice is the staple food. A typical meal consists of boiled rice, fried fish or pork, a vegetable, and fruit or desert.
- A wide variety of food is available in restaurants. Local dishes include *adobo* (a stew of chicken and pork in garlic, soy sauce, and vinegar) and *kare-kare* (a stew of meats and vegetables served in a peanut sauce). Meals are often skewered.

Gender Issues

- The Philippines is a good place for international businesswomen to do business. Filipino women generally enjoy equality with men and hold prominent positions in business and government.
- Filipino men often exhibit the Latin idea of *machismo*. For example, comments by men about women passing on the street are common (but should be ignored).
- Many Filipino women as well as men are educated in U.S. universities.

Also Remember This . . .

- Agriculture is the Filipino economy's backbone, employing about 40 percent of the labor force and providing about 20 percent of the gross domestic product.
- The Philippines is very diverse, having been influenced by the Chinese, Malaysian, Spanish, and U.S. cultures.
- Individual accomplishment tends to be less important than family considerations.

SINGAPORE

Fast Facts

Monetary Unit: Singapore dollar
Major Industries: financial services, petroleum refining, electronics, oil-drilling equipment

Primary Trading Partners: Malaysia, United States, Hong Kong, China, Japan, Taiwan, Thailand, South Korea

Key Exports: computer equipment, petroleum products, telecommunications equipment

Key Imports: machinery and equipment, petroleum, chemicals, foodstuffs

Major Cities: Singapore (cap.) (4.4 mil.)

Ethnic Groups: Chinese (77%), Malay (14%), Indian (8%), other (1%)

Primary Religions: Majority of Chinese are Buddhists or atheists; Malays are nearly all Muslim.

Languages: Mandarin Chinese, Malay, Tamil, and English are all official languages; English is the business language.

Reducing Communication Noise

Greetings

- Shake hands upon meeting and leaving, with an additional slight bow for the Chinese and older people.
- Address people as *Mr., Mrs.,* or *Miss* unless invited to do otherwise. For the Chinese, the family name is first, the middle name next, and the given name is last, so that Lee Tse Chen is Mr. Lee.
- Business cards are important.

Conversation

- Try talking about the wide variety of cultural arts, the progressive economy, Singapore's beauty, and the excellent shopping.
- Soccer, badminton, basketball, water sports, tennis, and golf are all popular.
- Gambling is also a popular pastime.

Sensitivities

- Avoid talking about religion or politics.
- Avoid telling jokes unless you know your counterparts well. Singaporeans are friendly, but are not great joke tellers or receivers. Humor is subdued.
- Finger gestures, such as the rounded "okay" sign or pointing, is considered rude.
- Don't touch people on the head.

Key Negotiating Pointers

- The business culture is largely British, combined with the Chinese reputation for driving a hard bargain.
- Make prior appointments and be punctual. Being late is considered rude.

- Expect fast-paced negotiations. Singaporeans have a reputation as an entrepreneurial and industrious people.

- Singaporean negotiators are generally more direct and open than those in many other Pacific Rim countries.

- The concept of *face* is very important. Public embarrassment would seriously damage, if not end, a potential deal.

- Be direct on money matters. Prices and schedules are generally key issues.

- To help counter the price issue, stress your organization's ability to produce fast deliveries and other indications of customer responsiveness.

- Expect Singaporean negotiators to remind you of the competition, and to keep the pressure on you to make concessions.

- Singaporeans tend to make concessions in an escalating pattern, beginning with a low amount and increasing it at each session.

- The new generation of Chinese have adopted many Westernized business practices, emphasizing facts, technical specifications, and detailed contracts. More traditional Chinese will consummate a deal based on trust, with simple, general contracts.

- Avoid even the hint of any action that might constitute bribery. The Singaporean government has a reputation for being squeaky clean in this regard.

Day-to-Day Pointers

Business Entertainment Guidelines

- Most business entertainment is done in restaurants.

- Singapore is one of the few non-Western countries where business can be discussed over a meal.

- If your counterpart is from the private sector, it is appropriate to invite him or her to dinner only after several meetings. Government officials are not allowed to accept invitations.

- Unlike the case in many Pacific Rim countries, gift giving is not a custom among businesspeople.

- In restaurants, the service charge is included in the bill and tipping is not expected. Modest tips for bellhops are the exception.

Table Manners and Food

- Don't use your left hand if with Malay Muslims.

- Try to use chopsticks.

- With its ethnic mix, Singapore offers a tremendous variety of superb cuisine. Every type of Chinese food (e.g., Cantonese, Mandarin, Szechuan) is available, and there are many Malay, Indian, and European restaurants.

- Rice is a staple of the Singaporean diet, and seafood and chicken are cooked in many ways. Hindus and Buddhists do not eat beef. *Dim sum* (Chinese dumplings) are popular snacks. All groups enjoy *roti prata*, an Indian dough-bread breakfast food.

Gender Issues

- Singapore is a good place for international businesswomen to do business.
- Singaporean women have equal employment, political, and educational rights, and are often highly educated and fill professional positions.

Also Remember This . . .

- This small island is considered an economic miracle by many, and is often rated as economically and politically safe as Switzerland.
- Singapore has the second-highest standard of living in Asia, trailing only Japan.
- Singapore is already effective at producing high-tech goods.
- Most Singaporeans have the opportunity to enjoy a high standard of living, and unemployment is low.

SOUTH KOREA

(Republic of Korea)

Fast Facts

Monetary Unit: won

Major Industries: electronics

Primary Trading Partners: China, United States Japan, Hong Kong, Saudi Arabia

Key Exports: semiconductors, wireless communications equipment, motor vehicles, computers, steel, ships

Key Imports: machinery, electronics and electronic equipment, oil, steel, transport equipment, chemicals

Major Cities: Seoul (cap.) (10.6 mil.), Pusan (3.8 mil.), Taegu (2.2 mil.), Inchon (2.4 mil.)

Ethnic Groups: All ethnic Korean, except for a small Chinese minority

Primary Religions: Christian (26%), Buddhist (26%), Confucianism and other (2%), no affiliation (46%)

Languages: Korean; many businesspeople speak both English and Japanese.

Reducing Communication Noise

Greetings

- Bow slightly and shake hands with men. The left hand may support the right forearm during the handshake to show respect. Women shake hands less often than men.
- A common greeting is *Annyong haseyo?* (Are you at peace?).
- Present and accept business cards with both hands after a handshake. Hand everything with two hands or support your right hand with your left, under the elbow or forearm.
- The majority of the population share only three family names: Kim, Park, and Lee. Address people by their title and family name, which comes first, so that Kim Won-Song is Mr. Kim.

Conversation

- Try talking about Korean culture and the country's economic success. Koreans are proud of these accomplishments.
- Soccer, baseball, boxing, and basketball are very popular sports. The martial art tae kwon do comes from Korea and is very popular. Mountain climbing and hiking are favorite pastimes.
- Koreans are very modest. Compliments are graciously denied.
- A person may respond by laughing when embarrassed.
- It is not unusual to see younger Korean men holding hands or walking with their hands on each other's shoulders. This is an expression of friendship.

Sensitivities

- Avoid discussions of politics.
- Don't give compliments. This could be very embarrassing to your Korean counterpart.
- Avoid making comparisons between Korea and Japan. Koreans are fierce competitors with the Japanese.
- Don't place your feet on a desk or chair.
- Personal space is limited in Korea. Pushing and shoving is common and usually not considered impolite.

Key Negotiating Pointers

- Koreans are tough negotiators. Be firm, consistent, but not aggressive.
- Eating and drinking precede getting down to business.
- Build a strong relationship. This will be vital to your success in Korea. Mutual trust and respect are highly valued.

- Be very diplomatic and gracious. Candor and bluntness could cost you the deal. Peace and harmony are important.

- Be patient. Results will be slow, but a proper investment in time can pay big dividends.

- Negotiations are likely to be repetitive. Be prepared to give detailed information.

- Don't be alarmed if you are asked questions that you may already have answered. The Koreans are trying to make sure they are correct in their decisions. A major mistake is cause for embarrassment, and the person might resign his job or be fired. Consistently repeated answers will help you more than fresh creative answers.

- Don't appear to be excessively proud of the accomplishments that you or your company have had.

- Listen carefully to your Korean counterpart. Koreans are seldom direct and open in their communication.

- Even though English is spoken, use an interpreter, particularly for big or sensitive deals.

- Get a government-approved agent. This is a tough market.

- Be aware that a written contract is subject to change and renegotiation.

Day-to-Day Pointers

Business Entertainment Guidelines

- Drinking large quantities of alcohol, usually *soju*, (the traditional Korean rice wine), is common at business dinners.

- There are likely to be several toasts. Raise your drink with your right hand and say *Gun-bei* (Raise cup).

- The meal usually comes before socializing.

- Wives are seldom included in business entertainment.

- Exchanging gifts is very common among businesspeople. Food or small mementos are appropriate. If you receive a gift, be sure to reciprocate. Open your gift in private.

- In restaurants, tipping is not expected. A service charge is usually included in the bill.

Table Manners and Food

- Use your left hand to support your right forearm or wrist when items are passed or drinks are poured.

- Chopsticks and spoons are the usual eating utensils.

- Korean food is generally spicy. Rice and kimchi (spicy pickled cabbage) are popular. Lots of fish is also eaten. A favorite delicacy is *pulkogi*, strips of mari-

nated and barbecued beef. *Pipimbap* is rice mixed with seasoned vegetables, usually with an egg on top and sometimes bits of meat added.

- Most meals are served with *soju*, an alcoholic drink, and barley tea. Fruit is a typical dessert.

Gender Issues

- Although few South Korean women are in management, South Koreans are quite accepting of international businesswomen—more so, for example, than are the Japanese.
- Women should try to use elevated titles.
- Touching members of the opposite sex is usually not appropriate.

Also Remember This . . .

- Japanese management practices prevail in South Korea.
- The big four South Korean firms are Daewoo, Hyandai, Samsung, and Gold Star.
- The *chaebol*, huge conglomerates that make up the bulk of Korean exports, are still run by their founding Korean families, such as Samsung, Daewoo, Sungyong, and Sangyong Group. These families concentrate in electronics, shipbuilding, and construction and industrial equipment.
- There are many rituals, courtesies, and formalities in Korean social relations, heavily influenced by Confucianism.

SRI LANKA

Fast Facts

Monetary Unit: rupee
Major Industries: processing of rubber, tea, coconuts, and garments; telecommunications, insurance, banking
Primary Trading Partners: United States, United Kingdom, India, Germany, Singapore, Hong Kong, China, Iran, Japan, Malaysia
Key Exports: clothing and accessories, tea, precious and semiprecious stones, coconut products
Key Imports: textiles, mineral products, petroleum and natural gas, foods, machinery and transportation equipment
Major Cities: Colombo (commercial cap.) (2.4 mil. metro area), Sri Jaygwardenpura Kotte (legis. and judicial) (118,000), Dehiwala-Mount Lavinia (214,000)

Ethnic Groups: Sinhalese (74%), Sri Lankan Moor (7%), Indian Tamil (6%), Sri Lankan Tamil (4%), other and unspecified (9%)
Primary Religions: Buddhist (76%), Muslim (9%), Hindu (8%), Christian (7%)
Languages: Sinhala (official and national) (74%), Tamil (national) (18%), other (8%)

Reducing Communication Noise

Greetings

- Sri Lankans are generally gentle, so expect a warm and hospitable welcome.
- Greetings vary among different ethnic groups and castes. Sri Lankan men usually shake hands with both men and women when greeting. Sri Lankan women are comfortable shaking hands with Westerners. Pressing the palms together in front of the chest with a slightly bowed head is widely used, however. This may be accompanied by the Sinhalese phrase *Ayubowan* or the Tamil *Vannakkam*, meaning, "May you be blessed with a long life." A Muslim greeting is *Assalumu alaikum* (Peace be upon you). If you are a Westerner, it is not expected for you to return these greetings, but it's a plus if you do.
- Titles are important to Sri Lankans, even among friends, so use the equivalents of *Mr., Mrs.,* and *Miss*. If speaking English, the title should precede the surname. For Sinhala and Tamil, the title follows the name.
- Other useful words are *oh-ooh* for yes in Sinhala, or *aam* in Tamil; *nay* for no in Sinhala, or *iral* in Tamil; and *bs-toothee* for "thank you" in Sinhala and *nandri* in Tamil.
- Sri Lankans indicate agreement by wagging their head from side to side.

Conversation

- Sri Lankans are generally tolerant if you don't know their local customs, but it's certainly a plus if you do. For example, Sri Lankans are proud of the ancient Buddhist ruins throughout the country.
- Theater and dance often promote traditional values, and are often accompanied by colorful costumes.
- Although the most popular sport is cricket in Sri Lanka, soccer, volleyball, and table tennis are also popular. Golf or tennis may also be a favorite sport of your negotiating counterpart.
- Sri Lankans enjoy both Western and Sri Lankan movies.

Sensitivities

- Don't be surprised if you see men holding hands in public, but not a man and woman holding hands in public.
- Avoid talking about Sri Lankan politics and religion. Political and religious upheaval is commonplace in Sri Lanka.

- General inquiries about one's family are appropriate.
- Sri Lanka suffered its worst disaster in 2004 when an undersea earthquake created tidal waves that killed more than 30,000 Sri Lankans and displaced hundreds of thousands of people.

Key Negotiating Pointers

- Deal with the highest-level person possible. Decisions are made at the top.
- Get a Sri Lankan agent. Knowing the right families is important, and an agent can be helpful.
- Sri Lankans are somewhat casual, and there are few routine courtesies.
- Be patient. Sri Lankan life generally moves at a slow pace, and so will your negotiations. Several visits will probably be necessary to get into serious business items. Expect many meetings as you weave your way through the multilayered levels of management. You may see this as inefficient, but don't tell this to your counterpart.
- Don't expect a direct no if your Sri Lankan counterpart disagrees with you. An emphasis on social harmony influences the negotiating process.
- Be reserved and controlled in your overall style and presentations.
- Sri Lankan managers generally have high security needs and work in very autocratic organizations. This means that middle-level managers with whom you negotiate will check and recheck decisions with various layers of management.
- Expect a lot of rules and regulations in the public sector, but much less so in the private sector.
- Contracts must be written in the local language as well as English.
- Dress modestly.

Day-to-Day Pointers

Business Entertainment Guidelines

- Husbands should be invited to bring along their wives to social functions. The exception is Muslims, where wives are to be kept from public view.
- Tipping is usually 5 to 10 percent of the total bill before the service charge and government tax has been added.

Table Manners and Food

- You will probably be offered tea sweetened with milk and sugar prior to the meal.
- Lunch is usually the main meal of the day. A typical lunch or dinner consists of rice or bread, then a *dahl* (lentils) or curry, and finally a vegetable such as carrots or cabbage. Scraped and spiced coconut (*pol sambol*) is popular, as is *Katta sambol*, a spicy mixture of chilies and fried onions.

- Foods vary widely in Sri Lanka according to culture, though rice and curry are staples. Fast foods are also readily available.
- Sri Lankans of all religions try to avoid spiritual contamination that might be derived from food entering the body that might be seen as a potential source of pollution. Strict Buddhists eat no flesh of any kind, though some Buddhists eat fish and eggs. Muslims do not eat pork, and Hindus do not eat beef.
- Pass food and eat with your right hand. The left hand is often used for hygiene purposes. When giving or receiving a gift, however, both hands are used.
- Though Sri Lankans will use cutlery in a business setting, they will use their fingers in informal settings. If you eat with your hands, use your thumb and fingers on your right hand to mix a convenient amount of food to eat.

Gender Issues

- Sri Lankan women do work outside the home and are involved in politics. Though a low glass ceiling exists, Sri Lankan women do occupy many professional ranks, and are sometimes entrepreneurs with their own companies.
- Western businesswomen may be accepted if they are seen as key to the negotiation.

Also Remember This . . .

- Sri Lanka has endured many invasions through the centuries, including the Romans and early Arabs, and various European powers. They were colonized alternately by the Portuguese, Dutch, and British from 1505 to 1948. The British defeated the last native ruler in 1815 and established the Crown Colony of Ceylon. The island peacefully obtained independence in 1948, but is still influenced by British conditions. The island was renamed Sri Lanka in 1972.
- Women earned the right to vote in 1931.
- There is a caste system in Sri Lanka, though it now plays less of a role than it historically has.
- Many modern-day engineers admire the ancient hydro-engineering techniques in Sri Lanka.

TAIWAN

(Republic of China)

Fast Facts

Monetary Unit: Taiwan dollar
Major Industries: electronics, petroleum refining, armaments, chemicals, textiles, iron and steel

Primary Trading Partners: China, United States, Hong Kong, Japan, South Korea
Key Exports: computer products and electrical equipment, metals, textiles, plastic and rubber products
Key Imports: machinery and electrical equipment, minerals, precision instruments
Major Cities: Taipei (cap.) (7.9 mil. metro area), Kaohsiung (1.5 mil.), Taichung (1.1 mil.), Tainan (756,000)
Ethnic Groups: Taiwanese (84%), mainland Chinese (14%), aborigines (2%)
Primary Religions: mixture of Buddhist, Confucian, and Taoist (93%), Christian (5%), other (2%)
Languages: Mandarin Chinese (official); Taiwanese, a variant of the Fukien dialect, is commonly spoken; English is spoken by many Taiwanese businesspeople.

Reducing Communication Noise

Greetings

- A smile and nod of the head, accompanied by a slight bow, are appropriate when meeting. Handshakes are usually reserved for acquaintances and friends.
- Stand when a guest, elderly person, or superior enters the room.
- First names are rarely used alone. Address people by a title with the last name.
- For Chinese names, the family name is first. It is common to have both an English and Chinese first name.
- Common greetings are *Ni hao ma?* (How are you?) and *Ching dzwo* (Please sit).
- Bring plenty of business cards, printed in both English and Chinese. (There are numerous printers in Taiwan who can fill such an order in two to three days.)

Conversation

- Polite inquires about health are considered appropriate. Also, show an appreciation for the significant economic gains that Taiwan has achieved.
- Movies, music, baseball, and hiking are popular pastimes. Taiwanese Little League champions consistently do well in the Little League World Series.
- Loud behavior is considered in poor taste.

Sensitivities

- Although it is a hot, open topic among Taiwanese, avoid discussion about mainland China or reunification with mainland China.
- Don't print simplified Chinese characters (used in Mainland China) on written documents.
- It is impolite to wink.
- Don't push a chair, door, or other objects with your feet (feet are considered dirty).

Key Negotiating Pointers

- Taiwanese negotiations are characterized by a soft sell and a hard buy.

- Take part in polite chitchat prior to discussions on content, but expect Taiwanese negotiators to get to the point faster than is typical in most other parts of the Pacific Rim.

- Give respect to the group as a whole in your comments, but try to determine the key decision maker. This person may or may not be at the negotiating table.

- Although the Taiwanese are competitive negotiators, bargain in the spirit of harmony and respect. Maintain friendliness in a reserved way. Taiwanese negotiators are generally quiet, refined, and friendly.

- Cultivate the relationship, even though business relationships are not as strong and close as they are in Japan.

- Taiwanese negotiators usually don't like to say no directly. Instead, they will give you a "soft no," or leave it unsaid.

- Avoid candor, abruptness, or criticism. Public embarrassment, or loss of face, can kill a negotiation.

- This is a very competitive market, and price is often a key sticking point. If the result is a slim profit margin, you may be able to make up some of it on margin in this large potential market.

- Many Taiwanese have been socialized to be very respectful of others, and to a Westerner, this can be perceived as being unassertive. This is not necessarily true of many of your negotiating counterparts, however—particularly those who work for Citibank, Dow Corning, and many other U.S. or Western companies. These individuals can be quite hard bargainers, and not at all shy about occasionally interrupting you and forcefully making their point, especially during the final stages of negotiations.

- Be patient—don't rush the negotiation. You might find the negotiations moving along faster than you expected, but let your Taiwanese counterpart take the lead.

- Be well prepared and consistent in your presentations.

- Common Taiwanese negotiating tactics are "take it or leave it," to remind you of your competition, and if you are the buyer, to remind you of their superior capabilities.

- Taiwanese tend to make concessions in a deescalating pattern—generous at first, and then tapering off.

- Detailed contracts are typical. Allow ample time for review by the Taiwanese negotiator, however.

- Many of your negotiating counterparts will speak some degree of English, though as a rule, it is important to speak simply and slowly. Don't be surprised

if many of your counterparts have worked or been educated in the United States or other Western countries.

Day-to-Day Pointers

Business Entertainment Guidelines

- The banquet is an important part of the negotiation. Taiwanese negotiators—particularly the men—like to entertain during the evening in restaurants. You are not expected to reciprocate.

- Business is not usually discussed during meals. If it is, let your host bring up the subject. Conversation during meals often centers on the meal itself—the ingredients and how the meal was prepared.

- Dinner usually begins about 6:00 p.m. to 7:00 p.m., and can easily continue for two or more hours as your host orders several courses of Chinese fare.

- Your Taiwanese hosts may drink a toast to you and then pass the empty glass. It will be filled by one of the hosts. You will be expected to toast your hosts and drink the whiskey or wine. The drinking sessions can carry on for many hours. Pace yourself.

- Bring a small gift to your counterpart.

- In most cases, tipping is not necessary. A 10 percent service charge is usually added to restaurant bills. It is appropriate, however, if you want to leave change when you pay the bill.

Table Manners and Food

- Food is placed in the center of the table. For a formal banquet, you will normally serve yourself. For a family type (or home) banquet, each person is given a personal bowl of rice in addition to the food in the center. The bowl is held near the mouth and chopsticks are used to eat the food.

- Eat sparingly—there will be lots of courses. Leave a small amount of rice at the bottom of the bowl when you are finished eating so that your bowl won't be refilled.

- Rice is eaten with nearly every meal. Soup, seafood, pork, chicken, vegetables, and fruit are commonly eaten. Many foods are stir-fried. Local Taiwanese cuisine, and Peking, Cantonese, Szechwan, and other cuisines are also available.

Gender Issues

- Taiwan is generally a good place for international businesswomen to do business.

- Although not common with local businesses, Taiwanese women do occupy professional positions in Western-owned or -managed businesses.

Also Remember This . . .

- Taiwan has maintained a dynamic economy for several decades, and holds large foreign reserves. Unemployment and inflation are characteristically low.
- Taiwan launched a $300 billion modernization program in the 1990s that made vast improvements in many aspects of the country such as roads, sewers, and schools.
- Taiwan has a highly skilled labor force. There is a strong middle class that is well educated and well off, and a market for consumer goods.
- Official diplomatic relations between the United States and Taiwan were severed in 1979, but active trade relations continue between the two countries.

THAILAND

Fast Facts

Monetary Unit: baht

Major Industries: tourism, textiles and garments, agricultural processing, beverages, tobacco, cement

Primary Trading Partners: United States, Japan, China, Singapore, Malaysia, Hong Kong, Taiwan

Key Exports: textiles and footwear, fishery products, rice, rubber, jewelry, automobiles, computers

Key Imports: capital goods, intermediate goods and raw materials, consumer goods, fuels

Major Cities: Bangkok (cap.) (6.3 mil.), Nonthanburi (305,000), Chiang Mai (176,000)

Ethnic Groups: Thai (75%), Chinese (14%), other (11%)

Primary Religions: Buddhist (95%), Muslim (5%)

Languages: Thai (official); those with advanced education often speak English.

Reducing Communication Noise

Greetings

- Westerners are greeted with handshakes. The most common greeting among Thais is a *wai*—placing the palms of your hands together, with fingers extended at chest level, and bowing slightly. The *wai* can mean Hello, Thank you, I'm sorry.
- In performing the *wai*, a man greets with *Sawasdee kraab* (Hello or Goodbye), while a woman says *Sawasdee ka*.

- Address people as *Mr., Mrs.,* or *Miss,* with the last name. Thais themselves use first names in everyday discussions, preceded by *kuhn*; they use surnames for formal occasions.

Conversation

- Thais love talking about their cultural heritage.
- Soccer, badminton, and volleyball are the most popular sports. Golf is gaining in popularity.
- Thai is a tonal language that is very difficult for most Westerners to speak. Try to learn a few basic phrases, however.
- Avoid telling your negotiating counterpart that you admire a particular object. Your counterpart may feel obligated to give it to you.
- There tends to be a lot of touching in Thailand compared to most other Pacific Rim countries. However, while good friends of the same sex may hold hands, men and women generally do not touch each other or show affection in public.

Sensitivities

- Avoid discussing drug trafficking or regional politics.
- Avoid any negative reference to the king or queen of Thailand. They are very respected by most Thais.
- It is considered offensive to cross your legs when sitting. Avoid stamping your feet, using them to move or point at objects, or pointing your feet at others. The bottoms of your feet are considered the least sacred part of your body.
- Avoid stepping on a doorsill of a private home or temple (*wat*). Thai tradition says a soul resides in the doorsill.
- Women should not touch or offer to shake hands with a Buddhist monk.

Key Negotiating Pointers

- Make prior appointments and be punctual. Punctuality is important.
- Be reserved, though a sense of humor and laughter are highly regarded.
- Bargaining is expected, but it should be done in the spirit of cooperation and friendship. Being loud or showing anger can cost you respect.
- Avoid comparisons to your country's approach. For example, Thais do not see development as a need to Westernize.
- Thais tend to make concessions in a deescalating pattern: generous at first, then tapering off.
- Contracts must be written in the local language as well as English.

Day-to-Day Pointers

Business Entertainment Guidelines

- If you are invited to a private home, it is not necessary to bring a gift unless your stay is an extended one.
- In restaurants, tips are not usually necessary, though a 10 percent tip for extremely good service is appreciated.
- Let your host bring up the subject of business during a meal.

Table Manners and Food

- Various dishes are placed at the center of the table, from which you choose foods to eat with rice.
- Thais use forks and spoons, except for chopsticks in Chinese homes and restaurants.
- Rice is the staple food of Thailand. It is usually served with very spicy dishes that consist of meat, vegetables, fish, eggs, and fruits. Curries and pepper sauces are popular.

Gender Issues

- Thailand is generally a good place for international businesswomen to do business.
- There are women in senior positions in many private Thai companies.

Also Remember This . . .

- Thais are proud of the fact that their country has avoided foreign rule (except for Japanese occupation during World War II).
- Buddhism deeply affects Thais' daily lives.
- Tourism is the largest source of foreign exchange.

VIETNAM

Fast Facts

Monetary Unit: dong
Major Industries: food processing, garments, shoes, machine building, mining, coal, steel, cement

Primary Trading Partners: United States, Japan, China, Australia, Germany, Singapore, United Kingdom, Taiwan, South Korea
Key Exports: crude oil, marine products, rice, coffee, rubber, tea, garments, shoes
Key Imports: machinery and equipment, petroleum products, fertilizer, steel products, raw cotton, grain
Major Cities: Hanoi (cap.) (2.5 mil. metro area), Ho Chi Minh City (formerly Saigon) (5.9 mil.), Haiphong (582,000), Da Nang (453,000)
Ethnic Groups: Vietnamese (86%), other (14%)
Primary Religions: Buddhist (9%), Catholic (7%), other (3%), none (81%)
Languages: Vietnamese (official); English is increasingly the second language; some French, Chinese, Khmer, and other languages are spoken.

Reducing Communication Noise

Greetings

- The Vietnamese usually shake hands when greeting and saying goodbye, using both hands to show respect for the other person.

- The handshake is usually accompanied by a slight bow of the head to show respect. Vietnamese women may bow their head slightly rather than shake hands.

- A basic greeting, combined with the given name and title, is *xin chao* (pronounced seen-chow). *Xin chao* could have six different meanings (only one of which is Hello) because Vietnamese is a tonal language. The Vietnamese respond warmly to visitors who can properly pronounce *xin chao*.

- Business attire is conservative but casual. Both men and women usually wear slacks with a casual cotton or knit blouse or sport shirt in everyday dress. Women wear the traditional *ao dai* (a long dress with front and back panels, worn over satin trousers, for special occasions.

- Bring plenty of business cards.

Conversation

- The Vietnamese have a lot of national pride, focusing on the future more than the past.

- The major holiday is *Tet*, the Lunar New Year, which comes in late January or early February. On this day, everyone becomes a year older. The *Tet* holiday runs for three days.

- Volleyball and soccer are popular team sports. Badminton, table tennis, swimming, and tennis are also popular sports.

- The Internet is active in Vietnam.

- The Vietnamese are generally interested in American products and lifestyles.

- Remember that southerners tend to be more jovial and less blunt than northerners.

Sensitivities

- Although the Vietnamese do not harbor anti-American feelings, avoid discussing the Vietnam War (known as the "American War" by the Vietnamese).
- Avoid patting another person on the back, or tapping an arm, to show friendship or emphasis. Especially, do not touch another person's head, which is considered the spiritual center in the Buddhist religion.
- Touching between men and women is minimized in business.

Key Negotiating Pointers

- An initial business meeting often begins with informal conversation over tea, coffee, fruit, or sweets.
- Wait for your Vietnamese counterpart to initiate business. You will probably be asked about your family and background. Respond with similar questions to your Vietnamese counterpart.
- Be prepared for a more-or-less win-win approach from the Vietnamese. Their education and upbringing is one where they try to beat the foreigner by outwitting the person.
- Expect to be involved in group rather than individual negotiations.
- Expect more generalities than specifics in answers to your questions. Similarly, talk in generalities before getting into specifics, thereby seeming less abrupt.
- Be patient. Expect your Vietnamese counterparts to use patience to wear you down. They hope that delays will win a concession from you.
- Don't become frustrated if you feel you aren't getting closure, or that you are wondering where you are in the negotiation. You are more likely to get a *maybe* than a *yes*.
- Remember that a preliminary agreement doesn't necessarily mean a final decision has been made. The Vietnamese usually negotiate with several suppliers.
- Don't mistake nods as a yes. This could mean, "I hear what you are saying," or even that they strongly disagree with you.
- When giving a presentation, find a good interpreter who has rehearsed it and knows the language nuances so that the audience gets the intended message.
- When using an interpreter, look at the person to whom you are speaking, and not the interpreter. Give your interpreter only two or three sentences at a time to translate.

Day-to-Day Pointers

Business Entertainment Guidelines

- Most business entertainment is done in restaurants, although a karaoke nightclub or golf outing are also possibilities.

- Try to find an air-conditioned restaurant, because it is often very hot, even in winter.
- Waiters do not expect foreigners to tip, though a 10 percent tip is appreciated.

Table Manners and Food

- The Vietnamese use chopsticks and rice bowls for most meals. It is considered rude to eat from a rice bowl on the table, so hold the rice bowl in your hand when eating. Spoons will be available for soup.
- You will select small portions from dishes of food that are placed in the center of the table. Don't leave any food in your individual rice bowl, and do not take remaining food in any of the dishes.
- White rice is the main food of Vietnam. *Nuoc mam*, a fermented fish sauce, is the main seasoning to flavor dishes.
- Vietnamese cuisine includes a wide variety of dishes and features excellent seafood. A typical meal includes rice, a salty dish such as *thit kho* (pork cooked in fish broth), *rau luoc* (boiled vegetables), and soup.
- Use both hands to pass food to another person.

Gender Issues

- International businesswomen will probably be dealing with men, and can expect good treatment.

Also Remember This . . .

- The Vietnamese lived under Chinese domination a thousand years, then a period of French Colonialism (1858–1954). Later followed a thirty-year period of civil war, which included the war with the United States.
- Though Vietnam is a communist state, there has been a policy of *doi moi* (renovation) since 1989. This includes private enterprise and trade, and an interest in tourism. A large number of unprofitable state-owned firms were shut down under *doi moi*, and new plants have opened, and underdeveloped industries have experienced growth with U.S., Japanese, and other Asian investment.
- The government's main goals have been to improve the poor infrastructure, low salaries, and corruption, and to improve the climate for foreign investment.

Negotiating in Sub-Saharan Africa

The Business Environment of Sub-Saharan Africa

The business climate of sub-Saharan Africa is undergoing radical changes as some of its countries try to become fully integrated international business partners while facing serious internal problems.

Sub-Saharan Africa is a very diverse area, covering countries such as Nigeria, South Africa, Zimbabwe, Zaire, Angola, Zambia, Tanzania, and Kenya. Much of the business environment of sub-Saharan Africa is affected by tribal influences and the European countries that colonized many of these countries. British influence can still be seen on the day-to-day business rituals in Nigeria, South Africa, and Zimbabwe.

The potential for productivity, diversity, and vitality characterizes the economies of many sub-Saharan African countries. Along with this potential for growth are challenges. There is a polarization of the rich and poor in most of sub-Saharan Africa. South Africa is the richest country in this region, but only a few people enjoy a high standard of living. Consequently, high unemployment, inflation, infrastructure development, civil strife, and the need for foreign investment must be addressed in many of these countries.

Cultural Factors That Affect Negotiating in Sub-Saharan Africa

Use of Time

Time in sub-Saharan Africa is generally quite precise, although it differs from country to country. Meetings are more likely to start on time, and negotiations move more briskly in South Africa and Zimbabwe than in Nigeria.

Too, schedules and agendas are likely to be present in this region of the world, though adherence to them will differ from place to place.

Individualism vs. Collectivism

There is a strong *we* orientation in most of sub-Saharan Africa, rooted in tribal affiliations. Many business counterparts in this part of the world see themselves as more related to their tribe than to nations or other political boundaries. Thus, status, language, and business associations are largely influenced by tribal roots.

Decision making is likely to be slowed by communication with, if not approval from, group members. Once made, decisions may be slowed by a cumbersome bureaucracy found in many sub-Saharan countries.

Role Orderliness and Conformity

There is a relatively high need for role orderliness and conformity in most sub-Saharan African countries. It would be difficult for negotiations to proceed without strong personal relationships. Doing business in person is essential for any important negotiation.

Formality and respect are key. Sending an older negotiator can be helpful, since wisdom is often connected with experience. Expect complicated governmental regulations in most sub-Saharan African countries.

Patterns of Communication

Verbal Communication

Verbal communication is likely to be animated and friendly. Verbal exchanges are on occasion quite direct and openly critical, but avoid statements that would offend your negotiating counterpart's dignity.

Nonverbal Communication

Expect physical space to be quite close, though there will be less hugs or other sustained touching than found in Latin America or Eastern Europe.

Direct eye contact is limited, particularly when addressing an older person or a person in a position of authority. Children are usually taught not to look at their elders directly in the eye because this is seen as disrespectful.

Sub-Saharan Africa is a good place to be warm and friendly, yet maintain a refined image.

HOW NEGOTIATIONS WORK IN
SUB-SAHARAN AFRICA

Negotiating Factors

1. *Pace of Negotiations* Moderate

2. *Negotiating Strategies*
 Opening Offers vis-à-vis Settlement High initial demands
 Presentation of Issues One at a time
 Presentations Informal
 Dealing with Differences Direct
 Concessions Slow

3. *Emphasis on personal relationships* High

4. *Emotional Aspects*
 Sensitivity Moderate
 Degree of Emotions Moderate

5. *Decision Making*
 Overall Method Group consensus
 Emphasize Concepts
 Emphasis on Group/Team Low: Decisions from top
 person
 Emphasis on Face Saving Extreme
 Influence of Special Interests on Decision Expected, condoned
 Makers

6. *Contractual and Administrative Factors*
 Need for an Agent High
 Degree of Contract Specificity Moderate
 Degree of Paperwork/Bureaucracy Moderate
 Need for an Agenda Low

NIGERIA

Fast Facts

Monetary Unit: naira

Major Industries: mining (crude oil, natural gas, coal, tin), processing industries (palm oil, peanuts, cotton), and manufacturing industries (textiles, cement, building materials, food products)

Primary Trading Partners: United States, Brazil, Spain, China, United Kingdom, the Netherlands, France, Germany

Key Exports: petroleum and petroleum products, cocoa, rubber

Key Imports: machinery, chemicals, transportation equipment, manufactured goods

Major Cities: Abuja (cap.) (590,400 metro area), Lagos (11.1 mil. metro area), Kano (3.3 mil.), Ibadan (3.1 mil.), Kaduna (1.5 mil.)

Ethnic Groups: more than 250 tribal groups; 29% are the Hausa and Fulani in the north, the Yorubas (21%) in the southwest, and Ibos (18%) in the southeast.

Primary Religions: Muslim (50%), Christian (40%), indigenous beliefs (10%)

Languages: English is the official language, although each ethnic group has its own language; less than half the population speaks English.

Reducing Communication Noise

Greetings

- Shake hands lightly when meeting and leaving. Handshakes are become more common in business.
- Address people by a title (such as *Mr., Mrs., Miss, Chief, Doctor*) with the last name. *Sir* and *Ma'am* are used if the individual's name is omitted.
- There is a wide variety of customs in Nigeria, and for that reason, English is widely spoken. *Hello, Good morning, Good afternoon*, and *Good evening* are common greetings. Be cheerful and courteous when greeting.

Conversation

- Nigerians enjoy talking about the cultural heritage of their particular ethnic group, Nigeria's industrial achievements, and plans for future development.
- Nigerians may want to discuss a recent movie they've seen, especially English-speaking ones.
- Soccer is the most popular Nigerian sport. Wrestling, polo, cricket, and swimming are also popular among the wealthy.
- Though English is widely spoken, avoid the use of jargon or colloquialisms.
- Try to get comfortable with the closer physical distance in Nigeria than in North America or Western Europe.

Sensitivities

- Avoid discussing religion and ethnic distinctions. There is a history of conflict among the different ethnic groups.
- Generally avoid discussing politics, although some Nigerians enjoy discussing the country's contributions to the Organization of African Unity (OAU) or Economic Community of West African States (ECOWAS).

- Avoid such words as *native*, *jungle*, or *witchcraft* that imply Nigeria is a backward country with half-dressed, spear-throwing people. This is why one would refer to a home (not hut) and clothes (not costume).

Key Negotiating Pointers

- Make prior appointments, particularly with government officials. Be punctual, even though you may be kept waiting.
- Allow plenty of time to reach your destination, since most modes of transportation are not timely.
- Start at the state government level rather than the federal government level. State officials generally want your business, are receptive, and can help you with their unique rules and regulations.
- Conduct business in person. Telephone or mail communication renders the matter trivial.
- Consider sending older individuals to do the negotiating or to be the chief spokesperson. Nigerians are very respectful of age, and connect wisdom with years of experience.
- Be patient. Nigerians are casual about time, and Nigerian bureaucracy is among the most cumbersome in the world.
- Be formal and respectful. Project a refined, confident image. Expect your Nigerian counterpart to be extraverted, friendly, and talkative. Be aware, however, that Nigerians are tough negotiators. Occasional open criticism is not unusual.
- Form a solid relationship in order to get and keep business. The concept of friendship is important in business dealings.
- Make good on delivery times, specifications, and quality. Failure to do so will be particularly harmful. Fulfillment of such promises helps maintain the mutual trust.
- Try to drink some of the tea, coffee, or soft drink that is sure to be offered to you. Refusal may be taken as an offense.
- Be sure to seek home office legal advice regarding gifts and payments for various services. The government officially discourages *dash* (payments) that resembles bribery, such as those for obtaining visas, clearing customs, and other government responsibilities. The practice remains widespread, however, and can enter into your business relationship if you are not careful.
- Get a Nigerian partner. Be sure to check that person's reputation carefully. One source is your embassy's commercial officer.

Day-to-Day Pointers

Business Entertainment Guidelines
- You may be invited to the home of your counterpart. If so, accept the invitation.
- In first-class restaurants, a service charge is normally included in the bill. A tip is given for many other services.

Table Manners and Food
- There is a large Muslim influence, so do not pass objects with your left hand.
- Nigerians usually eat hot, spicy food. Yams, cassava (a starchy root), and rice are traditional foods.
- Many Nigerians now eat continental meals as well.
- Hands are usually kept above the table.

Gender Issues

- International businesswomen doing business in Nigeria get a hearing if not total acceptance.
- Although there is a strong Muslim influence in Nigeria, local women have relatively more freedom in both the family and the marketplace than their Muslim counterparts in many other parts of the world.
- Women are quite independent in Nigeria, and are involved in politics and in running their own businesses in trading commodities within Nigeria.
- Many Nigerian businessmen are educated in North America or Western Europe or have experience with Western companies, and therefore have a heightened awareness of women's professional role in these countries.

Also Remember This . . .

- Nigeria became independent from the British in 1960.
- Nigeria's economy is one of the strongest in Africa, although corruption, poor planning, and ethnic tensions have hindered progress. Ethnic tensions have been characterized by coups, and both military and civilian governments. Nigeria's oil-rich Niger Delta region has experienced violence and attacks on oil production sites.
- Nigeria is a multicultural nation. Nigerians tend to define themselves first by their ethnic group, then religion, and then nationality. Muslims predominate in the north, the Christians in the south. Among tribal groups, the Hausa are practicing Muslims who are slow decision makers. The Yoruba tend to be outgoing, and have an "eat, drink, and be merry" philosophy of life. The Ibo are excellent businesspeople, hardworking, and conscientious, and they expect foreigners to conduct themselves similarly.

SOUTH AFRICA

Fast Facts

Monetary Unit: rand
Major Industries: mining, automobile assembly, metalworking

Primary Trading Partners: United States, United Kingdom, Japan, Germany, Italy, the Netherlands, China, France, Saudi Arabia
Key Exports: gold, diamonds, platinum, and other minerals and metals, food, chemicals
Key Imports: machinery, chemicals, transport equipment, petroleum products
Major Cities: Capetown (legislative cap.) (2.7 mil.), Pretoria (admin. cap.) (1.3 mil.), Durban/Pinetown (2.3 mil.), Johannesburg (1.7 mil.)
Ethnic Groups: black (76%) (mainly from nine ethnic groups; Zulus are the largest of this group at 23%), white (13%), Indian (3%), other (8%)
Primary Religions: Christian (69%; most whites and about 60% of blacks), traditional beliefs (28%), Muslim (2%), Hindu (1%)
Languages: Afrikaans (a Dutch derivation), English, and languages from the nine ethnic groups (such as Zulu, Xhosa, and Sotho) are all official languages; English is commonly used in business and is the primary language of instruction in secondary schools; Blacks speak a number of Bantu languages (such as Xhosa and Zulu), but more are learning English.

Reducing Communication Noise

Greetings

- Shake hands when meeting and leaving.
- Different greetings are used for different ethnic groups. Typical English greetings are *Hello* and *Good morning* (or afternoon or evening). *Goeie more* is used by Afrikaners and most people of color. The Zulu greet each other with *Sawubona* (literally this is, "I see you," and means "hello").
- Although using first names is increasingly common in business, wait until invited to do so. Until then, address your counterpart as *Mr., Mrs.,* or *Miss* with the last name.

Conversation

- South Africans like to discuss their country's natural beauty and culture.
- Soccer, rugby, and cricket are the most popular sports. Cricket and rugby is popular among whites, while Africans mainly follow soccer. Surfing and swimming are also popular. Those with club memberships may sail or play squash, or engage in lawn bowling, golf, sailing, or field hockey.

Sensitivities

- Avoid discussing political, religious, or racial issues.
- If you get trapped into a discussion on one of these subjects, be careful and do a lot of listening rather than talking.

Key Negotiating Pointers

- Make key connections before you go to South Africa. Decisions tend to be made at the top of organizations.

- Expect similarities between negotiations in South Africa and the United Kingdom. Many business dealings will be with people of British descent.

- Make prior appointments. Punctuality is strictly observed.

- Be friendly, but conduct yourself in a reserved, conservative style.

- Be patient. Bureaucratic delays are common in both the government and private sectors.

- A common tactic used by buyers asking for a lower price is to remind their counterpart of the competition, and to remind them that they "can do better than that." When asking buyers to pay more, South African sellers tend to have very high initial demands.

- The typical South African concession pattern is similar to that in the United States—slow and grudging.

- Contracts will be detailed.

Day-to-Day Pointers

Business Entertainment Guidelines

- Dinner is the main meal, usually eaten after 5:00 p.m.

- Expect to stay for one or two hours after the meal.

- Tipping is discretionary in restaurants.

Table Manners and Food

- South Africans generally use the continental style of eating, with fork in the left hand and knife in the right.

- Don't ask for food to be passed at the table.

- Typical foods include beef, mutton, curry, green vegetables, pumpkins, potatoes, and rice. Common beverages are wine, tea, and coffee.

- The *draaivleis* (barbecue) is popular during the weekend.

Gender Issues

- International businesswomen can generally conduct business in South Africa, although the Old Boy Network is alive and well.

- Gender is less an issue than race in doing business in South Africa.

- Women earn less than one-third of the nation's income.

Also Remember This . . .

- South Africa is the richest country in Africa, and has the best-developed infrastructure. Minerals and metals account for more than half of South Africa's export earnings. It is one of the largest producers of platinum and gold, and exports diamonds, chrome, and coal, while tourism and wine are fast-growing industries.

- South Africa is ethnically diverse, and there is a wide gap between the income of whites and others. The whites generally enjoy a high standard of living, but have a growth rate of zero. They are composed of English-speaking descendants of English, Irish, and Scottish settlers, and Afrikaans-speaking descendants of Dutch, German, and French settlers. People of color are mixed descendants of whites, settlers, native Hottentots, and imported slaves. Zulus are the largest of the black groups.

ZIMBABWE

Fast Facts

Monetary Unit: Zimbabwean dollar
Major Industries: mining, steel, wood products, cement, fertilizer, clothing, and textiles
Primary Trading Partners: South Africa, Switzerland, United Kingdom, China, Germany, Botswana
Key Exports: cotton, tobacco, gold, ferroalloys, textiles/clothing
Key Imports: machinery and transport equipment, manufactures, chemicals, fuels
Major Cities: Harare (cap.) (2.3 mil. metro area), Bulawayo (965,000), Chitungwiza (412,000)
Ethnic Groups: black (98%), mixed and Asian (1%), white (1%)
Primary Religions: Syncretic (part Christian and part indigenous beliefs) (50%), Christian (25%), indigenous beliefs (24%), Muslim and other (1%)
Languages: English is the official language and the most-used business language; Shona and Ndebele are also commonly spoken as a first language, especially in rural areas.

Reducing Communication Noise

Greetings

- Common greetings understood by all language groups are *Good morning, how are you?* or simply, *Hello*. Common Shona greetings are *Manguanani* (Good morning), *Masikati* (Good day), and *Maneru* (Good evening).

- A handshake usually accompanies the greeting. A polite handshake is to extend your right hand while grasping your right forearm with your left hand.
- Titles are sometimes used in urban areas, following the English tradition.
- Men wear suits for conducting business. Traditional African dress is reserved for special occasions or for performing.

Conversation

- Politeness is important in conversation. For example, don't refuse offers of refreshments.
- Soccer is Zimbabwe's most popular sport. Zimbabwe also has a lot of sports enthusiasts for tennis, boxing, rugby, cricket, polo, bowling, field hockey, squash, golf, and horse racing. Swimming is also popular, but does not take place in rivers or streams due to *bilharzia*, a dangerous parasite.
- Zimbabweans love to talk about their beautiful country, music, and arts. Their national parks are among Africa's finest.
- Watching television and going to movies are favorite pastimes.
- The main ethnic groups are the Shona, who occupy the north and east, and the Ndebele in the west.

Sensitivities

- Avoid discussions about the period of British colonization.
- Avoid long periods of direct eye contact; this is considered rude.

Key Negotiating Pointers

- Expect Zimbabweans to sometimes be somewhat cautious and reserved upon first meeting.
- Be on time for meetings.
- Avoid behavior that draws a lot of attention to yourself. Humility is held in high regard.
- Be sure to give a great deal of respect. Be polite when you encounter differences.
- Try to build a good relationship, but let your Zimbabwean counterpart take the lead in this.
- Make your presentations straightforward and factual.
- Find an agent who can help you make solid connections.

Day-to-Day Pointers

Business Entertainment Guidelines

- Although lunch is usually light, the five-star hotels usually have extravagant buffets. The main meal is the evening meal.
- Tea is popular with meals and in the office.

Table Manners and Food

- Water is often first provided for washing one's hands.
- *Sadza*, a porridge made from maize (cornmeal), is the main staple food of Zimbabweans, and is served at almost every meal. This is usually accompanied by vegetables.
- A more Western diet is usually eaten in the cities, including meat and potatoes, or rice, instead of *sadza*. Locally grown fruits, such as mangoes, bananas, melons, and papayas (*pawpaws*) are typical.
- Items are usually given and received with both hands.
- Leave a little food behind to show you are not greedy.

Gender Issues

- International businesswomen can expect some gender-based resistance in this male-dominated society, but can be effective nevertheless.
- A display of anger or frustration would be more hurtful to a woman doing business than it would be to a man.
- International businesswomen should dress conservatively (for example, avoid a sleeveless dress).
- Men sometimes have extramarital affairs with the knowledge of their wives to prove their virility. If you are an international businesswoman, you might be approached.

Also Remember This . . .

- Zimbabwe declared independence from Britain in 1965, after decades as a British colony and a civil war. Zimbabwe was officially recognized throughout the world in 1980.
- Zimbabwe is normally self-sufficient in food production, except in rare periods of drought. Agriculture employs about two-thirds of the labor force. Tobacco and cotton account for about 40 percent of all export earnings.
- Agriculture and mining are important parts of the economy. Corruption and mismanagement have hurt public services, hindered investor confidence, and severely damaged economic development.

References

Adler, Nancy J. *International Dimensions of Organizational Behavior*, 4th ed. Cincinnati, OH: South-Western, 2002.

Brunner, Borgna, ed. *Time Almanac 2008*. Pearson Education Company: Boston, MA, 2007.

Copeland, Lennie, and Lewis Griggs. *Going International*. New York: Random House, 1985.

CultureGrams™ 2007 World Edition. Provo, UT: ProQuest Information and Learning Company, 2006.

Harvard Business Review on Doing Business in China. Boston, MA: Harvard Business School Publishing, 2004.

Hendon, Donald W., and Rebecca Angeles Hendon. *World-Class Negotiating: Dealmaking in the Global Marketplace*. New York: Wiley, 1990.

Kremenyuk, Victor A., ed. *International Negotiation*. San Francisco: Jossey-Bass, 1991.

Moran, Robert T., Phillip R. Harris, and Sarah V. Moran. *Managing Cultural Differences*, 7th ed. Burlington, MA: Butterworth-Heinemann, 2007.

Rossman, Marlene L. *International Business of the '90s: A Guide to Success in the Global Market*. New York: Praeger, 1990.

Wright, John W., ed. *The New York Times 2008 Almanac*. New York: Penguin Group, 2008.

Index

Table Manners and Food

- Water is often first provided for washing one's hands.
- *Sadza*, a porridge made from maize (cornmeal), is the main staple food of Zimbabweans, and is served at almost every meal. This is usually accompanied by vegetables.
- A more Western diet is usually eaten in the cities, including meat and potatoes, or rice, instead of *sadza*. Locally grown fruits, such as mangoes, bananas, melons, and papayas (*pawpaws*) are typical.
- Items are usually given and received with both hands.
- Leave a little food behind to show you are not greedy.

Gender Issues

- International businesswomen can expect some gender-based resistance in this male-dominated society, but can be effective nevertheless.
- A display of anger or frustration would be more hurtful to a woman doing business than it would be to a man.
- International businesswomen should dress conservatively (for example, avoid a sleeveless dress).
- Men sometimes have extramarital affairs with the knowledge of their wives to prove their virility. If you are an international businesswoman, you might be approached.

Also Remember This . . .

- Zimbabwe declared independence from Britain in 1965, after decades as a British colony and a civil war. Zimbabwe was officially recognized throughout the world in 1980.
- Zimbabwe is normally self-sufficient in food production, except in rare periods of drought. Agriculture employs about two-thirds of the labor force. Tobacco and cotton account for about 40 percent of all export earnings.
- Agriculture and mining are important parts of the economy. Corruption and mismanagement have hurt public services, hindered investor confidence, and severely damaged economic development.

References

Adler, Nancy J. *International Dimensions of Organizational Behavior*, 4th ed. Cincinnati, OH: South-Western, 2002.

Brunner, Borgna, ed. *Time Almanac 2008*. Pearson Education Company: Boston, MA, 2007.

Copeland, Lennie, and Lewis Griggs. *Going International*. New York: Random House, 1985.

CultureGrams™ 2007 World Edition. Provo, UT: ProQuest Information and Learning Company, 2006.

Harvard Business Review on Doing Business in China. Boston, MA: Harvard Business School Publishing, 2004.

Hendon, Donald W., and Rebecca Angeles Hendon. *World-Class Negotiating: Dealmaking in the Global Marketplace*. New York: Wiley, 1990.

Kremenyuk, Victor A., ed. *International Negotiation*. San Francisco: Jossey-Bass, 1991.

Moran, Robert T., Phillip R. Harris, and Sarah V. Moran. *Managing Cultural Differences*, 7th ed. Burlington, MA: Butterworth-Heinemann, 2007.

Rossman, Marlene L. *International Business of the '90s: A Guide to Success in the Global Market*. New York: Praeger, 1990.

Wright, John W., ed. *The New York Times 2008 Almanac*. New York: Penguin Group, 2008.

Index